# IMAGES OF FAITH

MUSEUM OF CHURCH HISTORY AND ART

# IMAGES OF FAITH

## ART OF THE LATTER-DAY SAINTS

ESSAYS BY

RICHARD G. OMAN AND ROBERT O. DAVIS

Deseret Book Company, Salt Lake City, Utah

PHOTO CREDITS

*Except where listed below, all plates and figures are from photographs taken by the Museum of Church History and Art.*

Courtesy Archives Division, Historical Department, The Church of Jesus Christ of Latter-day Saints: Plates 47, 74, 75, 111; Figures 1, 3, 4, 9, 10, 12, 13, 14, 19, 22, 39.

Courtesy Visual Resources Library, The Church of Jesus Christ of Latter-day Saints: Plates 31, 86, 113, 119, 142, 145, 146, 149, 152, 178, 180, 192; Figures 17, 21, 26, 29, 33, 34, 63.

Courtesy Archives, Harold B. Lee Library, Brigham Young University: Plate 108.

Courtesy Utah State Historical Society: Plate 110; Figures 5, 23.

Courtesy Springville Museum of Art: Figures 6, 7, 8, 11, 15, 16, 30, 35, 37, 38, 42, 45, 46, 47, 49, 50, 51, 52, 59, 62, 64, 65.

Courtesy Library of Congress, Washington, D.C.: Plates 160 (Neg. # LC-USF34–1347–C), 162 (Neg. # LC-USF34–37376–D), 163 (Neg. # LC-USF34–37402–D).

Courtesy Museum of Art, Brigham Young University (© Museum of Art, Brigham Young University, all rights reserved): Plates 77, 85, 89, 117, 118, 120, 134, 135, 172, 187; Figure 61.

Plate 126: Photograph by Ansel Adams. Copyright ©1995 by the Trustees of The Ansel Adams Publishing Rights Trust. All rights reserved.

Plate 161: Copyright the Dorothea Lange Collection, The Oakland Museum, The City of Oakland. Gift of Paul S. Taylor.

Figure 73: Copyright Doug Martin Photography.

Joyce Athay Janetski, Plate 101. Elliott Fairbanks, Figure 20. Laurie Teichert Eastwood, Figure 24. Eugene Fairbanks, Figures 31, 32. Craig Law, Figure 48. Bethanne Andersen, Figure 53. Laurie Schnoebelen, Figure 54. Sallie Poet, Figure 55. Marcus Vincent, Figure 56. Brian Kershisnik, Figure 57. Jeanne Leighton-Lundberg, Figure 58. Judith Mehr, Figure 60. Leta Keith, Figure 68. Emma Allebes, Figure 70. Reid Parkinson, Figure 75. Ada Rigby, Figure 78. Ruben and Mary Ouzounian, Figure 80. Victor de la Torre, Figure 81. Tammy Garcia, Figure 85.

**Library of Congress Cataloging-in-Publication Data**

Oman, Richard G.
    Images of faith : art of the Latter-day Saints / Museum of Church
History and Art; essays by Richard G. Oman, Robert O. Davis.
        p.      cm.
    Includes bibliographical references and index.
    ISBN 0-87579-912-4 (hardbound)
    1. Mormon art—United States.  2. Art, Modern—19th Century—
United States.  3. Art, Modern—20th century—United States.
    I. Davis, Robert O. II. Museum of Church History and Art (Salt Lake
City, Utah) III. Title.
    N6510.042    1995
    704'.283'0973—dc20                                    95-16414
                                                          CIP

Printed in the United States of America

10   9   8   7   6   5   4   3   2   1

# CONTENTS

# LIST OF PLATES AND FIGURES

## FIGURES

W hen Brigham Young led the first Latter-day Saints out of Nauvoo and toward a new gathering place in the West, he endorsed an effort to create a museum for The Church of Jesus Christ of Latter-day Saints. The idea had surfaced first in Nauvoo, and it had the active encouragement of Philo Dibble in Winter Quarters. But it was not until 1869 that the Salt Lake Museum and Menagerie opened its doors. For most of the next half century, this fledgling institution, renamed the Deseret Museum, collected material from Utah and other regions of the West with which to educate students and the public. In 1919 the museum reoriented its focus and moved onto Temple Square, where it remained until 1976 as the LDS Museum, part of the Bureau of Information. During those years, the historical collection grew.

When the Temple Square museum closed, the collection became the responsibility of a newly organized Arts and Sites Division (later known as the Museum Division), whose stewardship expanded to include the Church art collection. That art existed mostly in temples, headquarters buildings, and meetinghouses. Over time, the collection grew to include new works of historical and contemporary art. Much of the art continues to serve its traditional functions in Church buildings. A broader international collection and newly acquired historical pieces find use in an expanded museum program at the Museum of Church History and Art.

Since its opening in 1984, the Church Museum has served a growing audience as it strives to preserve, care for, and interpret the historical and artistic legacy of the Church. In exhibitions at the Museum and in furnished buildings at key historic sites, the Museum works to build an understanding of the past for present and future generations. Interpretive exhibits utilizing art are an important part of that effort.

Visitors at the Museum have long expressed the desire for a published compilation of Museum holdings. This book responds, in part, to that need. It will expand the learning experience beyond the Museum's walls as individuals in geographically diverse areas study and enjoy the most important pieces from the Church art collection. Many important Latter-day Saint artists are not represented in that collection and thus are not found in this book. Nor can every artist whose works are in the collection be mentioned, because of space limitations. Their work is nonetheless part of the story told here.

Ongoing Church support of the Museum has made this book possible. Without a collection, there would be no book. Generous donors have also helped build the collection. Richard G. Oman and Robert O. Davis, art curators at the Museum, along with former curator Linda Jones Gibbs, have worked with artists, dealers, collectors, and donors to acquire the pieces represented in these pages. We are especially grateful to Florence S. Jacobsen, the former director of the Arts and Sites Division, whose vision for the potential of a new museum helped define our current programs. General Authorities who have served as advisors to and executive directors of the Historical Department, under which the Museum functions, have lent constant support. Especially appreciated are the efforts and suggestions of the current administration. Elder Stephen D. Nadauld, executive director, and Elder Alexander B. Morrison, assistant executive director (both of the Seventy), Richard E. Turley Jr., managing director, and Grant A. Anderson, acting director of special projects, have offered their ongoing encouragement.

The preparation of this book was a team effort, and we acknowledge the contributions of many willing hands. Curators Richard Oman and Robert Davis accepted the primary role of selecting the pieces to be included and of preparing the accompanying essays. Their willingness to devote much personal time to this effort is greatly appreciated. Several other staff members and Church service missionaries who serve as museum docents prepared the captions. Those contributors include staff members Marjorie D. Conder, Ray K. Halls, Glen M. Leonard, Jennifer L. Lund, and Mark L. Staker, and docents Mary K. Altizer, Lynnette P. Hanson, Elaine J. Homer, Colleen E. Johnson, Adelia H. Rushforth, and Suzanne N. Scruggs. Glen M. Leonard served as general editor, and Melinda Chisholm prepared headings for the captions and entered revisions to the texts. Most of the photographs were created by Ronald W. Read and Robert Davis, with others furnished by the Museum of Art at Brigham Young University, the Springville Museum of Art, the Visual Resources Library of The Church of Jesus Christ of Latter-day Saints, and the Archives Division of the Church's Historical Department (referred to herein as Church Archives). At Deseret Book, Sheri Dew, director of publishing, Kent Ware, designer, and Emily Watts, editor, have lent enthusiastic support from start to finish.

It is our hope that readers of this informative and handsome volume will gain a greater understanding of and a new appreciation for Latter-day Saint art.

*Glen M. Leonard*
*Museum Director*

# IMAGES OF FAITH

# INTRODUCTION

*by Richard G. Oman*

F or most of recorded history the vast sweep of world art has been religious. One particular religious art tradition, that of the members of The Church of Jesus Christ of Latter-day Saints over the last hundred and sixty years, is the subject of this book. Within this tradition can be found expressions of faith, religious commitment, and historical experience, portrayed through a wide variety of styles, forms, and mediums. In this book the authors have attempted to deal with five issues: What is Latter-day Saint art? How did it come to be? What are the finest examples of the tradition? Who made these works of art? and What does the art mean?

Almost all of the pieces used to illustrate and document this tradition are from the collection of The Church of Jesus Christ of Latter-day Saints. That collection is housed primarily in the Museum of Church History and Art across the street from Temple Square in Salt Lake City. Where works of art from other collections are used, the sources are carefully noted in captions that accompany the images.

The earliest Latter-day Saint art consisted of personally commissioned portraits of early Church leaders. Some of those paintings were borrowed for use in the Kirtland Temple. The founding of Nauvoo generated more portraiture, as well as the beginning of sculpture and documentary art. After the martyrdom and the move west, the Saints began to recognize the epic nature of their history. Historical paintings became the major focus of the Scandinavian emigrant artists in Utah. Meanwhile, the dramatic natural landscapes of the new Zion became prime subjects for the British emigrants. Those two groups provided most of the first-generation Utah artists. Members of both groups created portraiture and helped paint murals in meetinghouses, tabernacles, and temples.

With the Salt Lake Temple nearing completion, the Church sent several artists on study-missions to Paris to acquire the skills to paint murals in the temple. Those artists brought back the new impressionistic style and influenced a whole generation of Latter-day Saint artists as exemplars and teachers. They encouraged many of their best students to obtain advanced art training in Paris. The result was the development of a soft, impressionistic style that focused mainly on landscape painting and some portraiture. Some Utah artists also studied sculpture, creating a proliferation of classically inspired monuments celebrating significant events in Church history.

World War I closed the door to French study, and artists began to focus on New York City for their training. With this change came a new desire to create art depicting their own regions—art with strong Latter-day Saint overtones. The Mormon pioneer landscape with barns, villages, and rows of poplar trees became a favorite theme. Artists interpreted the historical experiences of the early Saints as examples of righteousness for the living.

The first half of the twentieth century was also the golden age of temple murals. Those commissions attracted some of the finest artists in the Church. With the elimination of murals in most of the temples in the second half of the century, an important focus of Latter-day Saint art ceased.

FACING PAGE:
**Come Follow Me,** 1922
JAMES T. HARWOOD (1860–1940)
OIL ON CANVAS, 51" x 41 1/2"
(129.5 CM X 105.4 CM)
MUSEUM OF CHURCH
HISTORY AND ART

*In this well-known painting commissioned by the Deseret Sunday School Union, Christ stands on the shores of the Sea of Galilee calling Simon Peter and Andrew to the holy apostleship. The two brothers listen in wonderment to the Savior's words, "Follow me, and I will make you fishers of men" (Matthew 4:19). The low angle of vision combined with the tilt of the figures' heads directs the viewer's gaze heavenward and suggests an attitude of humility before the Lord.*

*Little is known about the history of this impressive
likeness. It is similar to a signed grisaille portrait by
Weggeland that hung in the Cannon Sixth Ward
building in Salt Lake City. These two portraits, like
nearly all images that have attempted to depict
Joseph as he actually appeared, are derived from
three visual sources: the frontal portrait of unknown
date and maker now owned by the Reorganized
Church of Jesus Christ of Latter Day Saints, profile
portraits in formal and military dress by Sutcliffe
Maudsley, and the plaster death mask. This painting
was influenced by the mask and by Maudsley's
profiles. Weggeland produced several other
important portrayals of Joseph Smith for the Church.*

Brigham Young University developed as a center for art among the Saints with growing influence after 1950. Teachers and students eventually came together to generate the Mormon Arts Festival, which lasted for eighteen years. The festival once again encouraged artists to define and create a Latter-day Saint art.

Perhaps the most important event affecting Latter-day Saint art in recent years was the opening of the Museum of Church History and Art in 1984. This Church-sponsored institution collects, preserves, commissions, and exhibits Latter-day Saint art. The museum began to reach out to member artists all over the world. Through Churchwide competitions, artists were stimulated to produce art that celebrated their faith, history, and religious experiences. Museum visitors and readers of Church publications were exposed to this tidal wave of new artists and their art. Meanwhile, a number of major exhibitions and a few publications have documented the sweep of the Latter-day Saint art tradition over the past hundred and sixty years.

Most art officially commissioned by the Church is pedagogical rather than liturgical, used for education and inspiration rather than as a part of worship. Latter-day Saints do not have a highly structured liturgical tradition that demands religious art. Works of art are not used as objects of religious devotion. In recent years even the placing of paintings in chapels has been discouraged. But the separation of art and liturgy has probably helped maintain a certain amount of stylistic flexibility and openness in the art tradition. This opens the door to a vast range of artistic styles and gives the tradition the flexibility to adapt as Church membership expands throughout the world.

This is not to say that there is a totally flexible attitude toward art. But cohesion in the Latter-day Saint tradition rests in religious themes and functions, not stylistic continuity or development. The benchmark for this artistic tradition is faith, commitment, and religious understanding in depicting Latter-day Saint experience, history, and theology. Latter-day Saint art reinforces the identity of a religious community residing in over one hundred fifty different nations. It is a tradition in which religious ideas matter. The most useful way to approach Latter-day Saint art is not to compare artistic style but to look at subject.

The tradition of Latter-day Saint art is distinctive for three reasons. First, a flourishing tradition of religious art has been developed at the very time when most art traditions of the West have been moving away from religious art. Second, from its very beginning the tradition has drawn

PLATE 2: *Ascent,* 1993
DAVID LINN (1959– )
OIL ON CANVAS, 67" X 46 3/4" (170.2 CM X 118.8 CM)
MUSEUM OF CHURCH HISTORY AND ART

*Ascent was entered in the Museum's third Churchwide art competition, where it won merit and purchase honors. This work has quickly become a favorite of Church members for its instructive message and accomplished execution. The handling of the theme illustrates one way in which religious symbolism is employed by Latter-day Saint artists. David Linn explained, "Living the gospel demands that we help one another climb upward out of the darkness of the world into the light of truth. As the Lord's church, we form a living chain on the mountain of this mortal existence, drawing one another toward the veil and the presence of the Lord." Linn, an artist from northern California, studied painting at the Brigham Young University Department of Visual Arts.*

PLATE 3: *Mesa Arizona Temple Rug,* 1990
LETA KEITH, EDGEWATER CLAN (1923– )
HAND-SPUN WOOL, 52" X 71" (132.1 CM X 180.3 CM)
MUSEUM OF CHURCH HISTORY AND ART

*The tradition of Navajo pictorial rug weaving began in the late nineteenth century, allowing weavers to depict subject matter not possible with earlier patterned rugs. In this rug the rainbow figure arching over the temple is a traditional Navajo symbol of blessing. Sister Keith, who has served several times as Relief Society president in her ward located near Monument Valley, regularly travels more than two hundred miles to worship in the Navajo language in the Arizona Temple. About her beliefs, she stated: "The Old Ones long ago prayed . . . that they walk in hozho, which means: I will walk in beauty; I will walk with care; whatever I do I will do right; I will live righteously."*

from several different cultures. Third, it is a religious art tradition that has been amazingly egalitarian, nonelitist, and generally nonhierarchical. The creation of a religious art tradition combining such elements, especially within the last century and a half, is a significant achievement in world art history.

Over a century ago Charles Dickens questioned the founding of the Church with the query, "Visions in the age of railroads?" One might say of Latter-day Saint art, "A religious art tradition developing in the age of modern secularism?" Yet a religiously based art does exist and thrive in a secular age, testifying to the power of spiritual influences in the lives of Latter-day Saint artists and the religious community of which they are a part.

# THE FOUNDATION OF LATTER-DAY SAINT ART, 1835–1890

1

*by Richard G. Oman*

Portraits, architectural drawings, and historical art created between 1835 and 1890 laid the foundations for an important visual heritage for The Church of Jesus Christ of Latter-day Saints. During those beginning years, British and American artists helped define subjects and purposes for Latter-day Saint art that would continue in later periods. On a personal level, individuals hired itinerant artists to preserve their images on canvas, and some of those paintings served institutional needs. The Church employed architects and craftsmen to design and adorn temples. And artists began the work of documenting the places and events of Church history. Later generations would seek understanding and inspiration from those earliest images in the visual record of the Restoration.

## THE MIDWEST PERIOD

The first depictions of Latter-day Saints in art were privately commissioned portraits of Church leaders and their wives from the mid-1830s. Several such portraits of Church leaders serving in Ohio and Missouri hung for a time in the Kirtland Temple. Fewer than a dozen of them have survived.

In Nauvoo, the first Latter-day Saint artists created work especially for Church purposes. Some of that work focused on the Nauvoo Temple. The temple architect, William Weeks (1813–1900), drew meticulous renderings of the elevations and interior woodwork of the temple (FIGURE 1). The temple housed the first major sculptural work by Latter-day Saints: In 1841, Weeks designed and wood-carver Elijah Fordham created twelve life-sized wooden oxen for a temporary baptismal font. Four years later, twelve stone-carvers headed by William W. Player executed

FIGURE 1: NAUVOO TEMPLE ELEVATION

another set of oxen out of limestone. Only small pieces of that work remain. Completely lost is the angel weather vane made of gold-leafed tin by the Nauvoo Tinners Association, headed by Dustin Amy.

Several of the wonderfully carved symbolic stones from the outside facade of the Nauvoo Temple remain. The most dramatic of those are the so-called sunstones, which served as the capitals on thirty pilasters. The Museum of Church History and Art created an exact replica of the sunstone displayed at the Smithsonian Institution's

FIGURE 2: NAUVOO TEMPLE SUNSTONE

National Museum of American History (FIGURE 2). A second original, owned by the State of Illinois, can be seen at the temple site in Nauvoo, and a third, damaged sunstone is preserved in storage by the Reorganized Church of Jesus Christ of Latter Day Saints.

Nauvoo also saw the increased development of portraiture. Most of the painters were British converts who

*Facing page: Detail from*
**Handcart Pioneers**,
*by C. C. A. Christensen.*
*(See Plate 49, page 27.)*

PLATE 5: *Joseph Smith,* AFTER 1842
ARTIST UNKNOWN
OIL ON CANVAS, 25" x 21" (63.5 CM x 53.4 CM)
MUSEUM OF CHURCH HISTORY AND ART

*This profile portrait contains many elements common to the images of the Prophet done from life by Sutcliffe Maudsley, an English immigrant to Nauvoo. Because Maudsley worked only in watercolor and ink, it is more likely that another artist painted this oil portrait. The Prophet's diary mentions sitting for a portrait by "Brother Rogers" in September 1842. David W. Rogers was a professional artist in New York City. Some maintain that during his brief visit to Nauvoo he may have created the handsome front-view portrait owned by the Reorganized Church of Jesus Christ of Latter Day Saints, rather than this one. Both portraits have been attributed at times to Rogers.*

PLATE 4: *Hyrum Smith,* BEFORE 1837
ARTIST UNKNOWN
OIL ON CANVAS, 26" x 22" (66 CM x 55.9 CM)
ARCHIVES, HAROLD B. LEE LIBRARY
BRIGHAM YOUNG UNIVERSITY
GIFT OF ELDRED GEE SMITH

*This handsome portrait captures Joseph Smith's older brother in his midthirties, shortly before he was called as a counselor in the First Presidency in Kirtland, Ohio. Almost all nineteenth-century images of Hyrum Smith can be traced to this oil portrait, done from life. Profiles of Hyrum by Sutcliffe Maudsley in Nauvoo provided a second, less popular source for later artists. This oil painting and a companion study of Hyrum's first wife, Jerusha Barden Smith, who died in childbirth in 1837, are among the earliest surviving portraits of Latter-day Saint subjects. Portraits of Church leaders done in the 1830s hung for a time in the Kirtland Temple. Another selection of portraits, including this one, hung for several weeks in the celestial room of the Nauvoo Temple.*

focused on the Smith family and other Church leaders. The most influential of those early painters was Sutcliffe Maudsley (1809–1881), a convert from Lancashire, England, who had been trained as a textile pattern maker. Maudsley immigrated to Nauvoo in 1842 and lived near the Prophet. As a portrait painter, he was largely self-taught and drew simple profiles. Because they had been done from life, and hence were deemed accurate renditions of the Prophet and his family, Maudsley's works were used as basic source material by Latter-day Saint artists for many decades (PLATES 6, 7, AND 8). His early drawings and watercolor paintings and their derivatives are very important because no photographs of Joseph Smith are known to exist.

PLATE 6: *Lucy Mack Smith,* ABOUT 1842
SUTCLIFFE MAUDSLEY (1809–1881)
EGG TEMPERA AND INK ON PAPER, 12" x 7 1/2"
(30.5 CM x 19.1 CM)
MUSEUM OF CHURCH HISTORY AND ART
GIFT OF ALICE L. BOYD

*Lucy Mack Smith, the mother of the Prophet, was a deeply religious woman. She is shown here holding a copy of the Book of Mormon. Lucy often spoke of her son's role as translator of the ancient record. On the wall is an image depicting Facsimile Number One, a part of the Egyptian papyrus from which Joseph Smith translated the Book of Abraham. Lucy was custodian of the papyrus in Nauvoo and showed it to guests in her home. The artist's training as a fabric designer and pattern maker in Lancashire, England, can be seen in the distinct outlines and two-dimensional nature of this work. He added dignity to the painting through the inclusion of the fringed draperies and the richly patterned carpeting.*

PLATE 7: *Lieutenant General Joseph Smith,* ABOUT 1842
SUTCLIFFE MAUDSLEY (1809–1881)
EGG TEMPERA AND INK ON PAPER, 12" X 7 1/2" (30.5 CM X 19 CM)
MUSEUM OF CHURCH HISTORY AND ART

PLATE 8: *Emma Hale Smith,* ABOUT 1842
SUTCLIFFE MAUDSLEY (1809–1881)
EGG TEMPERA AND INK ON PAPER, 12 5/8" X 7 1/4" (32.1 CM X 18.4 CM)
MUSEUM OF CHURCH HISTORY AND ART, DONATED BY THE SILVER FOUNDATION

*Joseph Smith is shown here in his role as lieutenant general and commanding officer of the Nauvoo Legion, the militia of the city of Nauvoo. This is one of very few portraits done of the Prophet during his lifetime. Although the artist was not highly accomplished artistically, the profile likeness is considered to be quite accurate. This image is like the one (also in the Museum collection) described in the History of the Church, June 25, 1842: "Sat for a drawing of my profile to be placed on lithograph of a map of the City of Nauvoo."*

*In the companion painting, Emma is shown in a formal dress holding her ivory-handled riding crop. She owned this pair of portraits following the martyrdom of the Prophet Joseph and his brother Hyrum, and the pictures later passed to her son Alexander Hale Smith and his descendants. The artist joined the Church in England in 1840. His trade involved making patterns to reproduce pictures and designs for cloth, which aided him in making profile portraits of his clients. Immigrating to Nauvoo in 1842, Maudsley was engaged to create portraits of Church leaders and their wives. Several dozen of Joseph Smith are extant, most of them copies done by the artist from two or three of his original portraits.*

PLATE 9: *General Joseph Smith Addressing the Nauvoo Legion,* 1845
ROBERT CAMPBELL (1810–1890)
WATERCOLOR AND INK ON PAPER, 11 7/8" X 16 3/4"
(30.2 CM X 42.5 CM)
MUSEUM OF CHURCH HISTORY AND ART

On June 18, 1844, Joseph Smith climbed atop the frame of a partially built home across from the Mansion House and addressed the Nauvoo Legion in what was to be his last public discourse. The Prophet as mayor and lieutenant general of the city militia had just declared martial law in response to the inflammatory sentiment opposing him and the Church. Drawing his sword, the Prophet challenged the Nauvoo Legion to defend the city and their rights.

Robert Campbell, a clerk and lithographer who was renting the Joseph Smith Sr. log home next to the makeshift speaker's stand, witnessed the speech. In 1845, Philo Dibble commissioned this detailed sketch as seen from a second-story window in the Prophet's red brick store. William W. Major enlarged it for a mural. The mural was displayed in Nauvoo at the Masonic Hall, again in Winter Quarters, and for a number of years in early Utah.

PLATE 10: *Phoebe Carter Woodruff and Son Joseph,* 1845–1846
THOMAS WARD (1808–1847)
OIL ON CANVAS, 30" X 24" (76.2 CM X 61 CM)
MUSEUM OF CHURCH HISTORY AND ART
GIFT OF ROBERT NEEDHAM SEARS

This family portrait was painted while Phoebe's husband, Wilford, was president of the British Mission. The portrait held special significance for the Woodruffs. To them young Joseph was a "covenant" child because he was their first child born after they were sealed in the Nauvoo Temple. Less than a year later little Joseph died at Winter Quarters. Almost a year after this portrait was begun, Wilford Woodruff recorded in his journal that "Mrs. Woodruff took out of her family box her portrait to see the likeness of her little Joseph we had buried." The artist, Thomas Ward, was a friend and colleague of the Woodruffs from the mission office in Liverpool. Although he painted straightforwardly, the artist gave both mother and child an air of nobility important to British artists by using rich colors, a formal pose, and a drapery in the background. Ward used a traditional portrait composition for a mother and child in this piece. The portrait is primitive in style, but in it the artist achieved unity and harmony.

The death of Joseph and Hyrum Smith in June 1844 at Carthage Jail was the catalyst for some of the earliest Latter-day Saint historical painting. Under a commission from Philo Dibble, Robert Campbell (1810–1890), a British teacher who became a clerk in Nauvoo, created a posthumous scene showing Joseph Smith giving his last address to the Nauvoo Legion (PLATE 9). This small pen-and-ink watercolor was probably the first narrative painting by an LDS artist. Campbell drew a companion piece telling the story of the martyrdom. Those two paintings were the basis for murals painted by another British convert, William W. Major (1804–1854), from Bristol. Major also did portraits that were loaned temporarily to the Nauvoo Temple.

PLATE 11: *Joseph Smith and Friends,* ABOUT 1845
WILLIAM W. MAJOR (1804–1854)
OIL ON CANVAS, 23 1/2" X 31 1/2" (59.7 CM X 80 CM)
MUSEUM OF CHURCH HISTORY AND ART

*This group portrait depicts several members of the First Presidency and Council of the Twelve. They are, from left to right: Hyrum Smith, Willard Richards, Joseph Smith, Orson Pratt, Parley P. Pratt, Orson Hyde, Heber C. Kimball, and Brigham Young. The artist, William Major, joined the Church in England. He arrived in Nauvoo in 1844 and began the portrait during this time, but may have added images of the Pratt brothers later. Called the first professional artist in the Salt Lake Valley, Major actively painted portraits and landscapes until his untimely death in England while serving a mission.*

PLATE 12: *Brigham Young and His Friends,* ABOUT 1864

SARAH ANN BURBAGE LONG (1826-1878)
OIL ON CANVAS, 34" X 44" (86.4 CM X 111.8 CM)
MUSEUM OF CHURCH HISTORY AND ART

*This painting depicts several of Brigham Young's closest friends, advisors, and colleagues in the mid-1860s. From left to right they are: John V. Long, husband of the artist and Brigham's clerk; John Lyon, a writer and librarian; John Young, the apostle son of Brigham; Edwin Woolley, a successful Salt Lake businessman and bishop who lived across the street from Brigham; George A. Smith, an apostle and the Church historian, who worked next door to Brigham's office; Lorenzo Snow, an apostle and brother-in-law of Brigham; Heber C. Kimball, a close friend from Brigham's upstate New York days and Brigham's counselor in the First Presidency; Brigham Young himself; and Daniel Wells, another neighbor and counselor. Behind the group are images of deceased members of the First Presidency, from left to right, Jedediah M. Grant, Joseph and Hyrum Smith, and a bust of Willard Richards. The artist, a native of Kent, England, immigrated to Utah in 1854 and began teaching art classes in Salt Lake City. She was the first woman artist in Utah.*

PLATE 13: *Ruins of the Nauvoo Temple*, 1853
FREDERICK PIERCY (1830–1891)
ENGRAVING BY C. FENN FROM PIERCY'S DRAWING,
6 7/8" X 10" (17.5 CM X 25.4 CM)
CHURCH ARCHIVES

*This engraving was published in the book* Route from
Liverpool to Great Salt Lake Valley *in 1855. Here
Piercy captures the ruins of the Nauvoo Temple after the
building had been burned by an arsonist's fire and
destroyed by a tornado. Piercy commented on his feelings
while sketching this piece. "The first objects I saw in
approaching the city were the remains of what was once
the Temple, situated on the highest eminence of the city,
and which, in the days of its prosperity must have been
to it, what the cap or top stone is to a building. . . .
[The buildings] after being pillaged of all that was
valuable and portable, have been abandoned by
their ruthless destroyers, and are now monuments
of their selfish, jealous and contemptible hate."*

PLATE 14: *Early View of Nauvoo*, 1859
JOHANN SCHRODER
OIL ON METAL, 10" X 13" (25.4 CM X 33 CM)
MUSEUM OF CHURCH HISTORY AND ART

*The artist recorded this scene fourteen years after the
Saints had left the city. Only the facade of the temple
remained. It occupies a prominent focus in the painting,
while most other buildings lack specific identifying detail.
Schroder was one of the German immigrants who moved
into the vacated city. Among other new residents were a
religious group known as the Icarians; their name
appears under the artist's signature on the painting.*

By late 1846 the majority of the Nauvoo Saints had headed west by covered wagon. Nauvoo was left a deserted city. The temple, which was torched in 1848 by mobs and hit by a tornado two years later, was soon in ruins. Nauvoo, with its meteoric rise and tragic abandonment, caught the imagination of subsequent artists, Mormon and non-Mormon, who painted various scenes of the city over the next fifteen years. Two of the most dramatic are the drawing of the Nauvoo Temple in ruins by an English convert artist, Frederick Piercy, of London (PLATE 13) and a

panoramic view by a resident German artist, Johann Schroder (PLATE 14). Piercy visited Nauvoo in 1853 as part of an artistic documentary trip from England to Utah. During this trip he documented key sites along the route. His careful drawings were the basis for the engravings that illustrated the immigrant travel guide *Route from Liverpool to Great Salt Lake Valley*, which the Church published in 1855 in England to answer the questions many converts from Great Britain had about their upcoming trip to Zion.

## THE UTAH PERIOD

As the Saints moved west, Latter-day Saint artists migrated with them. The earliest Latter-day Saint artist in pioneer Utah was William Major. A member of the Winter Quarters high council, he worked on a painting of Brigham and Mary Ann Angell Young and their children that he had begun in Nauvoo, and he finally completed it in Utah (PLATE 15). This painting became Major's masterpiece. He painted other family portraits and some small landscapes of early settlements in Utah. His career was cut short when he died while serving a mission to his native England.

Within the first few years after settlement began in the Salt Lake Valley, photographers and artists from outside the area captured panoramic views of the new city and valley. One of the

PLATE 15: **Brigham and Mary Ann Angell Young and Their Children,** 1845–1851
WILLIAM W. MAJOR (1804–1854)
OIL ON BOARD, 25" X 33" (63.5 CM X 83.8 CM)
MUSEUM OF CHURCH HISTORY AND ART

*This painting depicts Brigham Young, his wife Mary Ann Angell, and their six children. The children, from left to right, are: Luna Caroline, Joseph Angell, Brigham Jr., Mary Ann, Alice, and John Willard. Mary Ann, standing behind the table, died two years before this painting was begun. Her twin brother, Brigham, hands her a white rose, perhaps symbolizing her youth and purity at death. In the nineteenth century deceased family members were commonly included in family portraits. The Latter-day Saint belief that family ties continue beyond the grave enhances the significance of the piece.*

*Although Brigham Young never lived in the palatial country estate setting depicted here, the artist has included exaggeration to show honor, as was common in British art of the nineteenth century. This was Major's way of expressing his respect for the Church President and his family. The painting, one of Major's finest, was begun in Nauvoo and completed in Salt Lake City.*

FIGURE 3: UTAH STONE IN THE WASHINGTON MONUMENT

best known is Frederick Piercy's drawing for his immigrant guidebook (PLATE 16). Later artists
would continue to celebrate with landscapes the first city's place in Utah and Latter-day Saint
history.

One of the greatest single accomplishments of the pioneer Saints was the construction of the
Salt Lake Temple. To help give the Saints a vision of what they were striving to build, Brigham
Young had William Ward, another English convert, create an architectural rendering of the
temple as it was originally conceived. An engraved print of this rendering was published in
England and inspired two generations of pioneer Saints who toiled to construct the Church's
most sacred building and its greatest visual symbol (PLATE 18).

Ward was a man of multiple talents. As an architect he designed Brigham Young's Lion House
in "English Cottage Gothic" style. As a sculptor he carved the lion that gave the home its name
(PLATE 20). As a draftsman he did much of the architectural drafting for the Salt Lake Temple.
As a stonecutter he supervised much of the stonecutting done by the Salt Lake Public Works
(FIGURE 3). The Public Works was the earliest industrial center in pioneer Utah. It was a collection of blacksmith, woodworking, and stonecutting shops manned by skilled craftsmen who were
usually recent emigrants from Europe. The Public Works provided support for the building of
the temple and other major structures and their furnishings.

PLATE 19: *Salt Lake City, Utah, Morning,*
ABOUT 1887

FREDERICK SCHAFER (1839–1927)
OIL ON CANVAS, 15" X 22" (38.1 CM X 55.4 CM)
MUSEUM OF CHURCH HISTORY AND ART

*The buildings on Temple Square, including the
nearly completed temple, and the nearby cityscape
document Salt Lake City in the late 1880s. But the
grandeur of the Wasatch Mountains in the
background show this German-born artist's interest
in spectacular landscapes. Frederick Schafer, who
left his native land and established himself in San
Francisco in 1877, was one of many itinerant
artists who painted in early Utah. These traveling
European artists were awed by the beauty of the
rugged plains and majestic mountains. Although
the city is important in this scene, the artist also
revealed the breathtaking beauty of the peaks and
vales that tower above.*

PLATE 20: *Lion House Lion,* 1855

WILLIAM W. WARD (1827–1893)
CARVED SANDSTONE, 26" X 54" X 18"
(66 CM X 137 CM X 46 CM)
LION HOUSE

*This stone lion, located on the roof of the Lion House
front porch, gave the building its name. The lion
refers to the biblical "Lion of Judah." William Ward
carved it to represent Brigham Young. The artist
was also a highly skilled architect and was involved,
along with Truman Angell, in designing the rest of
the Lion House, the Salt Lake Temple, and other
buildings in Salt Lake. Born in Leicester, England,
Ward was trained by his father in stonemasonry
when he was very young. When he was seven, he
became an apprentice architect in the English Gothic
tradition. He also spent years working with masters
in stonemasonry to hone his skills. In his later years,
Ward taught mechanical and architectural drawing
at the University of Deseret.*

PLATE 21: *Sunburst from Original*
*Salt Lake Tabernacle,* 1852
MAKER UNKNOWN
CARVED WOOD, 18" x 36" (45.7 CM X 91.4 CM)
MUSEUM OF CHURCH HISTORY AND ART

*This sunburst is reminiscent of the sunstones on the
Nauvoo Temple. In Latter-day Saint scripture the
sun is often symbolic of celestial glory—the glory of
God, of His abode, and of the highest of Latter-day
Saint aspirations. This rising sun probably
represents the restoration of the gospel of Christ as
"the dawning of a brighter day," or "the gospel light
breaking forth" eventually to fill the whole earth
with celestial glory. Carved from wood, the sunburst
looked down over the doorway on the south gable of
the first tabernacle on Temple Square. Close
examination reveals that the sunburst and
background were originally painted a bright
yellow, with rays painted orange to represent
the brilliance of a rising sun.*

PLATE 22: *Symbols of Peace and*
*Friendship,* EARLY 1900s
JOSEPH H. FISHER (1856–1940)
ENAMEL ON WOOD, 27 1/2" x 18 1/2" (70 CM X 47 CM)
MUSEUM OF CHURCH HISTORY AND ART

*These symbols of peace and friendship illustrate
the spirit of community sought for by many
Latter-day Saints. They were common symbols for
pioneer Saints. The pulpit of the Latter-day Saint
meetinghouse in Meadow, Utah, has a similar
carving. Comparable images of peace and
friendship are found in other early Latter-day
Saint art from gravestones to quilts. The folk artist
who carved this piece, probably in the early
1900s, was born in Fillmore, Utah, but traveled
around the state, from St. George to Salt Lake.
He died in Meadow, Utah.*

European emigrants provided the backbone of the skilled craftsmen in pioneer Utah. The beloved Eagle Gate monument was carved by English emigrant Ralph Ramsey, assisted by his fellow countryman and furniture maker William Bell. The actual design of the gate and its sculpture was by Hiram B. Clawson, an early convert from upstate New York. The graceful arches of the gate were crowned by a large, copper-covered wooden eagle perched atop a

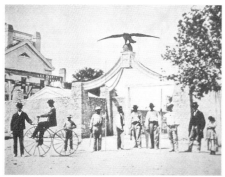

FIGURE 4: EAGLE GATE

beehive (FIGURE 4). The gate was originally the entrance to Brigham Young's farm. Ramsey also carved the beehive on Brigham Young's Beehive House and the original casing for the Salt Lake Tabernacle organ, but his major work consisted of crafting furniture.

One use of art in early Utah was to reinforce the faith of the Saints with visual images placed in their meetinghouses. Sculptures (PLATES 21 and 22) and other works (PLATE 23) appeared in chapels and tabernacles as reminders of the Church members' ideals and commitments. Other artworks, such as pottery (PLATE 24) and furniture, were more utilitarian.

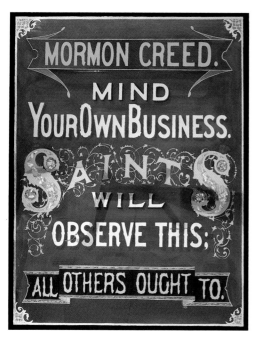

PLATE 23: **Mormon Creed,** ABOUT 1884
MAKER UNKNOWN
PAINTED AND GILDED GLASS, 36" X 28" (91.4 CM X 71.1 CM)
MUSEUM OF CHURCH HISTORY AND ART

*In 1975, this backpainted glass fixture was found stored in the Logan Temple. The phrase it illustrates was a common one among nineteenth-century Latter-day Saints. In the context of the temple it reminded the Saints not to divulge information about their sacred marriage covenants to federal officials who were in the area to prosecute polygamists. President John Taylor stated in reference to the Saints, "I tell them to keep their own secrets, and remember what is called the Mormon Creed, 'Mind your own business.'" The Americanism "mind your own business" was commonly used in New England in the early 1800s. Asael Smith, the Prophet Joseph Smith's grandfather, called it "the eleventh commandment," as did most other New Englanders. William Smith apparently was the first to publish this statement as the "Mormon Creed." He wrote in the Nauvoo Wasp: "Mormon Creed: To mind their own business, and let everybody else, do likewise. Publish this, ye Editors, who boast of equal rights and privileges." Latter-day Saints repeated the creed in various forms over the next fifty years.*

PLATE 24: **Mormon Pioneer Pottery,** ABOUT 1870
EARDLEY BROTHERS
CERAMIC, 9 1/2" X 8 1/2" (24.1 CM X 21.6 CM)
MUSEUM OF CHURCH HISTORY AND ART

*This pot was made from clay found locally, and its design emphasized function. It is attributed to the Eardley brothers, who operated potteries in several Utah communities in the late 1800s. The Eardleys' training in England helped them understand clay and types of firing before they arrived in Utah. During the colonizing of Utah, at least sixty potters set up shop in more than a dozen settlements across the territory. Most of them were immigrant converts from England and Denmark. Many Latter-day Saint potters received their training in the Potteries in Staffordshire, England, in Great Britain's fine china factories. Those factories proved inappropriate models for pioneer Utah; the high alkaline content of the Utah clay made it unsuitable for fine pottery. Thin pieces broke too easily, and the clay would not hold a sophisticated china glaze. Heavy pieces with simple glazes worked better, so the small shops of Denmark and Nauvoo became the pattern for early Utah pottery. By 1910 most people bought Mason jars, enamelware, or tinware instead of pottery, and traditional skills died out.*

PLATE 25: **Thomas Tanner Tombstone,** 1855
WILLIAM W. WARD (1827–1893)
CARVED STONE, 63" X 27" X 9" (160 CM X 68.6 CM X 22.9 CM)
MUSEUM OF CHURCH HISTORY AND ART

*Thomas Tanner served as superintendent of the Public Works blacksmith shop on Temple Square. When he died of an injury in 1855, his fellow workers took up a collection to provide a gravestone. It was carved by William Ward, who supervised the Public Works stonecutters. The gravestone depicts the tools and products of a blacksmith. The encircling chain symbolizes the links between this life and the next. The blacksmith apron is carefully laid on the anvil as a symbol of eternal rest. This is one of the finest examples of gravestone sculpture in pioneer Utah.*

## PINE FURNITURE

Latter-day Saints created a rich furniture tradition in the second half of the nineteenth century. The furniture was usually made of local pine, hand grained (painted) to look like fashionable hardwoods that were virtually unobtainable in pioneer Utah. Mormon craftsmen created furniture for homes, businesses, and Church buildings. The distinctiveness of Mormon furniture is found not so much in its style as in its religious context. A unique set of religious imperatives called the furniture into being. The tradition of Mormon pine furniture among Latter-day Saint pioneers in the West resulted directly from the Church programs of missionary work, gathering, and colonizing missions. The United Order and cooperative movement also played a part, as did the Latter-day Saint value of self-sufficiency.

Like many skilled craftsmen and artists in pioneer Utah, most of the furniture makers migrated from Great Britain and Scandinavia, where arts and crafts training was more readily available. Sought out by missionaries, these skilled workers obeyed the religious imperative to gather to Zion. Once in Utah, they were often called to help establish settlements from southeastern Idaho to northern Mexico. Church leaders made sure such towns included people with all of the skills necessary to establish a functioning community. This effort dispersed the pine furniture makers throughout the territory.

The Latter-day Saint cooperative movement and the United Order kept the pine furniture tradition going even after the completion of the railroad in 1869 brought increased competition from eastern factory-made furniture. Continued emphasis on Latter-day Saint self-reliance perpetuated the tradition even longer. All these factors resulted in a pine furniture tradition that arrived full blown from Europe, was widely dispersed, and lasted much longer than other American pine furniture traditions. Within this tradition there developed three distinctive geographical styles: the Salt Lake Public Works (which was mostly British), the Scandinavian Sanpete County, and the Brigham City United Order. In addition, general American furniture traditions of the time were expressed in Mormon pine furniture.

PLATE 28: **Drop Leaf Desk,** BEFORE 1831
BRIGHAM YOUNG (1801–1877)
CHERRYWOOD, 66 1/2" X 37" X 21 1/2"
(169 CM X 93.5 CM X 54.1 CM)
MUSEUM OF CHURCH HISTORY AND ART

*This desk was made by Brigham Young, an expert carpenter, painter, glazier, and blacksmith. He made the desk while he operated a carpenter shop and forge in Mendon, New York, a small town near Palmyra. In 1832, after reading the Book of Mormon, Brigham went with his neighbor Heber C. Kimball to Kirtland, Ohio, to meet Joseph Smith. They both joined the Church. Brigham Young never went back to his shop in New York, but he occasionally made fine furniture in Kirtland and later in Nauvoo. There are no known pieces of furniture made by President Young after 1847, but he continued to promote fine craftsmanship for temples, tabernacles, public buildings, and homes. He designed much of the furniture that others made for him. Brigham Young was also one of the biggest promoters and supporters of early Latter-day Saint artisans and home-produced work.*

PLATE 29: **Brigham Young's Desk,** 1850s
WILLIAM BELL (1816–1886)
AND SALT LAKE PUBLIC WORKS
POLYCHROME WOOD, 88" X 56" X 28 1/2"
(223.5 CM X 142.2 CM X 72.4 CM)
MUSEUM OF CHURCH HISTORY AND ART

*This is one of Bell's finest pieces of furniture. Made mostly of pine, it is grained to resemble mahogany, which was fashionable in Great Britain when Bell emigrated. The paint is applied to resemble even the direction of the wood grain of the mahogany veneers that would have been applied in London. The only actual mahogany in this piece is applied as a veneer around the writing surface. The desk was designed to be functional, with many shelves and drawers and several hidden compartments. Bell received his training as a furniture maker in London before joining the Church, immigrating to Utah, and becoming Brigham Young's family furniture maker. The shallow applied arch motifs became almost a signature for Bell's finest pieces.*

PLATE 30: **Washstand,** ABOUT 1863
WILLIAM BELL (1816–1886)
AND SALT LAKE PUBLIC WORKS
POLYCHROME WOOD, 35" X 31" X 18"
(89.4 CM X 78.1 CM X 46.3 CM)
BEEHIVE HOUSE

*This washstand, made in the Country Empire style,
was constructed of softwood painted to simulate
marble and walnut. In 1863 William Bell
submitted an invoice to Brigham Young for $18 for
six identical cupboard washstands that had doors,
columns, and a drawer. President Young purchased
the washstands for the private use of his large
family. William Bell had learned furniture making
from his father. He arrived in Utah in 1854 and
worked with the Public Works shop for fifteen
years. Bell's Country Empire style chairs were
renowned for their durability and fine finish.*

PLATE 31: **Detail from Salt Lake Tabernacle
Organ Case,** 1869
RALPH RAMSEY (? -1905)
UTAH PINE, ENTIRE ORIGINAL, 240" X 360" X 480"
(609.6 CM X 914.4 CM X 1,219.2 CM)
SALT LAKE TABERNACLE

*The organ case in the Salt Lake Mormon Tabernacle
was made of Utah pine painted and varnished to its
present "faux oak" appearance. The case is patterned
after the Boston Music Hall case for the Walcker
organ that was seen by Joseph Ridges, the Tabernacle
organ builder, and shown in Harper's Weekly in
1863. The Salt Lake organ case is more stylistic and
less ornate in design than the Boston case. There
were plans for Ramsey to carve ornate panels for the
lower half of the case, but for some reason this was
never done. In 1916, the organ was updated for a
second time and the case was expanded to encase
more pipes. The character, design, and materials of
the original were carried into the addition. Ramsey
spent most of his life working in wood. Originally
from the village of Leddlesfell, England, Ramsey
learned to carve at Newcastle-on-Tyne. The artist
came as a Latter-day Saint to Utah in 1856. He
carved wherever he went as he settled new areas
with other Saints. Ramsey died in the LDS settlement
of Snowflake, Arizona, in 1905.*

PLATE 32: **Cupboard,** ABOUT 1885
MAKER UNKNOWN
POLYCHROME WOOD, 86" X 49 1/2" X 20"
(218.4 CM X 125.7 CM X 50.8 CM)
MUSEUM OF CHURCH HISTORY AND ART

*This hand-grained cupboard from Malad, Idaho,
was painted with green base, then covered with
brown using a brush designed to give a more
fashionable oak-grain appearance to the wood. The
upper panels were painted to simulate white oak.
The design elements are Eastlake. This style of
furniture was common from the 1870s to the 1890s
after the transcontinental railroad was completed.
The fact that pine furniture continued to be made
when imported hardwood furniture was available
attests to the resilience of the ideas of home
manufacture and self-reliance in the Intermountain
West. When the pioneers settled Utah, the most
readily available wood was pine. Fashionable
hardwoods were commonly imitated by even the
wealthiest in the East and Europe. Pioneer
craftsmen followed that tradition. Although some of
those who handgrained the wood were trained
artists, the talent was widespread and used by
artisans with a wide range of abilities.*

PLATE 33: **Mormon Couch,** ABOUT 1875
CARL UCKERMAN (1842–1914)
POLYCHROME WOOD, 36" X 84" X 24"
(91.4 CM X 213.4 CM X 61CM)
MUSEUM OF CHURCH HISTORY AND ART

*This couch is attributed to Carl Uckerman of Ephraim, Utah. It was made of Utah pine painted to look like mahogany. The gold edging is decorative paint. The carving in the back of the couch has a grape leaf with various seed casings in front of it, including a pine cone and chokecherries. Of all the pine furniture made in early pioneer Utah, the Mormon couch is among the more distinctive because of its widespread use by Latter-day Saints. The couch served not only as a place to sit but also as a bed. It was occasionally known as a "Bishop's Couch" because it was popular with bishops who needed an extra bed when a guest was staying over. The front half of the couch and half of the wooden slats were often made to slide out, forming a double bed.*

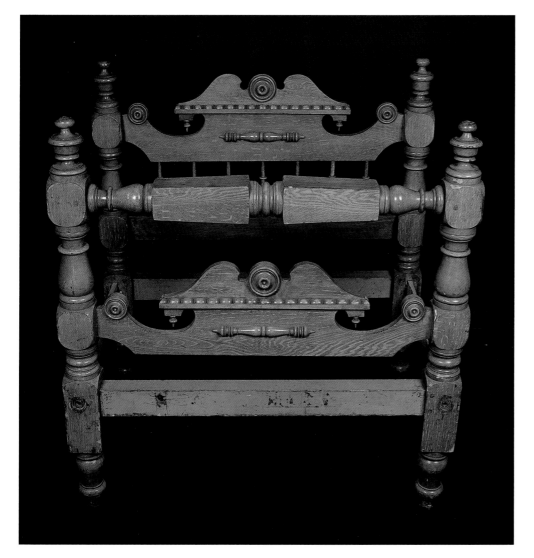

PLATE 34: **Mormon Pine Bedstead,** 1877
MAKER UNKNOWN
POLYCHROME PINE, 55 1/2" X 60" (141 CM X 152.4 CM)
MUSEUM OF CHURCH HISTORY AND ART
GIFT OF IRWIN CLAWSON

*This massive bed has superbly crafted turnings as well as a finely done polychrome finish of hand graining that replicates quarter-sawn oak. The headboard has an elaborately scrolled crest, and the footboard has a large turned rail over which extra quilts could be draped.*

## THE BRITISH ROMANTIC LANDSCAPE TRADITION IN PIONEER UTAH

Many of the early British converts to the Church came from the industrial cities and coal mining towns of the British Isles, environments like those described by Charles Dickens in such books as *Oliver Twist* and *David Copperfield.* They yearned for clean air, pure water, more open spaces, and better food. Those yearnings in Victorian England gave rise to English Romanticism, which celebrated the ideals with landscape painting and nature poetry. Many of the British Saints brought these ideas with them to pioneer Utah, where they gave them a particular Latter-day Saint perspective.

The literary and artistic works of these early British Saints gave voice to a union of English Romanticism and the gospel. For example, many hymns that speak of the mountains, such as "O Ye Mountains High" by Charles Penrose, were written by British converts. Almost all of the pure landscapes painted by the first generation of Mormon pioneers in Utah were done by British Saints. For these artists, the mountains, waterfalls, vast sunsets, and broad valleys of Utah symbolized purity, the majesty of God as seen through the vastness of his creations, the protection of Zion from the forces of "Babylon," and the literal fulfillment of Isaiah's prophecy that in the last days "the mountain of the Lord's house shall be established in the top of the mountains, . . . and

FIGURE 5: ALFRED LAMBOURNE

all nations shall flow unto it" (Isaiah 2:2).

Alfred Lambourne (1850–1926) (FIGURE 5), a leading exponent of this dramatic style, created his finest paintings, *Adam-ondi-Ahman* (PLATE 35) and *Hill Cumorah* (PLATE 36), for the Salt Lake Temple. For Lambourne, the beginning and ending of human life on this planet both take place in a garden, and the restoration of the gospel in this dispensation is also celebrated through a landscape. Lambourne enhances the drama of nature by artistic exaggeration; this is done to show the importance of the event and the power and majesty of the Lord as expressed in the natural world. Other leading Latter-day Saint artists of this tradition were John Tullidge (1837–1899) (FIGURE 6), Reuben Kirkham (1844–1886), H. L. A. Culmer (1854–1914) (FIGURE 7), and George Beard (1855–1944) (FIGURE 8). All these artists were born in England and migrated to Utah in the nineteenth century.

FIGURE 6: JOHN TULLIDGE    FIGURE 7: H. L. A. CULMER    FIGURE 8: GEORGE BEARD

PLATE 35: *Adam-ondi-Ahman,* 1893

ALFRED LAMBOURNE (1850–1926)
OIL ON CANVAS, 35" x 74" (88.9 CM x 188 CM)
MUSEUM OF CHURCH HISTORY AND ART

*Adam-ondi-Ahman was settled by the Saints during the late 1830s and then abandoned in the expulsion from Missouri. Lambourne enhances the geographic setting of this site to suggest its prophetic role as "the place where Adam shall come to visit his people" (D&C 116). Lambourne's works are often classified as prime examples of the Rocky Mountain School. That ignores the English roots of this British convert, who expressed his religious reverence for nature in his paintings and in fourteen books of essays, poetry, and history. All of his work as an immigrant in pioneer Utah reflects his immersion in English culture. This painting and the companion work of the Hill Cumorah were commissioned to hang in the newly completed Salt Lake Temple. Lambourne created two pairs of these scenes. One pair still hangs in the temple; the other is in the Museum collection.*

PLATE 36: *Hill Cumorah,* 1893

ALFRED LAMBOURNE (1850–1926)
OIL ON CANVAS, 35" x 74" (88.9 CM x 188 CM)
MUSEUM OF CHURCH HISTORY AND ART

*The Hill Cumorah is a familiar metaphor to Latter-day Saints, and one of the most sacred sites in Mormon history. In this emotionally charged portrayal the rising sun of the gospel's restoration dispels the dark night of religious error. By dramatically increasing the Hill Cumorah's elevation, Lambourne helps the viewer feel the spiritual stature of this place where the Angel Moroni delivered the ancient text of the Book of Mormon to Joseph Smith. At the age of ten, Lambourne emigrated with his family from Berkshire, England, to America. Although primarily self-taught, he took lessons from several teachers in Salt Lake City and painted scenery for the Salt Lake Theater.*

PLATE 37: **Logan, Utah,** 1892
CHRISTIAN EISELE (1847–1917)
OIL ON CANVAS, 25 1/4" x 83" (64.1 CM x 210.8 CM)
MUSEUM OF CHURCH HISTORY AND ART

*Christian Eisele's panoramic view of Logan, Utah, reveals that
Logan followed the pattern set forth by Joseph Smith in his original
plan for the "City of Zion" with religious buildings at the center.
Around the tabernacle and the city center are the homes and
gardens, with the farming area farther out. Eisele, an itinerant
painter from Essling, Germany, traveled to many states, but he and
his wife lived in Utah between 1887 and 1900. This panorama of
Logan hung in the council room in the Salt Lake Temple and later
in the Logan Temple.*

PLATE 38: **Temple Square at Sunset,
Looking Northwest,** 1892
CHRISTIAN EISELE (1847–1917)
OIL ON CANVAS, 20" x 44" (50.8 CM x 111.8 CM)
MUSEUM OF CHURCH HISTORY AND ART
GIFT OF NORMAN FALDMO SR. FAMILY

*This painting represents Temple Square as it was in 1892 just
after the capstone of the Salt Lake Temple was laid. The temple,
tabernacle, and Assembly Hall delineate the faith, determination,
commitment, and artistry of those early settlers of the wilderness
as they made the desert "blossom as the rose." Eisele has
captured the heightened mood of this sacred place by silhouetting
the uplifted spires against a magnificent Utah sunset above the
Great Salt Lake. The painting's visual impact reaffirms that here
indeed is "the mountain of the Lord's house."*

PLATE 40: *American Fork Canyon,* 1882
JOHN TULLIDGE (1837–1899)
OIL ON CANVAS, 40 3/4" X 26 1/2"
(103.5 CM X 67.3 CM)
MUSEUM OF CHURCH HISTORY AND ART
GIFT OF GARY SWENSEN

*In the mountains and canyons of Zion, British convert immigrants found symbols of the Lord's power protecting the Saints from physical and spiritual harm. This painting relies on massive imagery and dramatic counterpoint of light and dark. Tullidge's childhood days in Weymouth, England, shaped his love for the sea and sensitivity to the grandeur of nature. Although he had little formal art education, he had natural talent that drew from traditions of English Romanticism. After his family immigrated to Utah, Tullidge, who was already skilled in decorative painting, became a successful businessman.*

PLATE 39: *Canyon Landscape,* 1885
REUBEN KIRKHAM (1844–1886)
OIL ON CANVAS, 20" X 15" (50.8 CM X 38.1 CM)
MUSEUM OF CHURCH HISTORY AND ART

*This scene, probably done in Logan, Utah, where Kirkham settled, reflects the artist's ardent love of the sublime and picturesque in nature. Kirkham invites the viewer to feel the power of the Lord in the energy and movement of nature. A native of Lancashire, England, Kirkham immigrated to Utah in 1866. With no formal training, he began his art career as a scenery painter for the Salt Lake Theater before finally settling in Logan. A close friend of Alfred Lambourne, Kirkham collaborated with him in painting and touring with the "American Landscape" panorama. He also produced a very popular panorama of nineteen Book of Mormon scenes, which he exhibited throughout the territory.*

PLATE 41: **Shoshone Falls,** ABOUT 1900
HENRY LAVENDER ADOLPHUS CULMER (1854–1914)
OIL ON CANVAS, 15" X 30" (38.1 CM X 76.2 CM)
MUSEUM OF CHURCH HISTORY AND ART
GIFT OF WILLIAM HURST

*In this painting, Culmer depicts the largest natural
falls in the Intermountain West, located on the Snake
River near Twin Falls, Idaho. Shoshone Falls was a
favorite subject of many western artists. Culmer
brought out the grandeur of moving water, a frequent
metaphor for God's vastness and power. After
gathering with the Saints to Utah from his native Kent,
England, Culmer became a successful businessman and
newspaper publisher in Salt Lake City. Largely self-
taught, he became an artist later in life, and his works
reflect greater realism and less exaggeration than those
of his romantic-landscape contemporaries. Culmer
chose dramatic scenes like Shoshone Falls, allowing the
subject to convey the sublime.*

PLATE 42: **Black Rock, Great Salt Lake,** 1910
H. L. A. CULMER (1854–1914), OIL ON CANVAS, 30" X 96" (76.2 CM X 243.8 CM), MUSEUM OF CHURCH HISTORY AND ART

*The early Latter-day Saints found many parallels between the Utah landscape and that of Palestine, often comparing the Great Salt
Lake to the Dead Sea. From pioneer times artists have been drawn to the Black Rock landmark on the southeast end of the Great
Salt Lake. Nineteenth-century immigrant artists Alfred Lambourne, John Tullidge, and others romanticized their renditions of the
site, but Culmer, another English-born artist, has not exaggerated the height of the rock formation. The pale tonalities he used
convey the nature of the arid landscape. Culmer was a prominent businessman in the Salt Lake Valley with art as an avocation.
Largely self-taught, he traveled through the Wasatch Mountains with his artist friends in search of grandiose vistas to portray. He
had become acquainted with another English-born artist, Thomas Moran, and like him produced enormous landscape paintings for
wealthy citizens and public places. Toward the end of his life his style was more influenced by plein-air artwork, as in this piece.*

PLATE 43: **Reid's Peak and Baldy on
Grandaddy Lake Trail,** 1925
GEORGE BEARD (1855–1944)
OIL ON CANVAS, 40" X 65" (101.6 CM X 165.1 CM)
MUSEUM OF CHURCH HISTORY AND ART
GIFT OF LEGRAND RICHARDS

*In this scene from the Uinta Mountains of northern Utah,
Beard gives the viewer a wide-angle view of spectacular
scenery. The setting is uninhabited, as if the viewer has come
alone upon a sacred place. By contrasting the exaggerated
height of the mountains with the calm of the lake, Beard
communicates his passion for the sublime grandeur of a scene
unmarred by the presence of man. Beard grew up near
Sherwood Forest in England, where he loved to hike. He was
encouraged to sketch and paint from early childhood and
enjoyed landscape paintings displayed in art galleries in
Manchester. In 1868, his family immigrated as converts to
Utah and settled in Coalville. His mountain home provided
subjects to paint and photograph, and he also enjoyed camping
and exploring. While on his jaunts he gave names to some of
the Uinta sites, including Grandaddy Lake in this painting.
Although he lived until 1944, Beard always retained his
preference for romantic landscapes of the previous century.
"My idea of Art," he wrote, "is the picture which, when you
study it, produces a feeling which can be felt but not described."*

FIGURE 9: CARL CHRISTIAN
ANTON CHRISTENSEN

FIGURE 10: DANQUART
ANTON WEGGELAND

PLATE 44: *Bountiful Tabernacle Mural,* 1863
DANQUART A. WEGGELAND (1827–1918)
OIL TEMPERA ON PLASTER, 141" x 128"
(360 CM x 330 CM)
MUSEUM OF CHURCH HISTORY AND ART

*Brigham Young commissioned Weggeland to paint this mural of Joseph Smith for the new tabernacle in Bountiful. It depicts the bust of Joseph Smith looking out a window, symbolically viewing the new Zion that he had seen in vision. Various symbols depict the sacredness of the building, the doctrines that Joseph taught, and Joseph's role as translator of the Book of Mormon. Weggeland painted the mural in a "grisaille" style, using hues of gray to create the illusion of three-dimensional sculpture. He painted the wooden columns and plaster arch framing the piece to look like marble.*

## THE SCANDINAVIANS PAINT HISTORY AND DAILY LIFE IN PIONEER UTAH

The Scandinavian converts who left for Utah in the nineteenth century carried with them a profound respect for the nobility of the common man. They also saw the sweep of Latter-day Saint history in epic terms. They avoided painting vast, empty panoramas of nature and concentrated on painting scenes that documented the historical events of the Church and the colonization of the Mormon West.

Carl Christian Anton Christensen (1831–1912) (FIGURE 9) from Denmark and Danquart Anton Weggeland (1827–1918) (FIGURE 10) from Norway stand out as the main artists in this tradition. Both painted important scenes from early Church history, frequently after talking with eyewitnesses to the events. They also documented the epic trek across the plains and pioneer homesteading in Utah. Christensen's "Mormon Panorama" (PLATE 50) and other smaller studies of early Church history (PLATES 48, 49, AND 51) illustrate his dictum that "history will preserve much, but art alone can make the narration of the suffering of the Saints comprehensible for the following generation."

PLATE 45: *Handcart Pioneers,* 1908
DANQUART A. WEGGELAND (1827–1918)
OIL ON CANVAS, 32" x 41" (81.3 CM x 104.1 CM)
MUSEUM OF CHURCH HISTORY AND ART

*Most Latter-day Saints gathering to the Mountain West before 1869 joined Church-sponsored wagon trains. Leaders proposed handcart immigration as a fast and inexpensive method to transport Saints of modest means from Britain and Scandinavia to Utah. Emigrants joined handcart companies between 1856 and 1860, and used carts sporadically after that. Weggeland, himself a Norwegian emigrant of 1862, shows the European composition of the companies through the people's clothing. He depicts the pioneers participating in a variety of activities drawn from different times of the day, such as gathering wood, cooking, and marching. The American flag carried in the distance illustrates their enthusiasm for their new homeland.*

PLATE 46: **Joseph Smith Preaching to the Indians,** 1890

WILLIAM ARMITAGE (1817–1890)
OIL ON CANVAS, 120" X 192" (304.8 CM X 487.7 CM)
MUSEUM OF CHURCH HISTORY AND ART

In this painting the Prophet Joseph Smith, holding in his hand the Book of Mormon, is explaining to Native Americans the story of their ancestry and the promises made by the Lord to their people as related in that book. More than one hundred Sac and Fox Indians visited in Nauvoo on August 12, 1841. This painting was probably inspired by that visit, although the Prophet and other Church members met many times with local Indians. The Utah artist's portrayal of the Native Americans listening attentively to Joseph Smith's message follows the European custom of the day to romanticize the Indians. Also, with the mountains in the background, the artist has transformed a midwestern setting to one of the Rocky Mountains. Armitage's classical and well-drawn figures show the academic training he received at the Royal Academy of Arts in London. This, Armitage's best known painting, was commissioned by the Church for the Salt Lake Temple. It hung there with his Christ Appears to the Nephites for more than fifty years.

PLATE 47: **Christ Appears to the Nephites,** 1890

WILLIAM ARMITAGE (1817–1890)
OIL ON CANVAS, 142" X 213" (360.7 CM X 541 CM)
SALT LAKE TEMPLE
COURTESY CHURCH ARCHIVES

This early photograph of a hallway inside the Salt Lake Temple shows the magnificent dimensions of Armitage's artwork, hanging on the right-hand side. The huge painting depicts Christ's visit to his "other sheep . . . which are not of this fold" mentioned in John 10:16. Christ's appearance to the Nephites on the American continent after his resurrection elicited awe and reverence, as shown in the faces and body language of both the Nephites and the heavenly beings accompanying the Lord. The rich coloring of the Nephites and the subtle softness of the attending angels in the background show the coming together of heaven and earth. The color sense, atmospheric perspective, and classic figures portrayed show Armitage's European academic training. Although he was converted to the Church in 1853, he did not arrive in Utah until 1881.

PLATE 49: *Handcart Pioneers,* 1900
PLATE 49: *Handcart Pioneers,* 1900
C. C. A. CHRISTENSEN (1831–1912)
OIL ON CANVAS, 24" X 37" (61 CM X 93.9 CM)
MUSEUM OF CHURCH HISTORY AND ART

*To ensure that the courageous spirit of the Mormon
pioneers would be remembered, this master
storyteller in art recorded on canvas his own 1857
honeymoon trek with a handcart company on its
way to the Salt Lake Valley. It is a valued
documentary of the personalities, places, and
varied activities of these faithful, committed
pioneers. Compelled by an ardent desire to join
other Saints in the valley, they loaded their bare
essentials on small, two-wheeled carts that they
would push by hand the 1,300 miles from Iowa
instead of waiting until they could afford wagons
and oxen. Christensen's interesting details and
separate activities blend to make a complete picture
of this experience. Although the figures' anatomy
may seem primitive, Christensen's use of color and
composition show his native talent and his
academic training at the Royal Academy of
Art in Copenhagen, where he studied before his
conversion to Mormonism. As artist, poet,
journalist, historian, and missionary throughout
his life, Christensen expressed his zeal and love
for the gospel with his gifts of art and writing.*

PLATE 48: *Sugar Creek,* ABOUT 1885
CARL CHRISTIAN ANTON CHRISTENSEN (1831–1912), OIL ON CANVAS, 14 1/8" X 22 1/8" (35.8 CM X 56.1 CM)
MUSEUM OF CHURCH HISTORY AND ART, GIFT OF ETHEL T. CHRISTENSEN

*In February 1846, Latter-day Saints began their hasty departure from Nauvoo and shortly afterward camped nine miles
away in Iowa at Sugar Creek. Christensen sets the mood by painting a menacing landscape bare of everything but trees and
snow. The long shadows add to the feeling of urgency as the exiled Saints hurry to get over the icy creek before nightfall.*

PLATE 50: *Crossing the Mississippi on the Ice,* AFTER 1878

C. C. A. CHRISTENSEN (1831–1912)
TEMPERA ON CANVAS, 78" X 117" (198.1 CM X 297.2 CM)
MUSEUM OF ART, BRIGHAM YOUNG UNIVERSITY

*As persecution increased in Nauvoo, Latter-day Saints made
plans to move west. Church leaders decided to move in winter
and not wait until spring. Many thousands of Saints joined
the premature departure, often without adequate
preparations. By late February 1846 it was so cold that teams
and wagons could cross the frozen Mississippi. In this scene
from his "Mormon Panorama," Christensen gives a sense of
epoch drama to the event by depicting an endless line of
wagons and an expansive sheet of frozen ice. The newly
finished temple clearly visible in the distance is a dramatic
symbol of Nauvoo and all that the Saints left behind. The boy
pulling a load on his sled represents the sacrifice of play and
comfort as the Saints leave their homes.*

PLATE 51: *Missionaries Preaching in Denmark,* 1903

C. C. A. CHRISTENSEN (1831–1912)
OIL ON CANVAS, 6 1/2" x 9 1/2" (16.5 CM X 24.1 CM)
MUSEUM OF CHURCH HISTORY AND ART

*This scene of Christensen's native Denmark shows two
missionaries—one waiting by the road while the other talks to
a woman. The importance of the message they bring is
suggested by the nest with two storks on top of the farmhouse,
believed to be a sign of new life and good fortune.
Christensen's studies at the Royal Academy in Copenhagen
focused on realistic landscapes and people at their everyday
tasks. His art typically reinforces the faith, history, and
cultural identity of the Saints. Christensen created this
painting while helping to compile a history of the
Scandinavian mission. It documents an event from the first
four missions he served in his native Scandinavia.*

PLATE 52: **Second Day of Creation**, ABOUT 1886
C. C. A. CHRISTENSEN (1831–1912)
OIL ON CANVAS, 11 3/4" x 13" (29.8 CM x 33 CM)
MUSEUM OF CHURCH HISTORY AND ART
GIFT OF JOSEPH AND EDNA BEARD

*This sketch depicts the second day of creation described in Genesis 1:6–8. Christensen made a series of sketches before painting the interior walls of the Manti Temple. He shows the creation as an active process with a volcano creating a mountain out of the sea.*

PLATE 53: **Manti Temple**, 1889
C. C. A. CHRISTENSEN (1831–1912)
OIL ON CANVAS, 54 1/4" x 72 3/8" (138.5 CM x 183.5 CM)
MANTI TEMPLE

*This painting of the Manti Temple, commissioned by the Sanpete Stake Relief Society, was submitted to the 1893 World Columbian Exposition in Chicago. Earlier, Christensen completed murals on the walls inside the Manti Temple creation room and painted the exterior roof. This is the finest example of Christensen's ability to use perspective and render architecture. Someone later painted over the foreground terraces in green to reflect the large hill of lawn that replaced the terracing. The terraces and figures in the original painting were discovered and uncovered during conservation in 1983.*

The best way to understand the differences between the contributions made by British and Scandinavian artists in pioneer Utah is to compare the work of Scandinavian artists C. C. A. Christensen and Dan Weggeland with that of British artists Alfred Lambourne and William Major.

Christensen and Lambourne both painted large paintings for temples. Christensen's paintings for the Manti Temple show what Manti's temple hill looked like when the first pioneers arrived and what it looked like when the temple was completed (PLATE 53). For Christensen, the millennial imperative was literally to build Zion. That is why he and other Scandinavian Latter-day Saint artists documented the pioneering labors of the early Saints. Lambourne's paintings for the Salt Lake Temple show two scenes from nature, both devoid of people. One is the *Hill Cumorah* (PLATE 36) with the sun breaking through the clouds representing the gospel breaking through the clouds of error. The other shows *Adam-ondi-Ahman*, where Adam called his posterity together just before his death, also a prophesied site of future millennial events (PLATE 35). For Christensen, Zion and the New Jerusalem would be built through the toil and sweat of the Saints. The physical labor as pioneers was part of that process. For Lambourne, Zion was the return to the purity of Eden.

The setting for William Major's masterpiece, *Brigham and Mary Ann Angell Young and Their Children* (PLATE 15), is a fanciful scene reminiscent of the country estate of a member of the British House of Lords. In England, granting a noble title along with a grand estate was a symbol of respect and appreciation for a great act of service. Major visually rewards President Brigham Young in this impressive but totally imaginary setting.

PLATE 54: **Brigham Young's Backyard,** 1915
DANQUART A. WEGGELAND (1827–1918)
OIL ON CANVAS, 20" x 30" (50.8 CM X 76.2 CM)
MUSEUM OF CHURCH HISTORY AND ART

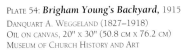

*This painting depicts Brigham Young's Salt Lake property as one looks south through his yard. The original version of the work dates from 1868; this copy was made thirty-eight years after President Young's death and after the rural appearance of this property in the heart of Salt Lake City had disappeared. With this painting, Dan Weggeland reflects his Scandinavian art training as he explores the shared activities of everyday life rather than the symbols of wealth or power. By depicting the backyard, the artist emphasizes the social closeness between Brigham Young and his fellow Saints. Eagle Gate, spanning State Street, marks the entrance to the property. To the left of the gate is the schoolhouse and to the right is the Beehive House. These become the background to the daily life of the farm yard.*

The family portrait by the English artist increased the distance between Brigham Young and the Saints in order to express respect. In contrast, the Scandinavian Dan Weggeland's painting *Brigham Young's Backyard* (PLATE 54) narrowed the distance in order to express approachability and affection. Weggeland emphasized facilities and possessions such as barns, ditches, haystacks, horses, and chickens that Brigham Young had in common with his fellow Saints.

PLATE 55: *Ice Skaters,* 1870
DANQUART A. WEGGELAND (1827–1918)
OIL ON CANVAS, 22" X 30" (55.9 CM X 76.2 CM)
MUSEUM OF CHURCH HISTORY AND ART

*This scene depicts a winter day at the corner of Fourth East and Sixth South near the artist's home in Salt Lake City. The painting develops a theme of a cross-section of the community having fun through recreation. Individuals and couples are enjoying skating and sleigh riding together. Some have considerable skill and others are just learning. Differences in wealth and age become irrelevant. The small cabin is a reminder of previous difficult times. The family has built a comfortable, two-story adobe structure next to their earlier home. The abstract figures at the left of this picture had been damaged by extensive overpainting. Rather than attempt to reconstruct them, the conservator removed the overpainting and left them as they appear here.*

PLATE 56: *Pelican Point—Utah Lake,* ABOUT 1916
DANQUART A. WEGGELAND (1827–1918)
OIL ON CANVAS, 14" X 22" (35.6 CM X 56 CM)
MUSEUM OF CHURCH HISTORY AND ART

*The homestead depicted in this painting belonged to the Holmstead family, friends and fellow Scandinavians of the artist. Weggeland painted the site several times. The family raised sheep and cattle and ran a part-time commercial fishing enterprise, sending trout and bass to Salt Lake from this spot near Lehi, Utah.*

PLATE 57: ***Bishop P. Madsen's Residence in Provo***, 1912

DANQUART A. WEGGELAND (1827–1918)
OIL ON BOARD, 12" x 18" (30.5 CM X 45.7 CM)
MUSEUM OF CHURCH HISTORY AND ART

*At Bishop Peter Madsen's home in Provo, Scandinavian Latter-day Saints held annual reunions during the late 1800s. The child walking away from the house is wearing a red hat with a white cross in the center representing the flag of Denmark. Feelings of unity and common heritage were strong among Latter-day Saints from Scandinavia. This painting, done when the artist was eighty-five years old, reflected on events that occurred in decades past.*

PLATE 58: *Peasant Girl in a Blue Jumper*, 1852
PLATE 59: *Old Man with Top Hat
and Walking Stick*, 1852
DANQUART A. WEGGELAND (1827–1918)
WATERCOLOR ON PAPER, BOTH 11 3/4" X 6"
(29.8 CM X 15.2 CM)
MUSEUM OF CHURCH HISTORY AND ART

*These portraits were completed by Weggeland in
the Hardanger region of Norway as part of a
Norwegian government project to document folk
costumes. Weggeland often depicted scenes of
common life focusing on recreation and labor. This
was part of the Scandinavian art tradition in which
he was trained. Norwegian by birth, Weggeland
was trained at the Royal Academy in Copenhagen,
Denmark. When he became a Latter-day Saint in
1855, he used his training to depict scenes related
to his new religious heritage. Weggeland has been
called the "father of Utah art" because of his great
artistic output and his influence as a teacher and
mentor to many later artists. Among the several
major pioneer artists in Utah, he alone derived his
income solely from his artistic production.*

PLATE 60: *Alice Melvina Rice Crookston,* 1883
DANQUART A. WEGGELAND (1827–1918)
OIL ON CANVAS, 34" X 28" (86.4 CM X 71.1 CM)
MUSEUM OF CHURCH HISTORY AND ART
GIFT IN THE NAME OF DEAN F. PETERSON

*This portrait shows Alice Crookston in her blue
wedding dress soon after her marriage. At the time,
Weggeland was staying with the Crookston family
while he painted murals for the Logan Temple. In
exchange for the portrait, Weggeland received
meals and lodging. The artist carefully depicts the
fine fabric of Alice's dress to give it a lifelike
quality. In terms of finish and detail, this is one of
Weggeland's finest portraits.*

FIGURE 11: GEORGE OTTINGER

George Ottinger (FIGURE 11) was the only major painter in pioneer Utah who was actually born in America. Like the pine furniture tradition, the early Latter-day Saint artistic tradition in Utah was almost totally dependent on European convert emigrants. Ottinger painted his portrait masterpiece of Brigham Young (PLATE 61) after a non-LDS artist from the eastern states came through Salt Lake City and received many portrait commissions. Ottinger set out to show that high-quality portraiture was available from local Latter-day Saint artists. Ottinger's historical masterpiece depicts the march of the Mormon Battalion in the deserts of the Southwest (PLATE 62). But perhaps Ottinger's most significant historical works were a series of small oil paintings done while he was actually crossing the plains in a covered wagon (PLATE 63). These little jewels are primary visual documents that depict the experiences of thousands of Latter-day Saint pioneers in their epic trek to Zion.

Like most artists in pioneer Utah, Ottinger struggled to make a living. He painted scenery in the Church's Salt Lake Theater, served as fire chief of Salt Lake City's volunteer fire department, and taught art lessons. Other early artists did a lot of "hand graining" of furniture and woodwork. Some, like C.C.A. Christensen, spent most of their time farming.

PLATE 61: **Brigham Young,** 1872
GEORGE M. OTTINGER (1833–1917)
OIL ON CANVAS, 30" X 25" (76.2 CM X 63.5 CM)
MUSEUM OF CHURCH HISTORY AND ART

*This painting of Brigham Young was done five years before the Church leader's death. The artist paid great attention to detail and accuracy in capturing the likeness of the prophet. After Brigham Young's death, Ottinger made a death mask and a cast of the President's hand to preserve an exact likeness for later reference. This is one of the finest portraits done by a Latter-day Saint artist in the pioneer period. Faced with competition from itinerant artists from the large cities of the East, Ottinger was attempting to prove that local artists could provide high-quality portraiture. It is perhaps fitting that one of America's most prominent religious leaders was painted by George Ottinger, the only prominent Latter-day Saint artist working at the time who had been born in America.*

PLATE 62: *The Mormon Battalion,* 1881
GEORGE M. OTTINGER (1833–1917)
OIL ON CANVAS, 33" X 65" (83.8 CM X 165.1 CM)
MUSEUM OF CHURCH HISTORY AND ART

*This painting depicts the Mormon Battalion arriving at Carrizo Creek in southeastern California. The battalion consisted of about five hundred Latter-day Saint volunteers. They were recruited by the U.S. government in 1846 to march from Fort Leavenworth, Kansas, to San Diego, California, in one of the longest infantry marches in recorded history. Although they never fought in the war with Mexico, they suffered extreme conditions of travel made worse by periods without adequate food, water, and other supplies. In this painting Ottinger captures that suffering, along with the rejoicing of battalion members at a creek after a particularly long waterless stretch of the march through the deserts of the Southwest. Ottinger won a silver medal for this work in the art competition at the 1881 territorial fair. He sold the painting to the Church for use in the Gardo House, the residence of President John Taylor.*

PLATE 63: *Chimney Rock, August 3, 1861,* 1861
GEORGE M. OTTINGER (1833–1917)
OIL ON CANVAS, 6 1/4" X 13" (15.9 CM X 33 CM)
MUSEUM OF CHURCH HISTORY AND ART

*George Ottinger traveled to Utah with his mother in 1861. This sketch was painted as the immigrant company passed Chimney Rock, the halfway landmark point on the Mormon trail. Ottinger's journal records: "I determined to start off in the morning, at daylight, to get a sketch of the Rock. I walked until nearly half past ten o'clock . . . at length I got near enough to the Rock to make a sketch. . . . After painting a sketch of the Rock, I caught up with the [wagon] train, only after it had gotten into camp that evening. We marched some seventeen miles that day." The artist captured the camp in the evening as the last rays of light still linger. Ottinger studied art at the Pennsylvania Academy of Fine Arts. In 1863, he became president of the short-lived Deseret Academy of Fine Arts, the first art school in the West.*

*This quilt was given to Bishop Elijah F. Sheets by the Salt Lake Eighth Ward Relief Society. Sheets served as a Latter-day Saint bishop for fifty years—longer than any other known person. The entire Relief Society helped make the quilt midway through his term of service. The center of the quilt features a beehive surrounded by bees—powerful symbols of community and industry. Above the hive is the all-seeing eye of God. Beneath the hive, the letters F.R.S. stand for Female Relief Society.*

PLATE 65: *Star of Bethlehem,* 1880

*Star pattern variations are common in quilting. The vibrant colors combined with the octagonal shape and eight-pointed star in this quilt create an illusion that the quilt is round instead of square. The makers used over three thousand pieces of diamond-shaped calico cotton to create this colorful, dynamic design. This quilt was made by patients at a Salt Lake City hospital for the mentally ill, operated by Dr. Seymour Bicknell Young. Dr. Young had purchased the hospital a few years after his graduation in 1874 from the College of Physicians and Surgeons of New York City. He brought back to Utah an advanced approach to the care of the mentally ill and incorporated in his treament occupational therapy such as gardening and needlework.*

## TEXTILE ARTS IN PIONEER UTAH

For women and girls, the textile arts in pioneer Utah offered a means of artistic expression. Textiles flourished in five main types: quilts, clothing, samplers, banners, and hair wreaths.

The most distinctive Latter-day Saint quilts celebrated important religious events. Among these were bishops quilts. These were made by a ward Relief Society and presented to the bishop, usually at the time of his release. The *Elijah Sheets Quilt* made by the Salt Lake Eighth Ward is a masterpiece of this genre (PLATE 64).

One piece of clothing that Latter-day Saint women loved to embellish, often with elaborate pleating and lace, was the blessing gown (PLATE 66). Mothers put these long dresses on their babies when the infants were given a name and a blessing. Often a single blessing gown was used to bless an entire family of children, sometimes for several generations.

PLATE 66: *Blessing Gown,* 1863

*Hanna Smith hand embroidered and decorated this cotton gown with cutwork while she traveled from England to Utah. She was engaged to marry John London, who had immigrated to Utah in 1862. She made the blessing gown in anticipation of the children they would have together. In the nineteenth century these gowns were worn by both male and female children when they received a name and blessing. In style and pattern, the gowns resemble those used for christening in some Catholic and Protestant churches. The cutwork and eyelet techniques popular during the period imitate expensive lace.*

Samplers were small textile panels usually embroidered with cross-stitch. Favorite themes included the alphabet, numbers, a short verse, or sometimes a picture. Not only did young girls learn useful needlework skills, but the patterns helped them learn to read, write, and do arithmetic. Personal and Church history subjects also occasionally showed up on samplers. One early sampler records in poetry the feelings of a young girl upon hearing of the martyrdom of Joseph and Hyrum Smith. She embroidered the poem with her own hair and the border with silk thread (PLATE 67). Another masterful sampler by Ann Eckford depicts the Nauvoo Temple after the Saints had abandoned their city and moved west. Surrounding the temple are the names of the members of the Quorum of the Twelve, who took up the leadership of the Church after the deaths of Joseph and Hyrum Smith (PLATE 68).

PLATE 67: *Martyrdom Sampler*, 1844
MARY ANN BROOMHEAD (1831–?)
TEXTILE AND HUMAN HAIR, 27" X 24" (68.6 CM X 61 CM)
MUSEUM OF CHURCH HISTORY AND ART

*This sampler by a thirteen-year-old has flowers embroidered with cotton thread and words embroidered with human hair. Although the verse mentions the sorrow of the Saints at the deaths of Joseph and Hyrum Smith, it concludes emphasizing their resurrection and eventual glory as "They will come with Christ the Lord."*

*Experimenting with hair in embroidery was common in France during the early nineteenth century. It was also occasionally done in the United States and England. The writer of a caption that accompanied an advertisement for hair jewelry in the United States wrote: "Hair is at once the most delicate and lasting of our materials and survive us, like love. It is so light, so gentle, so escaping from the idea of death, that, with a lock of hair belonging to a child or friend, we may almost look up to heaven and compare notes with angelic nature— may almost say: 'I have a piece of thee here, not unworthy of thy being now.'"*

PLATE 68: *Nauvoo Temple Sampler*, 1846–1849
ANN ECKFORD (1836–?)
TEXTILE, 18" X 12" (45.7 CM X 30.5 CM)
MUSEUM OF CHURCH HISTORY AND ART
GIFT OF MARY DAVIS ENGLISH AND JOHN L. KROESSER

*Ann Eckford probably began this sampler of the Nauvoo Temple in 1846 when she was ten years old and finished it in 1849. As she matured and married, Ann immigrated with her husband and daughter to Utah to join the main body of Saints. The design of the sampler may have been based on a plate made by the Twiggy Pottery Company near Swinton, Yorkshire, England. The plate was made to commemorate the dedication of the Nauvoo Temple in 1846. It features a picture of the temple surrounded by the names of the presiding Church authorities.*

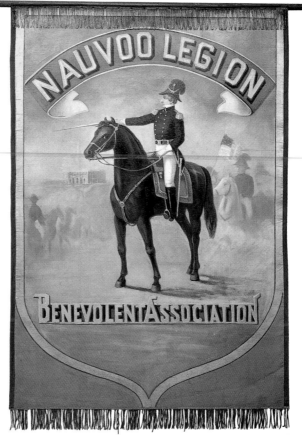

PLATE 70: **Nauvoo Legion Benevolent Association Banner,** 1903
DANQUART A. WEGGELAND (1827–1918)
SILK, METAL THREAD, AND PAINT, 60" X 44"
(152.4 CM X 111.8 CM)
MUSEUM OF CHURCH HISTORY AND ART

*The Nauvoo Legion Benevolent Association was a veterans organization celebrating the camaraderie and experiences of the Nauvoo Legion when it functioned as a city militia in Illinois and a territorial militia in Utah. The legion's founder, Joseph Smith, is depicted in full uniform as lieutenant general. Here he gives his final address to the Nauvoo Legion in Nauvoo nine days before his death. The artist, Dan Weggeland, joined the Church in Norway eleven years after General Smith gave his final speech. His painting is similar in many ways to one done in 1887 by his student John Hafen, but Weggeland shows a historically accurate unfinished Nauvoo Temple.*

PLATE 69: **Nauvoo Legion Snare Drum, Holiness to the Lord,** 1860s
ARTIST UNKNOWN
POLYCHROME WOOD, ROPE, AND LEATHER, 36" X 12 1/4"
(91.4 CM X 31.1 CM)
MUSEUM OF CHURCH HISTORY AND ART

*This snare drum was used by Utah's territorial militia, known as the Nauvoo Legion. It would have been used to beat a rhythm during military drills and for parades and other public events. The artist who painted this drum likely meant the eagle and shield to represent the national government and the beehive to represent the territorial government. The phrase "Holiness to the Lord" is a reference to the legionnaires' religious convictions and their dedication of all they had and did to the Lord. During this period, drummers typically painted their own designs, representing their own feelings and values, on the drums they used. It was not until after the Civil War that military symbols became more standardized.*

Latter-day Saint pioneers loved the annual celebrations commemorating the day that Brigham Young and other pioneers entered the Salt Lake Valley on July 24, 1847. Groups of people would often march in parades behind painted and embroidered banners declaring the particular pioneer group of which they were a part. These painted banners became important statements of pioneer identity and artistic expression.

Some widely practiced folk art traditions from the past may seem strange today. One such tradition is hair wreaths. These were meticulously constructed wreaths depicting flowers but made entirely of human hair. Frequently mothers or grandmothers would make such wreaths using hair from each member of the family. The masterpiece in the Church collection is a huge wreath made by the Relief Society in Manti to decorate the Manti Temple (PLATE 71).

PLATE 71: **Hair Wreath,** 1888
MANTI RELIEF SOCIETY
HAIR, 35" X 29 1/4" X 6 1/2"
(88.9 CM X 74.3 CM X 16.5 CM)
MUSEUM OF CHURCH HISTORY AND ART

*This hair wreath was made to decorate the Manti Temple. Working hair into jewelry and decorations was a popular craft among Latter-day Saint women in the late 1800s and was viewed as an economical, efficient, and very personal way to decorate. Making hairwork jewelry was already popular in Britain in the late seventeenth century. Toward the middle of the nineteenth century the fashion of wearing hair jewelry was at its height, and making pictures out of hair became popular as well. Watch chains made of hair were known as "Alberts," and a life-size, full-length portrait of Queen Victoria, made entirely of hair, was shown at the Paris Exhibition in 1855. Making items of hair became so popular that instruction manuals were written on the topic.*

Photography became widely used in America after the middle of the nineteenth century. Latter-day Saint pioneer photographers, most of them British emigrants, used photography to document the pioneer experience in early Utah. Among the most historically significant events recorded by those early photographers was the construction of the Salt Lake Temple (PLATE 72). In addition, they followed the growth of towns and cities in the mountain valleys and deserts of the Mormon West. The photographers did their best to record these scenes for posterity.

FIGURE 12: C. R. SAVAGE

PLATE 72: *Temple Foundation with Two Tabernacles*, 1871

CHARLES W. CARTER (1832–1918)
GELATIN SILVER PRINT, 16 1/2" X 21 3/4"
(41.9 CM X 55.2 CM)
MUSEUM OF CHURCH HISTORY AND ART
COURTESY CHURCH ARCHIVES

The foundation of the Salt Lake Temple barely rises above ground level in this 1871 photograph taken by Carter as part of a project to document the temple's construction year by year. The unfinished building forms a stark contrast with the newly completed Salt Lake Tabernacle dominating the background. The north end of the old tabernacle is shown on the left. The scene is carefully composed to emphasize the progress on the temple in comparison with the Tabernacle.

With a passion for history, Carter was an excellent documentary photographer. His images captured with exacting detail the growth and progress of the Latter-day Saints in the desert, leaving an invaluable record of the people and places of Utah. Carter immigrated to Utah in 1864 as a convert to the Church and worked briefly for C. R. Savage before opening his own studio in 1867. In addition to his series documenting the construction of the Salt Lake Temple, Carter is recognized for his photographs of Salt Lake City, local canyons, industry, transportation, Indians, and the military.

PLATE 73: *Rural Scene near Willard, Utah,* ABOUT 1890

CHARLES R. SAVAGE (1832–1909)
GELATIN SILVER PRINT, 20" X 24" (50.8 CM X 61 CM)
MUSEUM OF CHURCH HISTORY AND ART
COURTESY BRIGHAM YOUNG UNIVERSITY ARCHIVES

Savage was a commercial photographer who usually produced studio photographs, portraits, or landscapes that could be sold to the public. However, this photograph of a pastoral scene in northern Utah is an example of something Savage did less often: he manipulated a scene to create a documentary-style artistic photograph. The scene contains elements typical of the Mormon landscape—the poplar trees, the mountains in the background, the farmhouse, and the Mormon family doing chores and working the land.

After settling in Utah in 1860, Savage worked with early Utah photographer Marsena Cannon. Later Savage established a studio on Main Street in Salt Lake City, where he worked until he retired in 1906. His memorable works include views of Salt Lake City, the construction and dedication of the Salt Lake Temple, immigrating pioneer companies, and portraits of Church leaders. In addition, he photographed much of the western United States during his forty-year association with the Union Pacific Railroad.

# THE IMPACT OF FRENCH TRAINING ON LATTER-DAY SAINT ART, 1890-1925

*2*

*by Robert O. Davis*

The year 1890 signaled a fundamental change for the art of The Church of Jesus Christ of Latter-day Saints. On July 24, Pioneer Day in Utah Territory, three artists in their thirties—John Hafen, Lorus Pratt, and John B. Fairbanks—arrived in Paris to commence their artistic training. They were there as "art missionaries" called by Church leaders to develop their skills. Hafen explained his objective: "Being a firm believer that the highest development of talent is a duty we owe to our Creator, I made it a matter of prayer for many years that He would open a way whereby I could receive training which would befit me to decorate the holy temples and the habitations of Zion."[1]

In a letter home Hafen represented the attitude of the group: "As I beheld the grand boulevards of Paris, or strolled in the paradisiacal parks . . . or gazed upon the magnificent architecture of the Louvre, Madeleine, [and] Notre Dame . . . did I lose interest in the Gospel? No. For the Lord has predicted greater things than these for Zion; then it is we realize what a great work there is before us."[2]

The mission fulfilled its promise and much more, leading the artists and visual art of the Church into a new era. Pioneer artists of the previous generation shared the common bond of gathering to Zion from Europe. The unifying trait of artists of this era was their pilgrimage to the reigning world art capital to receive proper academic training for their chosen career. The Utah artists discussed in this chapter were born between 1855 and 1878 and studied in Paris, most at the Julian Academy. They produced a body of work significant enough to be called a regional "school," unified in purpose and style—an important tradition in the broader context of American art history. This work is among the most vital of any region of the country, and has many Latter-day Saint religious and cultural components.

## ART IN TEMPLES AND MEETINGHOUSES

Completing the Salt Lake Temple was the earliest and most important large project of the era. Church leaders called for the finest decorative arts and furnishings. The sacred rooms were adorned with several large art glass windows depicting Joseph Smith's first vision (PLATE 74), Joseph Smith receiving the gold plates (PLATE 75), and other themes. The windows were crafted by the Tiffany Glass and Decorating Company of New York, the premier glassmaker in the United States. Twenty years later, a window similar in design to the *First Vision* was installed in the Adams Ward building in Los Angeles, California (PLATE 76).

*Facing page: Detail from*
**Girl among the Hollyhocks**,
*by John Hafen.*
*(See Plate 79, page 46.)*

PLATE 74: **First Vision**, 1892
TIFFANY AND COMPANY
LEADED STAINED GLASS, 145" x 54"
(368.2 CM X 137.2 CM)
SALT LAKE TEMPLE
COURTESY CHURCH ARCHIVES

*The First Vision is the founding story of the
Restoration. This experience of Joseph Smith in the
Sacred Grove set in motion a new dispensation of
direct heavenly contact and numerous revelations
from God to mankind. This window was ordered
especially for the Salt Lake Temple shortly before
its dedication. After more than one hundred years it
is still the most spectacular piece of stained glass
depicting a Latter-day Saint subject. Tiffany and
Company of New York City was already
established as the most important producer of
stained glass when this window was commissioned.
This work set a precedent for a number of other less
elaborate art glass windows of the First Vision
produced for chapels in Utah and California.*

PLATE 75: **Joseph Smith Receives the Plates**, 1893
TIFFANY AND COMPANY
LEADED STAINED GLASS, 68" x 94"
(172.7 CM X 238.8 CM)
SALT LAKE TEMPLE
PHOTOGRAPH RALPH SAVAGE, 1911
COURTESY CHURCH ARCHIVES

*This magnificent stained glass art window in the Salt
Lake Temple is placed in the west sealing room, next
to the celestial room. The window and the furnishings
of the sealing room testify of how Church leaders
wanted to complete the House of the Lord. A visitor
recorded just prior to the dedication, "The majesty of
heaven was there, no cost has been spared to fit and
prepare this holy Temple for an offering to our God. . . .
The highest of all arts had been sought and obtained in
painting and adorning this beautiful Temple."*

*To create this and other windows in the temple, a
representative from Tiffany and Company, art glass
manufacturers from New York, visited Salt Lake City.
Company artists worked with interior architect Joseph
Don Carlos Young, who gave them detailed accounts
of Joseph Smith's first vision and his receiving the
plates from Moroni. He also gave input about gestures
of the subjects, the setting, and color, together with
details of the room and placement of the window. The
resulting art glass windows depicting those themes are
among the finest representations ever done.*

IF ANY OF YOU LACK WISDOM LET HIM ASK OF G
THAT GIVETH TO MEN LIBERALLY AND UPBRAIDETH NO
AND IT SHALL BE GIVEN HIM
JAMES 1-5 v.
THIS IS MY BELOVED SON HEAR HIM

"THIS IS MY BELOVED SON, HEAR HIM!"

PLATE 76:
*Joseph Smith's First Vision,*
1913

MAKER UNKNOWN
LEADED STAINED GLASS, 84" X 60"
(213.4 CM X 152.4 CM)
MUSEUM OF CHURCH
HISTORY AND ART

*The First Vision became a
popular theme for art glass
windows in Church
meetinghouses after the initial
one was created for the Salt
Lake Temple in 1893. The
story, with its references to light,
is especially suited to the stained
glass medium, which allows
sunlight to pass through and
illuminate the artwork. This
example is faithful to the
account given by Joseph Smith
in his history. The window was
manufactured in Los Angeles
and has similarities to earlier
examples that portray the First
Vision. Like many of the
windows from this period, the
scene is painted on the back side
of the glass. It was removed
when the Adams Ward
meetinghouse in Los Angeles
was razed in 1959, and later
reinstalled in the permanent
historical exhibition "A
Covenant Restored" at the
Church Museum.*

Pioneer artists had painted murals in temples at St. George, Logan, and Manti, but as the Salt Lake Temple was nearing completion in 1890, the Church sponsored training for the best of the new generation of Latter-day Saint artists. When they returned to Utah they were immediately engaged to produce the murals. Over the next two decades temples in Hawaii, Alberta, and Arizona also required the finest contributions of Latter-day Saint artists. In addition, these younger artists created murals and easel works for chapels and tabernacles.

It was largely through the efforts of John Hafen (1856–1910) (FIGURE 13) that the Church sponsored several men to study in Paris. Encouraged by pioneer artists, Hafen came to believe that in order to progress and be of greatest service, an artist had to receive training from masters at a major European academy. Early in 1890 he and Lorus Pratt discussed this with George Q. Cannon of the First Presidency and then submitted a formal proposal. It was accepted, and they were set apart as missionaries on June 3, 1890, leaving three weeks later. "There is a herculean task before me," Hafen wrote in France, "which if I accomplish in so short of time allotted for me to stay here, it will be through the miraculous power of God."[3] Hafen believed that by living gospel principles he could be a better artist. "Much depends upon character in obtaining excellence in art," he wrote. "Good art is also much dependent on truth. A man or woman who has wrong ideas of his or her individuality, of religion, of God, of duty, cannot become a great artist be they ever so gifted."[4] When the Paris art missionaries returned they were engaged along with Dan Weggeland, the "old master" of Utah art, to paint landscape settings extending completely around two ordinance rooms of the Salt Lake Temple. After these assignments, Hafen developed the "peaceable kingdom" theme of the garden room in a carefully composed mural for a chapel in Springville, and easel paintings such as *The Garden of Eden* (PLATE 77) for private clients.

A decade later Hafen was commissioned by the Church over a two-year period to expand its art collection. He was paid $100 per month in exchange for all of the artwork he produced. He had the option of redeeming the work, but he "expressed a wish that the church would keep this work and let it become a nucleus for some future gallery of paintings."[5] Hafen reported in a 1903 letter to President Joseph F. Smith that he had 153 paintings for the Church, mostly landscapes, with masterpieces like *Pastoral Scene near Draper* (PLATE 78) and *Girl among the Hollyhocks* (PLATE 79) and also portraits of General Authorities. He produced his excellent portrait of Elder Orson F. Whitney (PLATE 80) in 1907. President Heber J. Grant later wrote:

> I conceived the idea of hiring him for three years and agreeing to take his entire output. . . . [John Hafen] was by far the best landscape artist that Utah has ever produced. I am very fond of his paintings. After visiting art galleries from Scandinavia to Italy, I found upon my return that every one of my paintings by Hafen looked just as good to me as any that I saw in Europe.[6]

FIGURE 13: JOHN HAFEN

PLATE 77: **The Garden of Eden**, 1895
JOHN HAFEN (1856–1910)
OIL ON CANVAS, 44 1/2" X 116 1/4"
(113 CM X 295.3 CM)
MUSEUM OF ART, BRIGHAM YOUNG UNIVERSITY

*In 1890 John Hafen, sent by the Church to France, studied techniques to prepare for painting the Salt Lake Temple murals. The murals for ordinance rooms were to be part of the effort to beautify and edify the temple's interior. This study, closely related to the murals in the garden room of the temple, suggests the perfection of God's creations in the Garden of Eden. Hafen has used loose brush strokes of the impressionistic style and concentrated on light, color, and texture. A devout man, the artist recognized that God's creations were given to elevate God's children.*

PLATE 78: *Pastoral Scene near Draper, Utah,* 1900

JOHN HAFEN (1856–1910)

OIL ON CANVAS, 40" X 57" (101.6 CM X 144.8 CM)

MUSEUM OF CHURCH HISTORY AND ART

*This painting applies the pastoral technique of French artists, employing hazy tones and subtle values, exemplifying Hafen's tendency for painting intimate and often enclosed landscapes. The short brush strokes and the play of light and color of the Impressionists are expertly interwoven with the tonal harmony, restricted range of color, and poetic atmosphere of the Barbizon school influence. The brilliant effect of sunlight draws the viewer to the major area of focus at the midpoint of the composition. Hafen painted in the outdoors and wrote extensively about his feelings on art. He believed if one studied hard enough in God's outdoor temple, he or she would be shown a way out of human trouble.*

PLATE 79: *Girl among the Hollyhocks*, 1902
JOHN HAFEN (1856–1910)
OIL ON CANVAS, 36" X 41" (91.4 CM X 104.1 CM)
MUSEUM OF CHURCH HISTORY AND ART

*The young girl in this painting is the artist's daughter, Delia. She is standing among the flowers in the family's backyard. Hafen, who had to spend much of his life separated from his family while pursuing his art, expressed in this masterpiece his feelings about his family and home. Hafen immigrated to Utah with his family following their conversion to the Church in their native Switzerland. He was acquainted and studied with some of Utah's pioneer artists, including George Ottinger and Dan Weggeland.*

PLATE 80: *Orson F. Whitney,* 1907
JOHN HAFEN (1856–1910)
OIL ON CANVAS, 27" X 21" (68.6 CM X 53.3 CM)
MUSEUM OF CHURCH HISTORY AND ART

*Orson F. Whitney led a distinguished career as a historian, poet, and Church leader. He is best remembered for his four-volume series* History of Utah. *Although he served as an apostle for a quarter of a century, he always preferred the title of bishop. Bishop Whitney was called as bishop of the Salt Lake Eighteenth Ward at the age of twenty-three and served for twenty-eight years until his call to the Council of the Twelve in 1906. This painting was one of several official portraits of Church leaders commissioned from Hafen in the early 1900s.*

In a 1909 venture published by Ben E. Rich and German E. Ellsworth, Hafen illustrated Eliza R. Snow's famous Latter-day Saint poem and hymn "O My Father." Referring to the work in a letter to President Smith, Hafen maintained that art's proper purpose is "to interpret or reveal beauty in line and color" and to "express beauty in philosophy and principle."[7] Hafen's art is now widely appreciated, but during his lifetime his quiet, introspective landscapes were less understood. He believed that spiritual content is contained not necessarily in the subject of an artwork, but in the unlocking of an inner meaning or conveying of a sincere response through art. In Hafen's landscapes, one can sense deep spirituality and feel the artist's humility and integrity. "It is not the mission of art to ape or imitate," Hafen wrote. "Cease to look for mechanical effect or minute finish, for individual leaves, blades of grass . . . but look for smell, for soul, for feeling, for the beautiful."[8] He also testified about the power of art to lift the soul:

> The influence of art is so powerful in shaping our lives for a higher appreciation of the creations of our God. We should be as eager for its companionship [as we are] for food to sustain our lives, for it has as important a mission in shaping our character and in conducting to our happiness as anything we term necessities. Life is incomplete without it.[9]

Whereas Hafen had only a few institutional commissions, the noted American sculptor Cyrus E. Dallin (1861–1944) (FIGURE 14) devoted most of his energies to creating artwork for public places. A native of Hafen's hometown, Springville, Utah, at the age of twelve he modeled heads of Joseph and Hyrum Smith, prompting pioneer artist Philo Dibble to predict success for him. Though not a Latter-day Saint, Dallin was anxious to do artwork for the Church, and in 1884 made contact with President John Taylor seeking sponsorship (without success) for a statue of Joseph Smith. From 1888 to 1890 he was in Paris at the Julian Academy. In 1891, the artist again attempted to gain a commission for full-length statues of Joseph and Hyrum Smith for the two empty niches on the east wall of

FIGURE 14: CYRUS E. DALLIN

the Salt Lake Temple. Instead he was retained to complete three official portrait busts of the First Presidency: Wilford Woodruff, George Q. Cannon, and Joseph F. Smith. President Woodruff was pleased with his portrait and asked Dallin to create a new design of the *Angel Moroni* (PLATE 82) for the center east spire of the temple. Encouraged by his mother, Dallin agreed and quickly produced a model that was endorsed by the First Presidency. It shows strong influence of the French academic-classical tradition. On April 6, 1892, the twelve-and-one-half-foot gilded angel was lowered into place after the capstone ceremony at which tens of thousands of Latter-day Saints performed the grand "Hosanna Shout" and sang the hymn "The Spirit of God." President Woodruff asked Dallin if he now believed in angels. The artist replied, "I believe in angels because my mother is an angel."[10]

The next year a civic- and Church-sponsored committee, the Brigham Young Memorial Association, commissioned Dallin to create a $25,000, multifigure monument to Brigham Young and the pioneers. It was to be funded by contributions from many sources, but a nationwide depression and other problems delayed payment for seven years. The standing Brigham Young was cast for the Utah display at the 1893 Chicago World's Fair and was later set on a temporary pedestal on Temple Square. In 1897 the monument minus several figures was unveiled in the center of Main and South Temple Streets for the Pioneer Jubilee Celebration. Finally the artist was paid, the last figures were cast and installed, and on Pioneer Day, July 24, 1900, the completed monument was dedicated. Ninety-three years later it was moved north out of the intersection, providing better public access.

Dallin created scores of public monuments commemorating notable people, from Sir Isaac Newton to Christopher Columbus, Anne Hutchinson, Paul Revere, and Charles Lindbergh. He is best known, however, for his great Native American sculpture, including *Massasoit* at Plymouth, Massachusetts, and at the Utah State Capitol, and the "Epic of the Indian"—several thematic equestrian works cast in editions of several sizes. Two of them, including *Appeal to the Great Spirit* (PLATE 81), are in the Museum's collection.

PLATE 82: ***The Angel Moroni,*** 1891
CYRUS E. DALLIN (1861–1944)
GILDED PLASTER, 29" X 12" X 17"
(76.7 CM X 30.5 CM X 43.2 CM)
MUSEUM OF CHURCH HISTORY AND ART

*This is the original plaster model for the larger-than-life-size statue standing atop the Salt Lake Temple. It was produced under the encouragement of the President of the Church, Wilford Woodruff. A nationally prominent sculptor, Dallin was influenced by neoclassical techniques and artistic ideals. This powerful work exudes simplicity, dignity, and refinement with its smooth lines and pleasing aesthetic balance. Years later Dallin said, "I consider that my Angel Moroni brought me nearer to God than anything I ever did."*

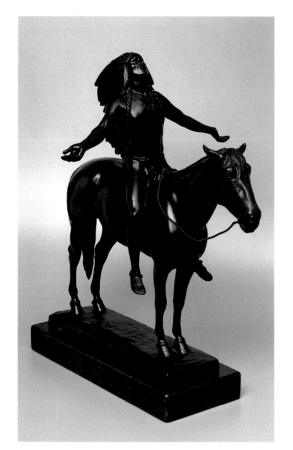

PLATE 81: ***Appeal to the Great Spirit,*** 1909
CYRUS EDWIN DALLIN (1861–1944)
CAST BRONZE, 21" X 21" X 14"
(53.3 CM X 53.3 CM X 35.6 CM)
MUSEUM OF CHURCH HISTORY AND ART

*Over a twenty-year period Dallin created his noble "Epic of the Indian" series of four works—Signal of Peace, Medicine Man, The Protest, and Appeal to the Great Spirit—depicting American Indians on horseback in subjects symbolizing their losing conflicts with the white expansionist culture. The sculptor's biographer, Rell Francis, stated: "The final stage of the Indian's plight is dramatically shown in Dallin's most famous statue, Appeal to the Great Spirit. The mounted Sioux chief, defeated in battle and in negotiations with the white man, now seeks divine assistance from the Great Spirit who rules the universe. This life-size equestrian, which stands in front of the Boston Museum of Fine Arts, was once almost as well known as the Statue of Liberty. Countless reproductions of this favorite work were made." (Cyrus E. Dallin: Let Justice be Done [Springville, Utah: Springville Museum of Art, 1976], 44–45.) This authorized modern casting was made by the Gorham Company, which owns the original molds.*

PLATE 83: *George Teasdale,* 1900
GEORGE HENRY TAGGART (1865–1959)
OIL ON CANVAS, 27" X 21" (68.6 CM X 53.3 CM)
MUSEUM OF CHURCH HISTORY AND ART

*George Teasdale (1831–1907), born in London, England, was one of the many early Latter-day Saint converts from the British Isles. A tireless and dedicated man, he served as a mission president and Mexican colonizer. On October 16, 1882, he was ordained an apostle. At the turn of the century, he became one of fifteen early Church leaders who sat for portraits by visiting artist George H. Taggart. Born in Watertown, New York, Taggart studied for nine years in Paris, then specialized in portraiture in his studio in New York. Around 1900 he spent two summers in Utah for health reasons and painted many well-conceived portraits.*

PLATE 84: *Emmeline B. Wells,* 1906
LEE GREENE RICHARDS (1878–1950)
OIL ON CANVAS, 42" X 36" (106.7 CM X 91.4 CM)
MUSEUM OF CHURCH HISTORY AND ART

*Emmeline B. Wells (1828–1921) worked for the advancement of women socially, politically, and economically. For almost forty years she edited the* Woman's Exponent, *the first and longest running women's newspaper west of the Mississippi. She also spearheaded a successful wheat storage project that eventually merged into the present system of Church welfare granaries. It was during her tenure as general president of the Relief Society (1910–1921) that the women's organization began a uniform course of study. Paris-trained artist Lee Greene Richards "owned" Utah's portrait business for decades. He painted in the style of eighteenth-century English painters Reynolds and Gainsborough, with softer edges. He received numerous commissions for portraits, including renderings of prominent Utah government and Church officials. Few have achieved keener figurative results than he did.*

## PORTRAITS OF CHURCH LEADERS AND MEMBERS

Before their Paris pilgrimage, several of the Utah artists were portrait painters who also generated side incomes by making charcoal-enhanced studio photographs of clients. After returning they were generally less involved in portraiture, but one artist, John Hafen, applied his new techniques with excellent results. Talented studio photographers in Salt Lake City such as C. R. Savage and C. E. Johnson filled much of the demand for portraits.

In 1900 portrait painter George Henry Taggart (1865–1959) from Watertown, New York, came to Utah for treatment of a lung ailment. While in Salt Lake City, he painted at least seven portraits of LDS Church Apostles, including his *bravura* portrait of George Teasdale (PLATE 83). Taggart produced paintings on assignment, entered fairs, and wrote about art. In a 1901 *Deseret News* article he maintained:

> There is not the slightest reason why great works of art should not be produced here in Utah; . . . this is already being done. The scenery of Utah has its own distinctive character as has the scenery of France and Holland. . . . The womanhood and the manhood, their home life, their very souls and character [are] as high and noble and as inspiring. Here are our themes; the way is open for the expression of the most profound thought and feeling.[11]

THE IMPACT OF FRENCH TRAINING ON LATTER-DAY SAINT ART, 1890–1925

PLATE 85: *Pioneer Mother,*
*Louisa Lula Greene Richards,* 1936
LEE GREENE RICHARDS (1878–1950)
OIL ON CANVAS, 38" X 48" (96.5 CM X 122 CM)
MUSEUM OF ART, BRIGHAM YOUNG UNIVERSITY

*This painting is a heartfelt tribute to the artist's*
*mother. The presence of poplar trees suggests a*
*narrative. Lombardy poplars, widely planted in*
*Salt Lake City during the pioneer era, had mostly*
*died out there by the middle 1930s when this work*
*was created. The artist may thus be recalling*
*memories of the past. Prior to her marriage, Louisa*
*Lula Greene Richards (1849–1944) was an editor*
*and journalist, and was called by Brigham Young to*
*be the first editor of the* Woman's Exponent
*magazine. Lee Greene Richards was gifted in art as*
*a youth and received excellent initial training from*
*his artist grandmother. When Lee Greene's mother*
*said, "Artists can never hope for riches," he replied,*
*"No, but they can be happy." Primarily known as a*
*portraitist, Lee Greene Richards was also a painter*
*of landscape. In some of his finest works, such as*
*this example, he has combined figures and*
*landscape to imply religious meaning.*

Today the Smithsonian's National Museum of American Art possesses thirty of Taggart's works, including a portrait of Teddy Roosevelt.

With the departure of Taggart by 1903, Lee Greene Richards (1878–1950) became the portrait artist of choice in Salt Lake City. He grew up with A. B. Wright, Mahonri M. Young, and other Latter-day Saint artists in his neighborhood, including George M. Ottinger, Alfred Lambourne, H. L. A. Culmer, and Jack Sears. Together they were called the "Twentieth Ward Group." "Lee has always known how to paint," reported Mahonri. "It was as easy for him to paint as for other boys to play."[12] Richards served a mission in England and traveled through Europe afterward. Later, in Paris he studied at the *Ecole des Beaux Arts* under Bonnat and Laurens. In 1904 he returned to Salt Lake City to open a portrait studio in the Templeton Building. One of his first engagements was to paint portraits of leaders of the Relief Society. *Emmeline B. Wells* (PLATE 84) was described by Alice Merrill Horne as "a poetic picture of a poet."[13] It displays Richards's reliance upon what he said was "my belief in the traditions of the past."[14] His portrait of his mother, *Louisa Lula Greene Richards* (PLATE 85), a niece of Brigham Young and early editor of the *Woman's Exponent* newspaper, is a fond tribute. With more than forty official portraits of LDS leaders painted from 1900 to 1948 now in the Church collection, Richards has been the portrait artist who has received the greatest number of commissions from the Church.

In response to the 1930 centennial of the organization of the Church, Richards created *Dreaming of Zion* (FIGURE 15), a beautiful and original masterpiece of Latter-day Saint art. The painting shows a young female pioneer, modeled by the artist's daughter, anticipating her new life as she is about to descend to the Salt Lake Valley. In 1934–1935 he designed the murals for the dome of the Utah State Capitol under sponsorship of the Federal Emergency Relief Administration. One segment depicts pioneers settling the Salt Lake Valley.

Four temples were designed and constructed between 1912 and 1945; Lee Greene Richards produced mural cycles for three of them. The best Latter-day Saint architects and artists were brought together at the Alberta Temple to produce a synthesis of religious architecture, furnishings and fixtures, painting and sculpture; Richards painted decorative murals for the garden

FIGURE 15: *DREAMING OF ZION*

PLATE 86: **_The Garden of Eden,_** 1920
LEE GREENE RICHARDS (1878–1950)
OIL ON CANVAS, EACH PANEL 108" x 65"
(274.3 CM x 165.1 CM)
GARDEN ROOM, ALBERTA TEMPLE

_Generally recognized as a portrait painter, Lee
Greene Richards demonstrated his diverse artistic
talent in this triptych. Created to set a reverent and
contemplative mood for Alberta Temple patrons in
the garden room, his paintings harmonize with the
unique and boldly modern design of the Canadian
temple. The artist's murals hint at an art nouveau
decorative style with curved trees, graceful
peacocks, and foliage, all popular at the turn of the
century. The postimpressionist techniques Richards
acquired in Paris are also evident in his use
of blue and purple shadows._

room. His beautiful wall triptych (PLATE 86) harmonizes rich, pointillistic color with inlaid wood patterns on the walls. Richards later executed more conventional mural work at the Arizona Temple, and at the Idaho Falls Temple in the early 1940s he produced magnificent allegorical murals with classically inspired figures.

## DEPICTING THE HISTORY OF THE RESTORED CHURCH

Artists, sculptors, and photographers of the late nineteenth and early twentieth centuries continued to commemorate the history of the Church in many works. The 1897 Pioneer Jubilee, for example, led to increased consciousness and new examples about the pioneer experience. Many of the younger native artists produced work alongside the immigrant pioneer artists who had made the trek west.

The last grandchild of Brigham Young born during the prophet's lifetime was Mahonri Mackintosh Young (1877–1957) (FIGURE 16). His heritage seemed to breed in him a deep sense of pioneer history, and he developed rapidly into a significant artist. Mahonri entered the Art Students League in New York City in 1899, but like most talented American artists of the time he crossed the Atlantic for art lessons, enrolling in the Julian, Colarossi, and Delecluse Academies in Paris. Early in his career Mahonri desired to express his history through sculpture: "I am going to use my art in erecting monuments to the Utah Pioneers. Back of the Mormon people there is a big idea: this as

FIGURE 16: MAHONRI
MACKINTOSH YOUNG

manifested in their life, migrations, and sufferings [has] always appealed to my imaginations, and they embody an infinite number of artistic themes."[15]

Mahonri realized his goals in the creation of several public monuments. In his Paris studio he worked up models for life-size sculptures of Joseph Smith and his brother Hyrum—_The Prophet_ and *The Patriarch* (FIGURE 17). These were enlarged, cast, and installed in their designated niches on the east side of the Salt Lake Temple, but soon they were moved to a more accessible spot on Temple Square. In 1912, now back in Utah, Mahonri was engaged to create on Temple Square the Seagull Monument, commemorating the miraculous intervention of seagulls that consumed hordes of crickets, thus saving the Mormon settlers' crops. Three relief panels and a title plaque on the base narrate with great power *The Plowing, Deliverance* (PLATE 87), and *The Harvesting*, while gilded seagulls cap the monument. In 1937 Mahonri commenced the sixty-foot-high *This Is the Place Monument* (FIGURE 18) east of Salt Lake City at the mouth of Emigration Canyon. His objective was to depict those who discovered and settled the Salt Lake Valley. Crowning the center pylon are Brigham Young, Heber C. Kimball, and Wilford Woodruff. President George Albert Smith dedicated the memorial on July 24, 1947, as part of the pioneer centennial.

Though he created many important sculptures in Utah, Mahonri spent most of his career in the East. In the late 1940s he commuted daily from his Connecticut studio to the New York hospital where his wife lay dying. He was working on the clay and plaster models for *Brigham Young Seated* (PLATE 88), the first step toward producing a statue of the most notable figure in Utah history for the Statuary Hall of the national capitol in Washington, D.C. Mahonri wrote his point of

FIGURE 17: *THE PATRIARCH AND THE PROPHET*

PLATE 87: *"Deliverance" Panel from the Seagull Monument,* 1912
MAHONRI M. YOUNG (1877–1957)
CAST BRONZE, 60" x 48" (152.4 CM X 121.9 CM)
TEMPLE SQUARE, SALT LAKE CITY, UTAH

*In the spring of 1848, Latter-day Saint crops were threatened with destruction by voracious crickets. Seagulls from the islands of the Great Salt Lake flew in to gorge themselves on the pests, preserving enough of the year's crop to ensure the pioneers' survival through the next winter. Latter-day Saints look on this event as evidence of the Lord's blessing, and the story has been related in numerous works of art, although nowhere more eloquently than in the Mahonri Young monument that stands on Temple Square. This panel depicting the gulls arriving to bless a pioneer family is one of four bronzes that relate the story. The panels are placed at the base of a granite shaft topped with a sculpture of two seagulls. One of the strongest aesthetic elements of this bas relief is the superb depiction of space on a basically flat piece of sculpture. Following study in Paris at the Julian Academy, Mahonri Young shifted back and forth between his native state of Utah and New York's art community. Young accepted several sculpture commissions during these years, including the Seagull Monument, completed early in his distinguished public career. Although a versatile artist who worked in bronze, marble, oil paint, pen and ink, and etchings, he was best known for his bronze sculpture.*

PLATE 88: ***Brigham Young,*** 1949
MAHONRI M. YOUNG (1877–1957)
CAST BRONZE, 22" x 11 1/2" x 14 1/2"
(56 CM x 28.6 CM x 36.8 CM)
MUSEUM OF CHURCH HISTORY AND ART
GIFT OF ROBERT AND PEGGY SEARS

*This table-sized bronze casting of President Brigham Young (1801–1877) was cast from the original model made by Mahonri M. Young in preparation for the large marble monument of his grandfather placed in Statuary Hall in the United States Capitol in 1950. The sculpture displays the artist's ability to carve vigorously textured surfaces into believable human figures. When Mahonri, the last of Brigham Young's grandchildren born while he was still living, heard that the state was going to place a statue of his grandfather in the nation's capitol, he immediately set out to win the competition. The state allowed the family to select the artist. Mahonri had long dreamed of portraying his grandfather as the great administrator and colonizer, "The Lion of the Lord." The family, however, wanted Brigham portrayed as a kindly, gentle patriarch. Mahonri deftly combined the two aspects into his model, and the 1944 family reunion awarded him the commission.*

view in a letter: "There was never a question in my mind how to represent Brigham Young. He should be seated. . . . He never walked when he could ride, and never stood when he could sit. He governed his world from his office chair. It was as a statesman, a leader and a prophet I felt he should be represented."[16]

Mahonri chiseled the heroic-size form in Italy from white Carrara marble. It was dedicated in 1950 in festivities that included members of the Young family, government dignitaries, and President George Albert Smith.

Mahonri Young's works appear in fifty museums around the world, including the Metropolitan Museum of Art in New York City. He is noted for images of prizefighters and workmen, and he modeled Hopi, Navajo, and Apache Indian groups for the American Museum of

FIGURE 18: THIS IS THE PLACE MONUMENT

PLATE 89: ***Isaac Chase and Brigham Young Home, Liberty Park, Salt Lake City,*** 1907
MAHONRI M. YOUNG (1877–1957)
OIL ON PANEL, 10" x 14" (25.4 CM x 35.6 CM)
MUSEUM OF ART, BRIGHAM YOUNG UNIVERSITY

*The eaves of the Isaac Chase home barely peek out through the trees in their Liberty Park setting. Chase built the home and gristmill in the 1850s and later sold it to his son-in-law Brigham Young. The property was later deeded to Salt Lake City for a public park, and the home and gristmill were left standing in the heart of the park as a memorial to pioneer family life and industry. This sketch is one of many examples by Mahonri Young picturing sites and life of Salt Lake City. These small works are gems of Utah art history. Young developed an energy-filled realism and became one of Utah's best-known artists. He spent much of his career in New York.*

Natural History. His work emphasizes strength and movement; though it is thoroughly American in theme, his modeling techniques have been compared to those of the great French sculptors Rodin and Maillol. His estate of thousands of works of art was bequeathed to Brigham Young University. Also a great teacher, whose classroom motto was "No Bunk,"[17] Mahonri taught courses at the Art Students League on and off from 1916 to 1943.

Mahonri gained worldwide recognition as a sculptor, but he was a very good painter and print artist as well. Early in his career he became skilled at creating quick, spontaneous sketches of slices of life, such as the *Isaac Chase and Brigham Young Home* (PLATE 89). Conscious of this versatility, one of his friends, illustrator Jack Sears, gave this evaluation: "[Mahonri Young is] an individual, sincere, a man with a splendid, well-balanced mind. A great draughtsman with a sound and large view of life and well-trained vision. I have walked with him, worked with him, lived with him, and I know he could do more things better than any living man today."[18]

Like Mahonri Young, John B. Fairbanks (1855–1940) (FIGURE 19) also depicted the Mormon pioneer epic. He was part of history in the making when he became the official artist and photographer for the Benjamin Cluff expedition to Central and South America, seeking evidences of the Book of Mormon. He painted the jewel-like *Magdelena River* (PLATE 90) on this trip. Ten years earlier Fairbanks had been a Paris art missionary. At the Julian Academy the missionaries were known for their dedication. Fairbanks wrote home, "If we do not excel it will not be for the lack of study." One artist noted that each day they were "the first to arrive and the last to leave."[19] Returning to Utah, Fairbanks painted the backgrounds in the garden room and the ceiling of the world room in the Salt Lake Temple. He roomed at the home of Joseph F. Smith and gave art lessons to one of his daughters. Twenty-four years later Fairbanks painted replacement murals in the world room of the St. George Temple.

Fairbanks, like his associate John Hafen, battled to earn a living for his large family with art and its associated pursuits. He turned to studio photography, made copies of old masters in New York museums, promoted national parks through art, and developed a stock of pretty living-room scenes that he copied again and again for customers. None of these projects earned much. His son J. Leo referred to this life: "My father's attitude, his willingness to sacrifice everything to his art had been an inspiration to me and I firmly believe has changed my whole career. Without his example I would undoubtedly have followed more lucrative employment."[20]

FIGURE 19:
JOHN B. FAIRBANKS

PLATE 90: *Magdelena River,* 1902
JOHN B. FAIRBANKS (1855–1940)
OIL ON CANVAS, 16" x 24" (40.6 CM X 61 CM)
MUSEUM OF CHURCH HISTORY AND ART
GIFT OF LEONARD AND DONNA MCKINLEY

*Fairbanks painted this South American river while on a two-year expedition. The group of scientists he accompanied visited Mexico, Central America, and Colombia, gathering specimens for their respective disciplines and searching for remains of Book of Mormon civilizations. The Magdelena River in Colombia, which some in the group believed to be the River Sidon mentioned in the Book of Mormon, was the final focus of the expedition. This painting has a soft, atmospheric quality that reveals French training. As one of the LDS art missionaries, Fairbanks studied in Paris, where he was influenced more by the Barbizon school than by the Impressionism that captivated his companions. Fairbanks's influence on Latter-day Saint art was far-reaching, both as a teacher and as the father of two prominent artists, J. Leo and Avard T. Fairbanks.*

After 1890 the younger artists began to abandon both the objective recording of rural settlement and the portrayals of the grandeur of the Rocky Mountains, and began to celebrate agrarian life, to seek the poetic beauty of nature, and to depict impressions of the rural landscape. In the finest of these priceless works are revealed the characteristics of the paradigmatic "Mormon Landscape." Local artists found increasing sales for these post-Paris pictures.

Soon after arriving in France to pursue art under Church sponsorship, Edwin Evans (1860–1946) of Lehi, Utah, began painting large works that were fundamentally different from rural landscapes produced by artists from Utah before that time. The pastoral painting *Grain Fields* (PLATE 91) became a model for paintings of the ideal landscape in the valleys of the Rocky Mountains. It was awarded a prize at the 1893 Columbian Exposition at the Chicago World's Fair Art Palace, which mounted an early exhibition of American Impressionism. Following study in Paris, Evans returned to work on murals for the Salt Lake Temple, producing detailed sketches for the garden room and working in collaboration with the other artists as they painted directly on the sealed plaster walls.

Always involved in art organizations, Evans was a charter member and the first president of the Society of Utah Artists. He also served as president of the Utah Art Institute for twelve years, for a time as art instructor at Brigham Young Academy in Provo and at LDS University in Salt Lake City, and finally as head of the University of Utah Art Department for twenty-two years. In

PLATE 91: *Grain Fields,* 1890
EDWIN EVANS (1860–1946)
OIL ON CANVAS, 39" X 58" (99.1 CM X 147.3 CM)
MUSEUM OF ART, BRIGHAM YOUNG UNIVERSITY

*The harvest was a natural theme for the Utah artists of this period, who for the most part had been raised on farms. The locale of this harvest scene remains unidentified. Evans's message suggests the continuing abundance of the earth as well as man's civilizing influence. The technique of Grain Fields reveals French Impressionist influence in the broken brush strokes, brilliant sunlight, and shadows painted in subdued bluish tones. Evans shows a heightened concern for composition; by placing the human figure in a subordinate position, he emphasizes the beauty of the landscape. Strong perspective lines created by the rows of grain stacks carry the viewer into the distance. Void of overt sentimentality, the painting conveys the relationship between man and nature as healthy and beneficial. Several paintings by Utah artists were included in the World Columbian Exposition in Chicago in 1893. Evans's Grain Fields was the only Utah painting to win an honorable mention.*

PLATE 92: **The Gleaners**, 1890
JAMES T. HARWOOD (1860–1940)
OIL ON CANVAS, 30" X 38" (76.2 CM X 96.5 CM)
MUSEUM OF CHURCH HISTORY AND ART

1918 President Joseph F. Smith hired Evans to paint murals in the Alberta Temple world room. These decorative compositions harmonized with the room design, which was paneled in figured South American walnut. In a Church publication Evans wrote about the interaction of his faith and art: "Art expresses character necessarily. 'Mormonism' tends to purify character. Hence, our faith would act in this way upon art and would thus show itself in the artist's work. On the whole, therefore, I should say that the influence of our religion on art would be wholesome and encouraging."[21]

Evans's boyhood friend from Lehi, James Taylor Harwood (1860–1940), had great natural gifts for portraying the landscape. Harwood took training from Alfred Lambourne and Dan Weggeland, studied at the California School of Design in San Francisco, and is also credited as the first Utah painter to study in France, entering the Julian Academy and in 1889 passing the stringent entrance requirements for the *Ecole des Beaux Arts*. The landmark painting *The Gleaners* (PLATE 92), painted in 1890, is also different in attitude and style from earlier Utah work. French influence is revealed in the academically ordered work theme derived from Millet's *Gleaners*. Fresh pastel colors and shadow effects rendered by broken brushwork show the effect of French artists and teachers who followed the Impressionists.

*This harvest scene from rural France, painted during Harwood's first stay in Paris, was strongly influenced by Millet's Gleaners, one of the most popular paintings of the nineteenth century. Both works express a theme of humble dignity that recalls the story of Ruth in the Old Testament. This painting typifies the Impressionists' fascination with light and color. Stalks of wheat are like strokes of light. Backlighting and contrasting colors help give the scene an atmosphere that seems alive. Although not one of the art missionaries, Harwood was the first Utah artist to study in Paris, and he encouraged others to join him. Unlike the other Utah artists in Paris, Harwood already had considerable professional training. In the years following his return to Utah, he was the major force behind the development of a regional school of Impressionism.*

PLATE 93: **The Wasatch Range, Salt Lake Valley,** 1895

JAMES T. HARWOOD (1860–1940)
OIL ON CANVAS, 32" X 64" (81.3 CM X 162.6 CM)
MUSEUM OF CHURCH HISTORY AND ART

*Utah's distinctive landscape encouraged artists to create regional paintings of the mountains and canyons and the Great Salt Lake. Harwood used the style of Impressionism, applying the effects of light to produce a hazy, subtle scene of the Wasatch Mountains. He used a thick application of paint and short brush strokes to create a natural, spontaneous scene. Harwood's hues appear pale, perhaps indicative of the bleached colors of the arid Utah atmosphere. He rendered shadows in the tones of purple that actually exist in nature rather than in the dull pigments used by earlier artists. Heber J. Grant raised funds to purchase this painting for the Salt Lake Temple soon after its dedication.*

PLATE 94: **The Salt Lake Valley with the Temple, Looking West,** ABOUT 1895

JAMES T. HARWOOD (1860–1940)
OIL ON CANVAS, 20" X 52" (50.8 CM X 132.1 CM)
MUSEUM OF CHURCH HISTORY AND ART

*In this picturesque rendering, Harwood depicted the breadth of the largest Latter-day Saint settlement in its valley setting. The placement of the Salt Lake Temple at the center of the panoramic view reinforces its importance as the spiritual center of Zion. The newly opened streets on the benchland and Anderson's Tower occupy space to the right, while the central business district and residential neighborhoods stretch to the left of the temple. Harwood had just returned from academic training in France and used his new skills to carefully render the effects of light. In this ambitious, backlit scene, the sun's rays emerge from behind the clouds, creating a glare on the lake and the sagebrush. Effects of atmosphere bathe the scene in soft tones, with the foreground in sharper focus.*

PLATE 95: *Church Public Works Blacksmith Shop, Salt Lake City,* ABOUT 1895
JAMES T. HARWOOD (1860–1940)
OIL ON CANVAS, 20" X 31 1/2" (50.8 CM X 80 CM)
MUSEUM OF CHURCH HISTORY AND ART

*In this valuable documentary painting, Harwood invites the onlooker to step back in time to see and feel a bygone era. The work depicts early Public Works shops built at the corner of State and North Temple streets. The constant flow of City Creek (depicted in the foreground) ran a water wheel that provided power for shop machinery used to produce tools. Harwood has captured the peace and serenity of this scene at dusk. His heightened concern for composition is evidenced in the more solid and well-defined forms of the buildings, while the sky and landscape are carried out with techniques of subdued, muted color and broken brush strokes. The diversified play of backlit light and shadows and changing sky creates a special warmth. Warm, glowing light radiates from the windows of the shop, while further evidence of industry ascends with the smoke rising from the chimneys.*

Harwood returned to Utah and opened a studio where he taught painting in the French manner. During the 1890s he completed picturesque, panoramic works of the Salt Lake Valley, typified by *The Wasatch Range* (PLATE 93). About that painting Harwood wrote: "A telegram came to us stating that one of my important landscapes had been sold for two hundred dollars. Heber J. Grant, [later] President of the L.D.S. Church, a good, kind, appreciative man, was instrumental in the purchase of a large oil 'The Wasatch Range' to represent me in the Salt Lake Temple."[22]

A similar work, *The Salt Lake Valley with the Temple* (PLATE 94), features the valley under the glare of the summer sun with the temple symbolically centered. Harwood portrayed the romance of older structures in *Church Public Works Blacksmith Shop* (PLATE 95), invoking a nostalgic mood in its shadowy landscape with glowing sky and the mysterious old building. Again, the piece relies upon French sources. These characteristics are also shown in *Dandelion Fields* (PLATE 96), in which the artist has brought out the vision and beauty of a pioneer farm in a manner recalling these words of Brigham Young:

> Make beautiful everything around you. Cultivate the earth and cultivate your minds. Build cities, adorn your habitations, make gardens, orchards and vineyards, and render the earth so pleasant that when you look upon your labors you may do so with pleasure, and that angels may delight to come and visit your beautiful locations.[23]

Harwood occasionally produced biblical works; the Church Museum's collection contains three of his finest: *Christ and the Woman Accused of Adultery, Christ Walking on the Sea of Galilee* (PLATE 98), and the widely reproduced *Come Follow Me*, commissioned by the Deseret Sunday School Union. His *Hattie Richards Harwood and Child* (PLATE 97) has a Madonna-and-child feeling to it.

PLATE 96: **Dandelion Fields,** 1913

JAMES T. HARWOOD (1860–1940)
OIL ON CANVAS, 25" X 39 3/8" (63.5 CM X 100 CM)
MUSEUM OF CHURCH HISTORY AND ART

*For both French and American Impressionists,
flowers were a popular subject, offering blazing
contrasts of light and shade, intense pure colors,
and decorative exuberance. Harwood's Dandelion
Fields is a notable example. This shimmering
depiction of a rural farm scene with its pastel color,
technique, and subject matter fits solidly within the
school of American Impressionism.*

PLATE 97: **Hattie Richards Harwood
and Child,** ABOUT 1900

JAMES T. HARWOOD (1860–1940)
OIL ON CANVAS, 32" X 24" (81.3 CM X 61 CM)
MUSEUM OF CHURCH HISTORY AND ART

*James and Harriett Richards Harwood were
married in Paris in 1891. In Utah, before their
marriage, Harriett had been one of Harwood's
drawing students. They spent their honeymoon
painting side by side at Pont Aven. This painting
shows Harriett with one of their five children.
Harwood often used them as models. As the only
woman from Utah represented in the women's
building at the World Columbian Exposition in
Chicago in 1893, Harriett was herself an
accomplished artist. She usually worked on small
canvases and particularly enjoyed painting still lifes.*

PLATE 98: **Christ Walking on the
Sea of Galilee,** 1930

JAMES T. HARWOOD (1860–1940)
OIL ON CANVAS, 29 1/2" X 24" (74.9 CM X 61 CM)
MUSEUM OF CHURCH HISTORY AND ART
GIFT OF PHILIP CLARK

*Created when Harwood was seventy years
old, this painting uses a kaleidoscopic
patchwork of rich color to render the
vibrating form of the Savior and the play of
reflections and light on the water. The artist
followed closely the scriptural accounts in the
Gospels. The brushwork technique reinforces
the story in which the disciples in the boat
incorrectly perceived Jesus to be a spirit. The
painting thus offers an accurate illustration
of the text combined with lasting artistic
value. Born in Utah, Harwood came from a
Latter-day Saint background, but there is no
record that he was baptized a member of the
Church. He created a solid body of work for
the Church, and the Museum's collection has
expanded to include his finest paintings
from all phases of his output.*

THE IMPACT OF FRENCH TRAINING ON LATTER-DAY SAINT ART, 1890–1925

59

PLATE 99: **Winter Light, Salt Lake Valley**, 1918
J. LEO FAIRBANKS (1878–1946)
OIL ON CANVAS, 24" x 36" (61 CM x 91.4 CM)
MUSEUM OF CHURCH HISTORY AND ART

*Painted on location, this work captures the light
and feeling of nature together with the rural
landscape of homes and farms nestled against the
Wasatch Mountains. The habitation of the Latter-
day Saints is seen as simple and serene against the
protective mountains to the east. The young J. Leo
pursued both painting and sculpture, carrying out
important projects in several temples. In his later
years he turned more to painting, executing
numerous landscapes of Utah and Oregon.*

PLATE 100: **Life Is the Reward of
Love and Labor,** ABOUT 1920
J. LEO FAIRBANKS (1878–1946)
OIL ON CANVAS, 24" x 48" (61 CM x 122 CM)
MUSEUM OF CHURCH HISTORY AND ART

*This mural sketch depicts how the values of the
pioneer past provide role models for the present.
The themes of marriage, family, affectionate
commitment, and hard work are depicted as the
basis of true living. The spring plowing, the
blossoming fruit trees, and the young couple and
small child living in the springtime of their lives
portray a scene of hope and optimism rooted in a
firm foundation of gospel values. The idyllic setting
in the Heber Valley east of the Wasatch Range
emphasizes the pioneer values of building Zion in
the land of promise. J. Leo Fairbanks was a
prominent muralist; however, the mural that was
to be based on this sketch was never executed.
Fairbanks served on the general board of the
Sunday School for many years and used his art to
teach a whole generation of young Latter-day
Saints about pioneers and the birth of the Church.*

J. Leo Fairbanks (1878–1946) (FIGURE 20) was noted for painting instructional work expressing ideas or history, but his pure landscapes done in Utah, Hawaii, and Oregon reveal his love of
nature and his enjoyment of his art. *Winter Light, Salt Lake Valley* (PLATE 99) uses the brighter
colors and layered brushwork of the American Impressionists to grasp nuances of light and
shadow on a bright winter day near a Mormon-settled farm. Fairbanks's gripping unfinished
mural study *Life Is the Reward of Love and Labor* (PLATE 100) shows how a similar idyllic rural
scene with a family could be turned into a lesson-filled commentary.

The oldest son of John B. Fairbanks, J. Leo studied at the Julian Academy in Paris twelve years
after his father. He was employed for nineteen years as art director for Salt Lake City schools,

THE IMPACT OF FRENCH TRAINING ON LATTER-DAY SAINT ART, 1890–1925

sponsoring classes for students of all ages. J. Leo strongly advocated community beautification, organizing the first Salt Lake City Planning Commission. He was an eloquent speaker with the ability to motivate others to high views and ideals. "Nothing is more delightful than creating lovely things and helping others to appreciate the beautiful," he said.[24] In 1923 Fairbanks became head of the department of art and architecture at Oregon State College (now University), where he remained the rest of his life. The fine turn-of-the-century arts building on that campus bears his name: J. Leo Fairbanks Hall. Two murals, *Learning by Tradition* and *Recorded Information*, were painted for the old library on campus—later Kidder Hall. The mural studies are now in the Church Museum collection. The English-style home he designed for his family is one of the most notable in Corvallis. He also delivered frequent addresses to organizations and spoke about art on radio programs.

Fairbanks participated in many Church projects. He designed the frieze on the Hawaii Temple and painted murals in the Salt Lake Temple. His stained glass windows, including *Salt Lake Temple and Elijah* (PLATE 101), were part of the "Eternal Progress" theme of the Church display at the Chicago World's Fair, 1933–1934. They were reinstalled at the California Pacific International Exposition of 1936 in San Diego and today are in the Salt Lake Temple annex. Fairbanks's illustrations appeared in Church magazines in the 1940s. His finest paintings unite religious narrative with serious art, as in *Jephtha's Daughter* and *The Journey of the Wise Men* (PLATE 102), reproduced in the December 1934 *Improvement Era* with his commentary:

> The picture represents the Wise Men approaching the city of Bethlehem to which strangers were directed by the heavenly symbol. As the lights of Jerusalem became visible, the men argued among themselves that the new King must be born in the City of the King; therefore the great city should be their destination. They turned in that direction only to find that the worldly wisdom had led them astray. After all, they had to go to the small city to which they were originally directed. "To Follow Divine Direction Even the Wisest Men Must Surrender Their Human Wisdom to God's Will." This is the inscription that goes with the picture.[25]

Throughout a lifetime of seeking the good, the true, and the beautiful, J. Leo Fairbanks put into practice the creed that he wrote for himself: "Art is for service; for making things beautiful as well as useful; for lifting men. . . . To me the purpose of art is to visualize ideas, to realize ideals, and to idealize realities."[26]

PLATE 101: *Salt Lake Temple and Elijah with Keys to Genealogy Work,* 1933
J. LEO FAIRBANKS (1878–1946)
LEADED STAINED GLASS, 72" x 48" (182.9 CM x 121.9 CM)
SALT LAKE TEMPLE

*The foundation of Latter-day Saint involvement in family history and temple building was marked by the appearance of Elijah to the Prophet Joseph Smith in the Kirtland Temple in April 1836, as prophesied by Malachi in the Old Testament. This image of Elijah restoring the sealing keys to the earth was originally created by Fairbanks for the Hall of Religion in the Century of Progress Chicago World's Fair in 1933–1934. J. Leo Fairbanks is part of a noted group of Latter-day Saint artists from the Fairbanks family.*

FIGURE 20: J. LEO FAIRBANKS

PLATE 102: *The Journey of the Wise Men,* 1933
J. LEO FAIRBANKS (1878–1946)
OIL ON CANVAS, 34 3/4" x 44 1/2" (88.3 CM x 113 CM)
MUSEUM OF CHURCH HISTORY AND ART

*J. Leo Fairbanks painted and sculpted numerous works with religious themes. This painting shows the wise men of the New Testament nativity, mounted on their camels and inspired by the new star shining in the eastern heavens, descending a treacherous mountain pass on their way to visit the newborn Christ child. Fairbanks also painted murals in temples, created a number of illustrations of the Book of Mormon, and portrayed epic pioneer scenes from Latter-day Saint history.*

PLATE 103: *John the Baptist Presents Christ before the People*, 1892
HERMAN H. HAAG (1871–1895)
CHARCOAL ON PAPER, 22" x 31" (55.8 CM x 78.7 CM)
MUSEUM OF CHURCH HISTORY AND ART

*Christ was introduced to John the Baptist's followers with the simple testimony, "Behold the Lamb of God, which taketh away the sin of the world" (John 1:29). Haag's careful composition helps illustrate this New Testament scripture. Christ, the light of the world, walks in a shaft of light toward John the Baptist. John, recognizing Christ, gestures to Him. John's followers, not yet knowing the Savior or understanding His teachings, stand in partial darkness. Haag received an award for this drawing in 1892 while studying at the Julian Academy in Paris. A German-born convert to the Church and immigrant to Utah, Haag had been one of James Harwood's students in Salt Lake City. In 1891, the two men journeyed together to Paris to study art. Haag was one of the few Paris-trained Utah artists who remained largely unaffected by impressionistic art. He died of a persistent lung illness shortly after his return to Utah.*

DEPICTING SCRIPTURAL STORIES AND PRINCIPLES IN ART

In 1890 the Deseret Sunday School Union sponsored a competition with cash prizes soliciting pictures that illustrated the life of Nephi. A circular was sent to "all the home artists known to the Board."[27] Two artists of the pioneer generation, C. C. A. Christensen and George M. Ottinger, were winners. The younger generation that studied in Paris depicted scriptural themes as fine art rather than illustration, but reproductions of their works were still sometimes published.

Herman H. Haag (1871–1895) was raised in Germany in a religious family that prepared him to be a good artist of scriptural themes. When he was born, his mother was reported to have chosen the three Hs of his name to remind him of "Holy, Holy, Holy is the Lord," and his father called him "Herman der Herzhafte" (the courageous).[28] Herman joined the Church with his mother and siblings and immigrated to Payson, Utah, when he was eleven years old. He spent his high school years at the Brigham Young Academy, where his artistic talent blossomed. Haag joined the art missionaries in France at the Julian Academy in June 1891, becoming the fifth artist sponsored by the Church. In a letter to his sister he contrasted the Sunday activity of

PLATE 104: *Nephi Obtains the Plates from Laban*, 1894
HERMAN H. HAAG (1871–1895)
OIL ON CANVAS, 47" x 36" (119.4 CM x 91.4 CM)
MUSEUM OF CHURCH HISTORY AND ART

*Haag's strengths as a visual storyteller are evident in this painting. Standing over the drunken Laban, Nephi contemplates the whisperings of the Spirit guiding him to obtain the sacred plates of brass in Laban's possession. With sword in hand, Nephi must decide whether to obey the Spirit and kill Laban, or let him live. Nephi's dilemma is enhanced by his position halfway in and halfway out of the bright moonlight. Haag, who preferred to work with narrative subject matter, accented the drama of the scene through strong lighting.*

PLATE 105: *Moroni Delivers*
*the Gold Plates,* 1923
LEWIS RAMSEY (1875–1941)
OIL ON CANVAS, 65" X 41" (165.1 CM X 104.1 CM)
MUSEUM OF CHURCH HISTORY AND ART

*In 1823, the Angel Moroni revealed the location of
the gold plates to the Prophet Joseph Smith. Joseph
returned as instructed to the same spot each year.
Finally, on September 22, 1827, Joseph received
the plates with instructions to translate them. This
painting depicts that event. The rays of sunshine
breaking through the clouds represent the dawning
of a new day through the restoration of the gospel.
Lewis Ramsey painted this scene in 1923, the
centennial anniversary of Moroni's first visit to
Joseph Smith. Ramsey studied art in Boston and
Paris. He became well-known as a landscape and
portrait painter and an art teacher in Utah and
California. He painted several copies of this
painting, including one that hangs in the Salt Lake
Eleventh Ward building, Ramsey's home ward.*

Parisians with that of Utahns, adding, "I know what I have come here for, and have it on my
mind continually to make the best use of my time."[29] His sensitive charcoal drawing *John the
Baptist Presents Christ* (PLATE 103) won an award at the Academy. He taught at Latter-day Saint
University and was an art instructor at the University of Utah in 1894 when he completed *Nephi
Obtains the Plates from Laban* (PLATE 104). Tragically, the life of this artist of great promise ended
when he was only twenty-three years old.

Lewis Ramsey (1875–1941) painted scriptural-historical works for Church meetinghouses in
Oregon and Utah. *Moroni Delivers the Gold Plates* (PLATE 105) hung at the Bureau of Information

on Temple Square and is now displayed in the entrance of the "Covenant Restored" permanent historical exhibit at the Church Museum. Ramsey was twelve years old when his family joined the Church in Illinois. He moved to Payson, where his early art interest developed into study with

J. B. Fairbanks and John Hafen, and he graduated from Brigham Young Academy in 1891. Ramsey joined the long line of Latter-day Saint artists who enrolled at the Julian Academy in Paris. In 1903 he returned to take a position at LDS University in Salt Lake City, instructing future teachers in the rudiments of art. His early work for the Church was posthumous portraiture of early leaders. His famous 1910 portrait of Joseph Smith (FIGURE 21) was praised by the Prophet's cousin-by-marriage Bathsheba Smith. Around this same time Ramsey did numerous illustrations for Church magazines and for a book, *From Plowboy to Prophet*. In about 1915 he

FIGURE 21: PORTRAIT OF JOSEPH SMITH

was called to paint preliminary murals in the Hawaii Temple, fulfilling a prediction Manti Temple President Daniel H. Wells had made years before. His later work consists of landscapes painted on location at national parks, among them *Grand Canyon*, now in the Church collection.

## LATTER-DAY SAINT LIFE IN ART

Latter-day Saint life as portrayed by local artists from 1890 to 1925 centered on the rural environment, and the topics and style were influenced by the academic standards of the French salon. During this period the documentary photography of C. R. Savage and especially George Edward Anderson expressed the wider range of Mormon life in the family, community, and Church.

PLATE 106: *The Harvest, Salt Lake County*, 1896
LORUS PRATT (1855–1923)
OIL ON CANVAS, 30" x 48" (76.2 CM x 122 CM)
MUSEUM OF CHURCH HISTORY AND ART

*This work is one of a series of three paintings Pratt created on the different stages of the grain harvest, all taking place in the same southwestern part of Salt Lake Valley. The farmers, enveloped in rising clouds of dust, load sheaves of grain into a threshing machine. Others pitch the straw, load the wagons, and watch the horses. Pratt was influenced by popular French landscape artists while studying at the Julian Academy in Paris. After returning to Utah, he continued using French landscape techniques in his paintings. The Harvest is particularly impressionistic in its emphasis on sunlight and atmosphere and in short, choppy brush strokes. Also indicative of the more modern French influence is the artist's attempt to record an "impression" of a fleeting moment in time, an ordinary yet vital slice of rural life.*

PLATE 107: *Jordan River Landscape,*
*Salt Lake Valley,* 1901
LORUS PRATT (1855–1923)
OIL ON CANVAS, 28" x 51" (71.1 CM X 129.5 CM)
MUSEUM OF CHURCH HISTORY AND ART

*After the turn of the century, Lorus Pratt*
*repeatedly painted the Jordan River, which flows*
*through west Salt Lake City into the Great Salt*
*Lake. Though he frequently painted in the brilliant*
*impressionistic mode, Pratt sometimes used a more*
*subdued Barbizon style, as seen in this pastoral*
*scene along the Jordan. Elements of the Mormon*
*landscape are evident in the setting: the tall,*
*straight poplars, the dry rolling hills in the*
*background, and the irrigated fields along the*
*riverbanks. Lorus Pratt, son of Apostle Orson Pratt,*
*was one of the five Paris art missionaries who*
*studied at the Julian Academy in the early 1890s.*

Professional artist Lorus Pratt (1855–1923) (FIGURE 22), a son of Elder Orson Pratt, did conventional landscapes and portraits for the Latter-day Saint market through the 1880s. After Paris

study, Pratt developed a half-dozen large, panoramic landscape compositions about life on the land. Forms such as haystacks are placed in rows to direct the eye to the work activity, as in *The Harvest* (PLATE 106). Here, short strokes of thickly applied paint simulate the play of light over the landscape. Another artful work, *Jordan River Landscape* (PLATE 107), was influenced by Pratt's French academic teachers. He copied this painting again and again for customers. Pratt helped establish the French Art Mission when he and

FIGURE 22: LORUS PRATT

Hafen made initial contacts with Church leaders, and part of the correspondence from the First Presidency was directed to him. George Q. Cannon wrote to the artists in Paris:

> We feel deeply interested in your success. We want you to become good artists, and to avail yourselves of all the advantages which the French government has so liberally put within the reach of students. . . . We want to see our young men qualified in every direction, so that the Lord's name may be glorified and his cause advanced through their labors and their proficiency in all the arts.[30]

When the missionaries returned, the Salt Lake Temple murals became the joint effort of five artists. Lorus Pratt assisted with the backgrounds.

The photographs done by George Edward Anderson (1860–1928) (FIGURE 23) provide a remarkable fifty-year visual record of Mormon life in rural central and southern Utah. After apprenticing with C. R. Savage, Anderson set up a studio in Salt Lake City but soon moved to Springville. About 1880 he equipped a wagon with a photographic lab and tent studio, creating a portable facility for producing pictures of people in their own villages. Besides taking regular gallery photographs, Anderson also recorded people before their homes, on their farms, in their shops, at work, and at play. People were at the heart of his photographs, and they appear natural

FIGURE 23: GEORGE
EDWARD ANDERSON

before the camera. *Ether Blanchard Family* (PLATE 108) is a statement about place and time, the

**Ether Blanchard Family Cutting
Grain near Springville, Utah,** 1902

GEORGE EDWARD ANDERSON (1860–1928)
GELATIN SILVER PRINT, 16" X 20"
(40.6 CM X 50.8 CM)
MUSEUM OF CHURCH HISTORY AND ART
COURTESY BRIGHAM YOUNG
UNIVERSITY ARCHIVES

*"Most boys like Achilles Blanchard, at
right, were kept out of school when
necessary to assist with farm work,"
photography historian Rell Francis said
of this piece. Ether insisted on
harvesting the hay and grain on his
thirteen acres with the outmoded cradle
scythe. The grain shocks were hand tied
with cords made of wheat stalks. With
a passion for documenting the events of
daily life, turn-of-the-century
photographer George Edward
Anderson photographed many scenes
like this one. A large number of
Anderson's photographs detail what
Mormon life was like in rural Utah in
the late nineteenth and early twentieth
centuries. In 1877, at the age of
seventeen, Anderson went into business
for himself by setting up a photography
studio in Salt Lake City. He had
worked as an apprentice for three
years with early Utah photographer
Charles R. Savage. For most of his
career, Anderson worked out of his
studio in Springville, Utah.*

PLATE 109: **Sister Manwaring and
Children at Prayer,** 1903

GEORGE EDWARD ANDERSON (1860–1928)
GELATIN SILVER PRINT, 15 1/2" X 19 1/2"
(39.4 CM X 49.5 CM)
MUSEUM OF CHURCH HISTORY AND ART

*Albert Manwaring, in England serving
a mission for the Church, received a
copy of this photograph from his
family. It shows his wife and daughters
praying for his success and protection.
Though Anderson preferred on-site
documentary photography, his studio
photographs often tell a story. In this
case, instead of merely recording the
appearance of a missionary's wife and
children, Anderson has captured the
love and concern they have for the
absent husband and father. To increase
business, Anderson traveled to rural
towns in Utah, setting up a portable
tent studio to photograph the local
residents. He was a personable man,
skilled at making people feel
comfortable in front of the camera.
His portraits reveal the character
and personality of his subjects.*

identity and roles of the subjects, and a way of life. The organization of the elements in this picture enables the viewer to understand clearly the story of life on a farm. Telling a story is also the intent of the beautiful photograph of *Sister Manwaring and Children* (PLATE 109), and its message about prayer is movingly conveyed. In 1881 Anderson opened a studio in Manti and began recording the building of the great Manti Temple. Olive Lowry, a young woman he photographed in his "Temple Bazaar" gallery, became his wife in May 1888; they were the second couple to be sealed in the recently completed temple. Anderson's classic *Manti Temple* composition (PLATE 110) was taken several years later, with the temple standing as a sentinel to the community.

After serving as bishop of the Springville Second Ward, Anderson was called on a mission to England in 1906. Before crossing the Atlantic, he spent one year with permission of Church leaders shooting with a view camera the significant Church historical sites in Vermont, New York, Pennsylvania, Ohio, Missouri, and Illinois. Anderson's poetic picture of the *Sacred Grove* (PLATE 111) has become likely the most recognizable image of this site where young Joseph Smith experienced his first vision. In 1909 the Deseret Sunday School Union published many of Anderson's photographs in *The Birth of Mormonism in Picture*, a booklet used to teach Church history. After completing his proselyting mission Anderson again traveled to Vermont to record Joseph Smith's birthplace and nearby sites associated with the Smith family. By taking upon himself the largely unsolicited task of documenting Latter-day Saint history, he left to his wife the role of family provider. After seven years he finally returned to Springville. One of his friends noted that while other Utah photographers "were in the business for money, Anderson was in it for art and history. That was his failure."[31]

PLATE 110: *Manti Township with the Temple, Looking North*, ABOUT 1895
GEORGE EDWARD ANDERSON (1860–1928)
GELATIN SILVER PRINT, 15" X 21" (38.1 CM X 53.3 CM)
MUSEUM OF CHURCH HISTORY AND ART
COURTESY UTAH STATE HISTORICAL SOCIETY

*The boys posed on a hilltop pull the viewer into this expansive view of Manti, Utah. Details such as house styles, barns, fences, trees, and irrigation ditches are clearly evident, creating an exacting record of a Mormon settlement. George Edward Anderson, a second-generation Utah photographer, captured many elements of Latter-day Saint settlement and social life during his productive career. His aesthetic intuition helped him create masterpieces of historic documentation.*

Throughout his days, Anderson took memorable photographs of Latter-day Saint activities and life, recording baptisms in the country, old folks' dinners, Church meetings, Primary and MIA festivals and parades, patriotic celebrations, Relief Society projects, Church building projects, and many other topics—usually without prospect for financial return. He traveled from town to town "without purse or scrip," trading photos for meals or lodging. He caught a ride to Cardston, Alberta, to record the completion of the temple there, and was in Mesa to record the Saints and the completion of the Arizona Temple in 1927, near the end of his life. Rell Francis wrote of George Edward Anderson's commitment to his work and its consequences:

> His quest to document church subjects as beautifully as possible was a demanding mistress. . . . The uniqueness of his pictures . . . includes their timely regard for ordinary events of human life that are now a part of history. They exist for us because George Edward Anderson was there. He had little practical or monetary reason for making many of these exposures, but some imperative force caused him to stop, set up his cumbersome camera, and record telling images.[32]

## SUMMARY

George Edward Anderson learned through practical experience how to illuminate and "paint" his photographic subjects with natural light. By contrast, the Latter-day Saint artists who studied in Paris in the 1890s completely changed their approach to artwork as a result of their training and contact with French Impressionism. By working in the open air they learned how sunlight and atmosphere envelop the landscape, and how to render form by utilizing short brush strokes of bright pigment. They turned away from the grand, dramatic landscape to eagerly embrace quiet and intimate views, fleeting effects of light and color, and a spiritual focus. The essence of a scene was now grasped in one or two sittings on site rather than in laborious studio work. John Hafen and James T. Harwood continued working in this mode the rest of their lives; they were the finest artists among the group of regional Impressionists who worked in Utah during the era lasting from 1890 to 1925.

Hafen's *Bluffdale Landscape* (PLATE 112) sums up what the artists gained abroad. Light vibrates across this painting in bursts of fresh color, and a silvery atmosphere bathes the valley and mountains beyond. This new painting manner reinforced Hafen's religious convictions and his fervent beliefs as "an ardent and sincere student of nature. . . ; he communes with it, he loves it. God is the author of nature. Anything which He has created is elevating and refining."[33]

PLATE 112: *Bluffdale Landscape*, 1902
JOHN HAFEN (1856–1910)
OIL ON CANVAS, 16" x 24" (40.6 CM X 61 CM)
MUSEUM OF CHURCH HISTORY AND ART

*This painting was among the more than 150 artworks that Hafen produced for the Church when he was hired to paint over a two-year period. In France, Hafen learned how to render effects of light and shade in landscape, and he now sought out subjects illuminated in unusual ways. In this backlit scene, brilliant highlights outline the man's left side, the fence rails, and the tops of the trees. Hafen avoided black and grey pigments, instead rendering the shadow areas in soft lavender and bluish hues. Here man, as steward of God's creations, has created an idyllic Eden of order and beauty, and one can feel the artist's contentment and joy in beholding such a scene. The added human element seems to represent the artist surveying what is before him.*

# DEVELOPING A REGIONAL LATTER-DAY SAINT ART, 1925–1965

3

*by Robert O. Davis*

I n a 1933 letter to the *Improvement Era*, the great Latter-day Saint landscape artist LeConte Stewart wrote: "The Church has been the real patron of the arts in Utah, and I owe a great deal to the opportunities given to me."[1] During this period many artists received assignments from the Church to produce a wide variety of works; some projects, including decorating entire temples, took years to complete. Explicit commissions were often given, while in other cases artists planned works and then submitted them to the Church for approval. Responding to current trends, artists of the Church—in this era working mainly in Utah—established a unique regional and religious identity in their choices of subject matter. The generation of artists who served the Church from 1925 to 1965 was the first to be trained in the United States, and their work was specifically American in approach. Several prominent artists and photographers who were not Church members also created significant work about Latter-day Saint life during this era.

This forty-year period saw great expansion of Church building efforts. Five new temples required extensive programs of painting and sculpture, and murals were added to rooms in earlier temples. In the hundreds of meetinghouses built during this era, religious artwork was sometimes part of the interior design, and Church architects worked closely with artists. Artwork was sometimes bestowed as a gift, or was acquired at the request of influential people or ward committees. During this period the Church developed key historic sites, including the Hill Cumorah in New York and the Winter Quarters Cemetery in Nebraska, and artists had major roles in designing commemorative monuments. The Bureau of Information on Temple Square made use of the Church collection, and visitors' centers employed extensive illustrative work in their educational programs. Several leaders, including President Heber J. Grant, expanded the Church collection by personally patronizing artists.

## ART IN CHURCH BUILDINGS

During and immediately after World War I, the new temples at Hawaii and Alberta needed art for their interior walls. The finest young artists in the Church were called upon, and their work was in harmony with the progressive intentions of the architects and advisors. Twenty-five years later, Minerva Teichert and Robert Shepherd completed mural cycles in the Manti Temple, built the previous century. By the end of this era, with the 1964 dedication of the Oakland Temple, murals were no longer painted in ordinance rooms.

In Utah, Lynn Fausett (1894–1977) is best known for three murals. He studied art at Brigham Young Academy from 1910 to 1912, and eventually landed in New York City, where he became associated with the Art Students League as a student and later as president. Returning to Utah in 1938, he carried out a large Works Progress Administration-sponsored mural in Price depicting the pioneer history of the region. The commemorative *Founding of the Primary* (PLATE 113), commissioned for the Farmington Ward chapel, is a work grounded more in ordinary life than in the ideal or the beautiful. Fausett expressed in 1959 the scope of the experience of the Mormon pioneers in another mural at the This Is the Place Monument Visitors' Center. It conveys an immense amount of information through its minute detail.

*Facing page: Detail from*
**November Hills, Eden, Utah,**
*by LeConte Stewart.*
*(See Plate 137, page 92.)*

PLATE 113: **The Founding of the Primary Association, August 25, 1878**, 1941
LYNN FAUSETT (1894–1977)
OIL ON CANVAS, 96" X 300" (243.8 CM X 762 CM)
ROCK MEETINGHOUSE, FARMINGTON, UTAH

*Children of Farmington, Utah, have come together for the first Primary gathering, where they will be instructed in obedience, honesty, faith, prayer, punctuality, and good manners. Lynn Fausett, a talented and experienced muralist, documented and gave form to this important event on the organization's sixty-third anniversary. Using portraits and photographs of the original members, Fausett captured the spirit and the times of the people. His talent for design endows the mural with sculptural forms expressed through rich primary colors. The small girl in yellow invites the viewer into the room's activity.*

FIGURE 24: MINERVA
KOHLHEPP TEICHERT

In contrast, the murals of Minerva Kohlhepp Teichert (1888–1976) (FIGURE 24) reduce detail to emphasize the main point. Teichert was dedicated to the lofty goal of creating a distinctly Latter-day Saint art for the walls of LDS meetinghouses and temples, and she relentlessly pursued this mission as she raised a family, managed a large cattle ranch, and served the Church and community. The artist summed up her life in 1947:

> I married my cowboy sweetheart, which was right. My first son was born while my husband was serving in France. I painted stage scenery to pay for his birth. I painted what I loved for the Pocatello Tabernacle—Not Alone—got thirty-eight dollars for it. . . . For the next ten years I helped in the hay fields. My first three little boys grew up beside a haystack. . . . When the American Falls Dam went in I was the last white woman out of the Snake River Bottoms. . . . I spent most of the mornings for the next fifteen years in the milk house. The children must be educated, etc. I painted after they were tucked into bed at night. I *must* paint. It's a disease.[2]

Minerva Teichert considered painting religious-historical murals to be her mission. She was born of pioneer stock whose trek west provided experiences that could be put to canvas, and she also knew the scriptures intimately and had an innate sense of how to portray their stories. Raised on humble dirt farms in Utah and Idaho, young Minerva possessed a natural gift for drawing animals and an indomitable will to succeed. After graduating from Pocatello High she taught in one-room schoolhouses, earning money to finance her studies at the Chicago Art Institute and the Art Students League. At the League in 1916 her mentor, the famous American artist Robert Henri, gave the diminutive, charismatic woman a mandate to go home to her people and tell through art "your great Mormon story."[3] She returned to Pocatello to open a studio.

After marrying in 1917, Minerva was commissioned by local Church leaders to paint the mural *Not Alone,* a work about pioneer sacrifice. Her painting was curtailed during the 1920s as she helped to develop the ranch along the Snake River Bottoms, and as she bore her five children. Moving to a large ranch near Cokeville, Wyoming, she resumed painting in the 1930s when Alice Merrill Horne, her agent, helped local school districts and wards acquire murals. Salt Lake City's Garden Park Ward, for example, installed four large biblical paintings in the chapel, and the nearby Yalecrest Ward put a mural in the foyer.

Teichert created artworks to teach the gospel and edify the viewer. She foresaw a great future for Latter-day Saint art. "We must paint the great Mormon story of our pioneers," she wrote. "This story thrills me, fills me, drives me on. . . . We will develop a style distinctly our own. We'll tell our stories on the walls."[4] The religious art she advocated should be "rich in story and backed by a great faith."[5] Themes were portrayed as epics—larger than life. Teichert believed that art should extend beyond mere enjoyment to perform a higher function: it must motivate people; it had to help build Zion. These concepts are reflected in *Handcart Pioneers* (PLATE 114). Here the pioneers are clearly in charge of their lives, with a heroic woman, head held high, rejoicing at the first sight of the Salt Lake Valley.

PLATE 114: **Handcart Pioneers,** ABOUT 1940

MINERVA K. TEICHERT (1888–1976)
OIL ON CANVAS, 68" X 51" (172.7 CM X 129.5 CM)
MUSEUM OF CHURCH HISTORY AND ART

*Poised at the edge of the Salt Lake Valley, the female figure in this painting turns to wave encouragement to her*
*trail-weary companions. The emotion of the moment is that of a "triumphal entry" to Zion. The woman, heroic in*
*expression, wears a dress decorated in a bird-of-paradise motif from fabric owned by Sara Bundy Wade, Minerva's*
*great-grandmother, who died at Winter Quarters in 1846. While studying at the Art Students League in New York,*
*Teichert accepted Robert Henri's charge to return home and paint the "great Mormon story." She painted hundreds*
*of canvases that narrated stories of pioneering, settlement, and the scriptures.*

*The Mormon trek, the subject of this grand example of narrative painting, remains an event of central importance to Latter-day Saints. The artist reinforces its enduring value by portraying her father as the pioneer on horseback, her son as the boy in the wagon, and a family as the focus of the trek. The wagon hoops draw compositional attention to the new mother in the wagon, revealing the artist's emphasis on women in Church history. The infant in the mother's arms and the stars in the early dawn complete the title's allusion to the birth of Jesus, ennobling the role of motherhood. Minerva Teichert's career reached its height during the decade of celebrations surrounding the centennial of the Mormon trek west. With an appreciation for her heritage and her own pioneering spirit, she memorialized the pioneers in hundreds of large canvases. She considered* Madonna of 1847 *to be one of her finest works. For days she painted at dawn to properly capture the early morning light as viewed through the east-facing window of her living-room studio (see Figure 25).*

Teichert's eleven-foot-wide mural *Madonna of 1847* (PLATE 115) was originally hung in a Cache Valley middle school to educate students about the pioneer history of their region. The figures, painted with bold and aggressive brushwork, fill the entire picture, with massive, straining oxen and a horseman directly approaching the viewer. *First Plowing* (PLATE 116) and *Indian Night Raid* (PLATE 117) also utilize these techniques.

The compassion of Jesus was a favorite Teichert theme, as in *Christ Teaching Mary and Martha* (PLATE 118), in which He is placed in an ordinary kitchen. Reed Dayton, Teichert's bishop and stake president, related: "I have posed for the Christ in some of her paintings. . . . I was deeply impressed as she told me she never undertook a painting without first seeking the help of the Master Artist."[6]

In 1947 the artist completed several paintings celebrating the centennial of the first pioneers' arrival in the Salt Lake Valley, and that summer she was commissioned to paint the immense *Pageant of History* murals (PLATE 119) on the four walls of the world room of the Manti Temple— more than four thousand square feet of surface. Teichert completed the project in just seven weeks, depicting "the world" as a great pageant with people and nations interacting.

Another favorite subject was the role women played in the work of the Lord. Teichert searched the scriptures and LDS history for stories in which women were involved in the action. *Queen Esther* (PLATE 120) is a fine example.

Teichert used art to enrich people. She brought relatives and townfolk into her living-room studio (FIGURE 25) to pose; as she worked, she shared the stories she was painting with her models and visitors, thus connecting the past with the present. She gave floral paintings as gifts on holidays, as

PLATE 116: *First Plowing,* ABOUT 1935
MINERVA K. TEICHERT (1888–1976)
OIL ON CANVAS, 45" X 68" (114.3 CM X 172.7 CM)
MUSEUM OF CHURCH HISTORY AND ART

*The first plowing and planting in the Salt Lake Valley becomes a religious act in this painting. Heads of both men and beasts are bowed as if in prayer, and the seagulls, a symbol of God's goodness, hover above in seeming blessing. In this sacred scene, the temporal acts of farming are interpreted as spiritual contributions to building the kingdom. This fine work illustrates Teichert's command of human and animal anatomy, yet it is also beautiful in its color harmonies. The power and boldness in this image indicate that Teichert was totally removed from the "pretty," highly detailed still lifes and landscapes painted by most women artists of the period. This piece is a statement of her natural inclinations toward expressing the strength and drama inherent in those who work with and are close to the earth.*

PLATE 117: *Indian Night Raid,* ABOUT 1935
MINERVA K. TEICHERT (1888–1976)
OIL ON CANVAS, 45" x 68" (114.3 CM X 172.7 CM)
MUSEUM OF ART, BRIGHAM YOUNG UNIVERSITY

*Under the cloak of night, Indians raid a pioneer camp, rustling a herd of horses without detection. Teichert seems to honor the Indians' skill and cunning as she makes them the heroes of this scene. Teichert was masterful in her portrayal of animals, Native Americans, and frontier life, partly because she experienced all of those firsthand. She could handle a horse or herd cattle as well as she could paint them, and the Shoshone Indians of the American Falls region of Idaho were her friends. Teichert helped her husband with the work on their Wyoming ranch, and retreated to painting only in the evenings or early mornings.*

wedding presents, or as condolences at funerals. Under an arrangement with Brigham Young University, Teichert exchanged artwork for tuition scholarships for her children and many others, especially those who needed assistance. As a result, the university now possesses a large collection of her works, many of them on public display. Late in life Teichert donated to BYU a series of about forty-five paintings of Book of Mormon themes. Faith resonates through these works and in her writings, as in this excerpt from an autobiographical sketch:

> Eternity seems very real to me. It's just a continuation. I want a touch of red in my heaven and [to] be able to paint after I leave here. . . . As the children grow more responsible and I find more freedom I do not care for bridge or teas or clubs, but the story of building a mountain empire, and the struggles of my people drive me on.[7]

Teichert saw the prospect for a golden age of Latter-day Saint art, telling the story of the Church and faith of its people in a distinctive style. "The next great art of the world will be Mormon," she confidently stated.[8] She sought that dream with deeds as she produced her artistic legacy.

FIGURE 25: MINERVA TEICHERT'S LIVING-ROOM STUDIO

PLATE 118: *Christ Teaching Mary and Martha,* 1941
MINERVA K. TEICHERT (1888–1976)
OIL ON CANVAS, 36" X 48" (91.4 CM X 121.9 CM)
MUSEUM OF ART, BRIGHAM YOUNG UNIVERSITY

*In this domestic scene, Teichert captures the depth of Christ's compassion and empathy for the humble and honest. Many of Minerva Teichert's religious works feature women of the scriptures. Perhaps she felt keenly drawn to this particular domestic theme because it reflected a part of her own life—that of teaching the gospel to her family while creating her paintings in her home in Cokeville, Wyoming.*

PLATE 119: *The Pageant of History,* 1947
MINERVA K. TEICHERT (1888–1976)
OIL ON CANVAS,
NORTH WALL 266" X 714" (675.6 CM X 1813.6 CM),
WEST WALL 266" X 282" (675.6 CM X 716.3 CM)
WORLD ROOM, MANTI TEMPLE

*The Church commissioned Teichert to create this mural for the Manti Temple world room. In it, she depicted the world through an interaction of peoples. Processions of explorers and conquerors are driven by their quest for wealth and power, while prophets and pilgrims search for religious and other personal freedoms. They converge on a wall dominated by a twelve-foot Indian representing America, and a City of Zion resembling the Salt Lake Valley. This immense undertaking, loosely painted and lacking in detail, reveals Teichert's personal manner of draftsmanship.*

PLATE 120:
**Queen Esther,
Portrait of Betty Curtis,**
1937

MINERVA K. TEICHERT
(1888–1976)
OIL ON CANVAS
(UNSTRETCHED),
63" x 45 1/4"
(160 CM x 114.9 CM)
MUSEUM OF ART,
BRIGHAM YOUNG UNIVERSITY

*The courage and determination of the biblical Queen Esther are captured in this portrait. Rather than narrating the story, the artist has tried to illuminate the elements of Esther's character that led her to save her people. Esther in her idealized beauty is reminiscent of period cinema posters, but, unlike most of those, she is an image of chaste modesty. The model for Esther was Teichert's Cokeville, Wyoming, friend and neighbor Betty Curtis. Teichert's paintings are filled with images of family and friends whom she cajoled into sitting for her. Their cooperation allowed her to keep up a vigorous painting schedule, although isolated from studios and professional models on a ranch in western Wyoming.*

Like Teichert, Edward Grigware (1889–1960) painted in heroic scale, but his manner is more illustrative. His work for the Church includes two large mural groups. The Cody, Wyoming, LDS meetinghouse features a complex circular mural cycle that portrays the history of the Church through eight presidential administrations, concluding with that of George Albert Smith. He was also commissioned to produce murals for the Los Angeles Temple (FIGURE 26). The Church Museum possesses his fluent preliminary watercolor sketches, including the peaceful *Garden of Eden* (PLATE 121).

PLATE 121: *The Garden of Eden,* 1955
EDWARD GRIGWARE (1889–1960)
WATERCOLOR ON PAPER, 20" X 23 1/2"
(50.8 CM X 60 CM)
WORKING SKETCH FOR GARDEN ROOM MURAL,
LOS ANGELES TEMPLE
MUSEUM OF CHURCH HISTORY AND ART
GIFT OF LLOYD TAGGART FAMILY

*Edward Grigware prepared this watercolor study for the Los Angeles Temple garden room mural. Grigware created a sense of being in the Garden, and reproduced God's creations with an intense feeling for beauty and accuracy. Grigware, a successful artist and muralist, had a flair for colorful composition. His use of dark shadows contrasts dramatically with brilliant light glowing through the trees. Not a member of the Church, Grigware studied its doctrine, which helped him to paint with knowledge and skill.*

FIGURE 26: LOS ANGELES TEMPLE

## PORTRAYING THE PEOPLE

In this period Church leaders continued to have official portraits done for display in the Salt Lake Temple and other locations. Further commissions were given to Lee Greene Richards of Salt Lake City, with several also going to John Willard Clawson (1858–1936) of California, a top artist and grandson of Brigham Young. Portraits of members of the Quorum of the Twelve were formal and uniform, life-size, usually on 28-by-22-inch canvas, showing the head and upper body on a slightly variegated background. Portraits of Church presidents were usually larger and more ambitious, often done by nonlocal artists.

Gordon Cope (1906– ), primarily a landscapist, also produced fine portraits. In the 1930s he completed the official portrait of Utah governor Henry Blood, and his painting of Elder J. Golden Kimball (PLATE 123) brings out Kimball's great wit. After receiving training from LeConte Stewart, Cope traveled overseas to study at the Julian Academy in Paris. He returned to head the art department at LDS University in Salt Lake City. Cope was a leading rural landscapist in Utah, but later moved to California. Throughout a long career his style has been direct; his philosophy

PLATE 122: *George Q. Morris,* 1961
EMIL KOSA JR. (1903–1968)
OIL ON CANVAS, 30" x 24" (76.2 CM x 61 CM)
MUSEUM OF CHURCH HISTORY AND ART

*Church portraits preserve for posterity the likenesses of Church leaders and recognize them for their significant service. Emil Kosa Jr. created this work shortly before the death of Elder Morris, a member of the Quorum of the Twelve from 1954 to 1962. A Paris-trained artist and accomplished portrait painter, Kosa is well-known for his representational watercolors. The deep green background of the portrait reflects his romantic nature and his love of the old master painters.*

PLATE 123: *J. Golden Kimball,* 1933
GORDON NICHOLSON COPE (1906– )
OIL ON PANEL, 31 1/2" x 24" (80 CM x 61 CM)
MUSEUM OF CHURCH HISTORY AND ART

*J. Golden Kimball (1853–1938), son of early Church leader Heber C. Kimball, was a member of the First Council of the Seventy from 1892 to 1938. Beloved by many, he became known for forthright speeches delivered in a high-pitched voice, and for his insightful sense of humor and often salty vocabulary. The latter two characteristics were rooted in his early years as a sheepherder and mule skinner. Artist Gordon Cope began his art education in Salt Lake with A.B. Wright and LeConte Stewart. In 1924 he traveled to Europe, where he studied extensively. Cope's portrayal of J. Golden Kimball is painted with muted colors and subdued lighting, reminiscent of Depression Era, American Scene Movement art of the 1930s.*

*Because no known photographs exist of Joseph
Smith, artists of various abilities and cultural
backgrounds have based their likenesses on early
paintings, the Prophet's death mask, and verbal
accounts of his appearance. In 1959 President David
O. McKay commissioned Alvin Gittins to paint his
impression of the Prophet. It quickly became a
popular image used widely in the Church. Born in
England, Alvin Gittins joined the University of Utah
faculty in 1947 and developed into Utah's most
dominant portraitist. Gittins was adept not only at
painting the likenesses of his subjects, but also
unveiling their unique "signatures" or personalities.
His portraits are bold and authoritative, often
capturing the individual at a dramatic moment.*

*This life-size portrait bust conveys President Young's
resoluteness and the qualities that led George Bernard
Shaw to write, "Brigham Young lived to become
immortal in history as an American Moses by leading
his people through the wilderness into an unpromised
land." It is one in a series of commemorative busts of
early Church leaders by the sculptor. Ortho Fairbanks,
a member of the noted Fairbanks family of artists, has
produced many works of public sculpture. His work for
the Church includes a large bronze relief of Christ in
the temple for the Highland View Ward in Salt Lake
City and a painted mural for the ward meetinghouse in
Halawa, Hawaii. After graduating from the University
of Utah, Fairbanks taught at several institutions
including the Church College in Laie, Hawaii. His
marble and bronze portraits of notable people include
seven of Church leaders in the Museum collection.*

of art and life are also revealed directly in his own words: "The language of paint has little need of the verb crutch, having a singleness of approach and purpose peculiar to itself. . . . If it is true that a picture is worth a thousand words, why require a thousand words to illustrate the picture?"[9]

After World War II, Church commissions were divided among several artists. Emil Kosa Jr. (1903–1968), a non-LDS painter from southern California, was skilled at bringing out character traits, as in his warm and friendly portrait of Elder George Q. Morris (PLATE 122). Portraiture of this era was largely defined by Alvin Gittins (1922–1981). Arriving from England after the war, he painted the official portrait of General Relief Society President Belle Spafford. After graduating from Brigham Young University in 1947, he joined the faculty of the University of Utah, where he spent the rest of his life teaching and creating portraits of university dignitaries. The Museum collection contains a dozen Gittins portraits of Church leaders, including four of President David O. McKay. His *Joseph Smith* (PLATE 124) is perhaps the finest idealization of the Prophet.

Ortho Fairbanks (1925– ) also produced posthumous portraits, but in sculpture form, such as his bronze *Brigham Young* (PLATE 125). He continued the tradition of public work on Mormon themes developed by his uncles J. Leo and Avard T. Fairbanks. His heroic bronze statue of

*This is a portrait of strength and wear. Martha Heaton Porter (1883–1969), her face bundled by the creases of seventy-eight years, is framed by the unyielding lines of her porch. The dominant porch post, also showing the effects of aging, matches the strength of this woman, who spent her entire life in the community of Orderville—at one time a model for the United Order. Birth and death had been Martha's constant companions. A midwife's helper and mother of eleven, she made the burial clothes for all the men who died in her community after making them for a four-year-old son who was killed in an accident. Driving into Orderville, Ansel Adams noticed her working in her garden and stopped to take her picture. Martha wanted to clean up first, but he prevailed, taking several pictures of her in her plaid work dress on the back porch of her home. Her son, Elbert Porter, said, "I can detect in her firmly set jaw some of the effects of the 'tussle' she had with Adams."*

*Impressed with the "straight photography" of Paul Strand, Ansel Adams had turned from hobbyist to professional photographer some thirty years before taking this picture.*

FIGURE 27: UTAH STATE CAPITOL

General Thomas Kane, friend to the Latter-day Saints, is located in the rotunda of the Utah State Capitol (FIGURE 27), while nearby, in front of the Daughters of the Utah Pioneers Museum, is the Eliza R. Snow Monument. Karl G. Maeser, first president of Brigham Young University, is also portrayed at the Provo campus in a heroic-size monument by Ortho Fairbanks.

Some of the finest portraits of Latter-day Saints were created by noted American photographers. Ansel Adams (1902–1984) was a landscape photographer who applied peerless technique to visualize nature in terms of sound composition and a range of tonal values. Adams's portraiture shares these traits and probes the personalities of his subjects as well. In Orderville he took his classic study of *Martha Heaton Porter* (PLATE 126), where the sturdy, no-nonsense woman of pioneer stock is juxtaposed with an element of her home that conveys something of her heritage. Adams had become acquainted with the small southern Utah towns on his trips to Zion National Park in the 1930s. In stunning but unpublished photographs, he brought out the picturesque beauty of Glendale in shots of the old Mormon meetinghouse and of the fall harvest of hay in regular stacks, juxtaposed with forthright Mormon pioneer homes. Twenty years later he collaborated with Dorothea Lange to photograph Mormon land and life in three southern Utah villages. His striking panoramas reveal how the villages sprang from a hostile desert setting.

Between 1925 and 1965, key events in the early history of the Church, such as the restoration of the priesthood and the pioneers' trek west, were commemorated in centennial celebrations. This great history provided a rich stock of themes to interpret and was the basis of the development of a distinctive Latter-day Saint art. Many artists from this era were directly descended from people close to those events.

The *Handcart Monument* on Temple Square, cast for the centennial of the Mormon pioneers' arrival in the Salt Lake Valley in 1947, is one of the best-known sculptures in the Church. It was created by Torlief Knaphus (1881–1965) (FIGURE 28), a reliable and dedicated Church sculptor. Twenty years earlier, his original one-third-size version (PLATE 127) was unveiled by President Heber J. Grant at the Bureau of Information.

As a youth in Norway, Knaphus came to art through working as an apprentice in his father's paint and decorating business. In Oslo he copied the old masters at the National Gallery and concurrently began his study of the Church, joining it in February 1902. His knowledge of old family legends led to a lifetime of service as a family historian, genealogist, and temple worker. After receiving training at the Julian Academy, Knaphus sailed to the United States in 1906, where he enrolled in the Art Students League in New York City. He then dedicated his professional career almost exclusively to executing Church commissions. At the Hawaii Temple he assisted youthful Avard Fairbanks in casting the baptismal font oxen. He was given full responsibility for the fonts with their twelve supporting oxen for the Alberta, Arizona, and Idaho Falls temples. His relief sculpture of *Jesus at the Well* for the exterior of the Alberta Temple was recast for several ward meetinghouses in Salt Lake City. Around 1925, Knaphus made an architectural frieze in eight parts for the exterior upper walls of the Arizona Temple (FIGURE 29), depicting different nations gathering to the Rocky Mountains. The *Angel Moroni Monument* on the Hill Cumorah memorialized the site where the gold record was retrieved by Joseph Smith. In addition to the nine-foot figure of Moroni atop the granite shaft, there are four bronze panels at the base expressing the coming forth of the Book of Mormon. When it was unveiled in 1935, Knaphus expressed the hope that "whoever sees this monument will investigate and accept the Gospel message as I have done."[10]

FIGURE 28:
TORLIEF KNAPHUS

FIGURE 29: ARIZONA TEMPLE

PLATE 127: *Scandinavian Handcart Pioneers,* 1926
TORLIEF KNAPHUS (1881–1965)
CAST BRONZE, 36" X 28" X 48"
(91.4 CM X 71.1 CM X 121.9 CM)
MUSEUM OF CHURCH HISTORY AND ART

*Knaphus's interpretation of the handcart story captures the values of religious devotion and family solidarity exemplified by the experiences of the handcart pioneers. The family struggles against the weight of their meager belongings, which they are taking to their new homeland. These pioneers accomplished their "gathering to Zion" with their own hard physical labor. As a twentieth-century emigrant from Norway, Knaphus readily identified with the hundreds of Scandinavian emigrants who pulled handcarts to Zion. Knaphus created this piece in 1926 on a commission from the Daughters of the Handcart Pioneers. This casting was exhibited on Temple Square until 1947, when a larger version was unveiled as part of the pioneer centennial celebration.*

*Trail-weary pioneers pause at the edge of the Salt Lake Valley in this painting. Although the figures are bowed, particularly the elderly couple in the center, the vibrant colors and the aggressive execution evoke a joyful mood. There is no doubt that these Saints, with their trials behind them, are grateful to be in Zion. Calvin Fletcher made his most lasting impact on the Latter-day Saint art community during a forty-year career as a professor of art at Utah State University. He received his own training at Brigham Young University, the Pratt Institute in New York, and Columbia University, as well as through private study in London and Paris.*

DEVELOPING A REGIONAL LATTER-DAY SAINT ART, 1925–1965

Calvin Fletcher (1882–1963) painted landscapes and themes from the settling of Utah's Cache Valley. Together with his wife, Irene Fletcher, H. Reuben Reynolds, David Howell Rosenbaum, Everett Thorpe, and others, Fletcher developed a bold regional style that expressed community values. In 1927 Fletcher, a bishop and art department head at Utah State Agricultural College, came to the conclusion that Utah artists were behind the times. Anxious to remedy this, he brought in leading contemporary artists as visiting professors. Birger Sandzen of Kansas introduced Fletcher and his students to bright color, thick impasto paint, geometrical form, and expressive gestures as means to interpret subject matter. Openness and experimentation were encouraged. These attitudes are visible in Fletcher's art done after this time. *The End of the Journey* (PLATE 128) is filled with dramatic gesture and bright, rich color—a typical work that shows the distinctive new regional style.

Whereas Fletcher and his colleagues emphasized local characteristics in their works, other artists leaned toward a more idealized, universal approach. One such person was Avard T.

FIGURE 30:
AVARD T. FAIRBANKS

Fairbanks (1897–1987) (FIGURE 30), who served his religion as an artist for three-quarters of a century. He set a high standard of Latter-day Saint sculpture, portraying the noblest endeavors and greatest events relating to Church history and doctrine. After an early stint at the Art Students League in New York City, he went to Paris to study. On his return, he and his brother J. Leo were called by the Church to create a frieze that extended completely around the upper outside walls of the new temple in Laie, Hawaii (FIGURE 31). The work represents four scriptural dispensations using 123 life-size prophets and figures. Avard's free-standing sculpture at the temple includes *Lehi Blessing Joseph* (FIGURE 32) and the baptismal font with its twelve oxen. Visitors approaching the temple see a series of pools fed by water from the beautiful fountain *Hawaiian Motherhood*. This sculpture is an impressive accomplishment for a youth who had just turned twenty.

Returning to the mainland, Fairbanks commenced his distinguished teaching career at the University of Oregon. After receiving his doctorate, he worked as a professor for eighteen years at the University of Michigan, and finally served as Dean of the College of Fine Arts at the University of Utah. During the Michigan years Avard and J. Leo created a mammoth artwork grouping for the Church's display in the Hall of Religion, "Century of Progress," at the Chicago World's Fair in 1933–1934. Here sculptures by Avard were combined with inscriptions of LDS religious principles. The exhibit also included two stained-glass windows of the First Vision and return of Elijah, along with murals depicting events from Church history—all by J. Leo Fairbanks. The presentation demonstrated the scope of Latter-day Saint religious experience in a unified artistic whole.

FIGURE 31: HAWAII TEMPLE

FIGURE 32: LEHI BLESSING JOSEPH

PLATE 129: **The Tragedy of Winter Quarters,
Nebraska**, 1933

AVARD T. FAIRBANKS (1897–1987)
CAST BRONZE, 36" X 25" X 25"
(91.4 CM X 63.5 CM X 63.5 CM)
MUSEUM OF CHURCH HISTORY AND ART

*With dignified pathos, a mother and father silently
pause while burying their infant. This scene was
enacted numerous times in Winter Quarters, a
temporary Latter-day Saint settlement founded in
1846 on the western shore of the Missouri River.
Although better planned than most frontier towns,
it faced epidemics brought on by the primitive living
conditions. Hundreds died there and in surrounding
campsites, many of them infants and children. A
heroic-size version of this sculpture is the focus of a
memorial Fairbanks created for the Winter
Quarters Cemetery in Omaha, Nebraska. The
scene is a modern echo of the artist's own
grandfather, who buried his infant son in the
prairie sod while migrating west.*

Avard Fairbanks's Winter Quarters Cemetery monument, with *The Tragedy of Winter Quarters* (PLATE 129) as the central sculpture, is a Latter-day Saint masterpiece. Erected to memorialize those persons who perished there during the winter of 1846–1847, it poignantly presents grief, but it is also noble and affirmative. Its significance was well expressed by Eugene Fairbanks, the artist's son: "The memorialization of Winter Quarters Cemetery at Florence, Nebraska, is more than a monument; it is the expression of a people that the sufferings of their pioneer ancestors were not in vain nor will they be forgotten. Since three of the sculptor's great grandparents lie buried in this cemetery, one can understand the great pains he has taken to create a tribute for those who lie resting in the hallowed ground."[11]

Some of the most important sculpture commissioned from the finest sculptors in the Church is erected at Temple Square in Salt Lake City. Avard Fairbanks contributed three monuments. His first work is the 1926 Monument to the Three Witnesses of the Book of Mormon (FIGURE 33), containing oval portraits of the witnesses and two narrative panels in bronze. His second is the beautiful and intricate

FIGURE 33:
THREE WITNESSES MONUMENT

monument erected in 1942 to commemorate the centennial of the organization of the Women's Relief Society in Nauvoo. Bronze panels narrate Relief Society work and qualities of Latter-day Saint womanhood. The tower houses the bell from the Nauvoo Temple, which rings hourly. The third monument depicts the restoration of the Aaronic Priesthood (FIGURE 34). The heroic-size figures of John the Baptist ordaining the Prophet Joseph Smith and Oliver Cowdery are idealized with a classical symmetry that conveys the solemnity of this event. Fairbanks also designed the eighteen-foot figure of the Angel Moroni on the spire of the Washington Temple (PLATE 130). The angel with trumpet, holding the gold plates of the Book of Mormon, alights on an orb representing the earth.

FIGURE 34: RESTORATION
OF THE AARONIC PRIESTHOOD

PLATE 130: **The Angel Moroni,** 1972
AVARD T. FAIRBANKS (1897–1987)
CAST BRONZE, 51 1/2" X 12" X 17"
(130.7 CM X 30.5 CM X 43.2 CM)
MUSEUM OF CHURCH HISTORY AND ART
GIFT OF EMIL B. FETZER

*When the gilded Angel Moroni statue was installed atop the Salt Lake Temple in 1892, this figure blowing his trumpet came to symbolize for Latter-day Saints the restoration of the gospel to all the earth. In the early 1970s, a Churchwide competition was launched to provide a new design of the Angel Moroni for the newly completed temple in Washington, D.C. Avard Fairbanks's winning entry was then enlarged and cast into a colossal, eighteen-foot-high statue in Pietrasanta, Italy, finished in gold leaf, shipped across the Atlantic, and installed on the temple with a giant crane. Over the next few years, slightly smaller versions were installed on temples in Seattle, West Jordan, Denver, and Mexico City.*

PLATE 131: *The Eternal Family,* 1940
AVARD T. FAIRBANKS (1897–1987)
CAST BRONZE, 19" X 12" X 12"
(48.3 CM X 30.5 CM X 30.5 CM)
MUSEUM OF CHURCH HISTORY AND ART

*Fairbanks depicts a pioneer family as an inspirational
role model for families today. The figures symbolize
courage, dedication, and faith. He said, "Don't ask me
when I first started work on the Pioneer Family. How
can a poet say when his poem began?" The artist
believed that art should ennoble the struggles of life.
Fairbanks was born in Provo, Utah, the youngest of ten
children. He studied in New York, Paris, and Italy and
did many works of art celebrating Church history.*

PLATE 132: *George Albert Smith,* 1950
AVARD T. FAIRBANKS (1897–1987)
CARRARA MARBLE, 18" X 15" X 12"
(45.7 CM X 38.1 CM X 30.5 CM)
MUSEUM OF CHURCH HISTORY AND ART

*George Albert Smith (1880–1951), Church President
from 1945 to 1951, was known as a generous
humanitarian who stayed involved in a remarkable
variety of civic affairs in addition to his Church
responsibilities. He is remembered for his work with the
Boy Scout program and special love for the Native
Americans. At the end of World War II, after consulting
with President Harry S. Truman, he administered
shipments of Church welfare commodities to the people of
war-torn Europe, assisting and bringing hope to
thousands.*

*Sculptor Avard T. Fairbanks, who rejected the modern
abstractionism of his era, preferred to work in the realm
of realism. It was his desire not only to represent his
subject, but when possible to inspire, as in this portrait
bust of President Smith. Here, Fairbanks deftly carved
the eyeglass-clad, angular face of his subject, subtly
capturing in stone his inner qualities of kindness, wisdom,
and compassion.*

Fairbanks also expressed Latter-day Saint themes in many smaller scale sculptures for museum
and home display. Notable are *The Eternal Family* (PLATE 131), sculptures of the Savior and of
Brigham Young, and his portrait bust of President George Albert Smith (PLATE 132). His dramatic *Joseph Smith's First Vision* (PLATE 133), a life-size rendition in Carrara marble, is displayed at
the Church Museum.

Fairbanks wrote: "The Arts are created for contemplation and edification, the expression of the
highest ambitions and the spiritual hope of a people. These produce a culture that lives on to uplift
subsequent generations."[12] Art of timeless beauty springs from profound ideas and noble intentions.
Fairbanks taught high ideals: "A sculptor must comprehend a significant civilization. . . . The hope of
the world lies in our faith and in our spiritual ideas. Such ideas we express in material form. . . . For the
great, inspiration comes to souls whose thoughts turn in the direction of the eternal things of life."[13]

Avard Fairbanks is also nationally known for his sculpture of noted historical figures, particularly Abraham Lincoln. In Statuary Hall, near the rotunda of the capitol at Washington, D.C.,
where each state has contributed sculpture depicting major figures in state history, Washington,
Wyoming, and North Dakota all are represented by large bronze statues by Fairbanks.

PLATE 133: **Joseph Smith's First Vision**, ABOUT 1958
AVARD T. FAIRBANKS (1897–1987)
CARRARA MARBLE, 42" X 34" X 28"
(106.7 CM X 86.4 CM X 71.1 CM)
MUSEUM OF CHURCH HISTORY AND ART

*In this portrayal of Joseph Smith's First Vision, Fairbanks
has focused on the fourteen-year-old Joseph kneeling in
prayer at just the moment when the two heavenly beings
appeared to him. One hand is pressed to his chest to
indicate the deep-felt emotion, while the other
hand lies open to represent his open mind.
The medium of white marble strikingly
communicates the purity and innocence
of the young Joseph and the holiness of
the moment. Nurtured by his artist
father and brothers, Avard Fairbanks's
youthful talent flourished. At the
age of fourteen he was awarded a
scholarship to the Art Students
League in New York. He had
a distinguished career as a
professor and nationally
recognized sculptor.*

## SHARING A LOVE FOR THE LAND

For many professional artists of the Intermountain West, landscape painting was a means of expressing with meaning and affection the scenes before them, besides receiving recognition and compensation. Landscape painters were drawn to the unique rural habitation established by the Latter-day Saints, where agrarian-religious principles influenced the appearance of the landscape. Compared to earlier artists who brought out either the romance of spectacular mountain scenes or the subtle and intimate views of nature, this American-trained group working from 1925 to 1965 was more prone to express the reality of the regional landscape.

As he painted the West, Maynard Dixon (1875–1946) moved from site to site seeking new subject material. Some of his favorite areas were settled by Latter-day Saints, including Carson City, Nevada, and the Utah towns of Springdale, Toquerville, and Orderville near Zion National Park. Dixon produced excellent paintings of the Mormon farms and accompanying landscape, such as *Empty House, Carson City, Nevada* (PLATE 134). In 1937 Dixon's friend Herald R. Clark acquired for Brigham Young University eighty-five works from all phases of the artist's output, including excellent images of the Mormon Landscape. From 1939 to 1945 Dixon and his third wife, Edith Hamlin, made their summer residence near Mount Carmel in Kane County, Utah.

PLATE 134: *Empty House, Carson City, Nevada,* 1935

MAYNARD DIXON (1875–1946)
OIL ON CANVAS, 30" X 25" (76.2 CM X 63.5 CM)
MUSEUM OF ART, BRIGHAM YOUNG UNIVERSITY
HERALD R. CLARK MEMORIAL COLLECTION

*This image interprets a scene along the road near Carson City, Nevada. Colors, mostly earthen tones, relate to the barren land and the harshness of life for its inhabitants. Wallace Stegner called lombardy poplars "Mormon trees." "Wherever they went the Mormons planted them," Stegner wrote. "They grew boldly and fast, without much tending, and they make the landscape of the long valleys of the Mormon Country something special and distinctive" (Wallace Stegner,* Mormon Country *[New York: Bonanza Books, 1942], 21, 22). Empty House reveals elements of the visual landscape Stegner wrote about. Even though not a Latter-day Saint, Dixon was familiar with "Mormon Country." He was acquainted with LeConte Stewart and drove through Utah several times. He spent the summers of his final years at his home near Mt. Carmel, Utah, not far from Zion National Park.*

His generous Mormon neighbors helped build his home and studio, and shared stories about settling the country years before. During this time Dixon completed his study for an unrealized mural in the Utah County Courthouse, *The Hand of God* (PLATE 135), a work using the earth colors of the Southwest.

Louise Richards Farnsworth (1878–1969) (FIGURE 35), a native of Salt Lake City, was known for her bright, expressionistic color. She was trained at the Art Students League and in Paris and then began her bold, individualistic paintings of the Rocky Mountains. She exhibited at New York's Montross Gallery, and her work was reviewed favorably in the *New York Times*. The three paintings in the Church collection, represented by *Snow on the Wasatch* (PLATE 136), show her to be somewhat modernist in outlook.

FIGURE 35: LOUISE RICHARDS FARNSWORTH

PLATE 135: ***The Hand of God,*** 1940
MAYNARD DIXON (1875–1946)
OIL ON PANEL, 16" X 34" (40.6 CM X 86.4 CM)
MUSEUM OF ART, BRIGHAM YOUNG UNIVERSITY

*This is a study for an unrealized mural for the Utah County Courthouse in Provo. It depicts the reclaiming of the desert through irrigation by Mormon pioneers. God's presence is symbolized by the hand in the form of a cloud. Maynard Dixon is known for his easel paintings of the American West, but throughout his life he also painted murals in public and private buildings. Dixon made southern Utah his home for several years near the close of his life.*

PLATE 136: ***Snow on the Wasatch Mountains,*** 1929
LOUISE RICHARDS FARNSWORTH (1878–1969)
OIL ON CANVAS, 15" X 22" (38.1 CM X 55.9 CM)
MUSEUM OF CHURCH HISTORY AND ART

*The crisp days of autumn are captured in this landscape typical of the season in Utah. The mountains, already cloaked in their winter dress, contrast sharply with the warm autumn colors of the trees and hillside. The power and serenity of the scene evokes nostalgia for "Our Mountain Home So Dear." Although Louise Farnsworth spent most of her adult life in New York, she continued to paint the Utah landscape. Her bold use of color corresponds with the vibrant forms of the mountains and canyons of her home state. She studied at the Art Students League in New York and the Julian Academy in Paris.*

PLATE 137: *November Hills,*
*Eden, Utah,* ABOUT 1930

LECONTE STEWART (1891–1990)
OIL ON CANVAS, 24" X 30" (61 CM X 76.2 CM)
MUSEUM OF CHURCH HISTORY AND ART
GIFT OF LUCILLE E. STRONG

*In this painting Stewart honors the legacy of Mormon pioneers who founded several hundred communities and created a distinctive rural landscape in western North America. This village, with its appropriate religious title, "Eden," lies protected in its northern Utah mountain home. The composition of this painting is typical of Stewart's approach to rural landscapes, with a field in the foreground and the humble homes and outbuildings of Mormon farms set against the mountains. Stewart strove throughout his career to capture the "Mormon Landscape" of his upbringing with its distinctive features of irrigation ditches, fences, unpainted barns and outbuildings, wide roads, and chapels set against the open landscape.*

LeConte Stewart (1891–1990) (FIGURE 36) was one of America's foremost landscape artists. For eight decades he portrayed with affection in untold thousands of works the appearance and character of Utah's land, primarily the farms and villages settled by the Latter-day Saints. Born and brought up in Sevier County, he said he couldn't remember a time when he was not sketching. After graduating from Ricks Academy, he traveled in 1913 to New York for study under master artists at the Art Students League schools in Woodstock and New York City. He then returned to Utah to express the regional landscape using the tonal-impressionistic style he acquired.

FIGURE 36:
LECONTE STEWART

LeConte Stewart's achievements arise from his ability to respond with great feeling to landscape. "I try to get the essential character of the subject," he said. "To me art is an expression of the sense of the thing rather than a reproduction of it."[14] He also wrote, "Art is a matter of caring—of being moved."[15] Stewart ordered the aesthetic elements using artistry with design, color harmony, and shapes. He created art that is faithful to how one's mind processes, summarizes, and understands visual information. Finally, Stewart realized the essence of the subject. "Painting is more than expressing the

appearance of things, it is expressing the spirit of things," he said. "When you know and love a tree you can paint its spirit, the quality God gave it."[16] All of these physical and spiritual components are in balance, not conflicting with one another, working together to create living, integrated artwork. *November Hills, Eden* (PLATE 137), *Grey Day, Winter, Farmington* (PLATE 138), and *Springtime in Peterson* (PLATE 139) are masterpieces that embody these concepts. As a result they speak on many levels—one can learn of the land they portray and sense the artist's deep feeling for it, or relish the harmony of subtle colors and forms.

LeConte Stewart faithfully recorded what has been called the "Mormon Landscape"—the distinctive features of the land settled and cultivated by the Saints. These include roadside irrigation ditches, Lombardy poplar trees in rows, fruit orchards on east-facing bench land set against mountains, solid pioneer homes of stone and adobe brick, and simple, unpainted barns and outbuildings. In one portrait of an aged pioneer dwelling, *Eyes Wide Open* (PLATE 140), the windows seem to open to the soul of this house, which has an almost living quality to it. Abandoned buildings always attracted Stewart, especially during the 1930s when he responded to the visual feeling of the Great Depression. The year he painted *LDS Meetinghouse, Clearfield* (PLATE 141),

PLATE 138: ***Grey Day, Winter, Farmington, Utah***, ABOUT 1930

LECONTE STEWART (1891–1990)
OIL ON PANEL, 24" X 30" (61 CM X 76.2 CM)
MUSEUM OF CHURCH HISTORY AND ART

*The grey skies hovering over this scene of a northern Utah village cloaked in winter are offset by the brilliance of the snow. The rock home in the foreground and the sturdy barns evoke a sense of security and peace; this typically Mormon townscape holds its own against a grim winter environment. Stewart, who usually painted on site, was acutely aware of the characteristics of the seasons as they unfolded on the valleys of northern Utah. He was particularly fond of the winter season, "not alone for the mood it creates, but for the tonal and color quality it possesses. The lavender of the hillsides and brush, orange of the scrub oak and maple, the patches of snow that take on the color of the sky are all of great interest to me. There is within such a scene an infinite number of color variations" (Robert O. Davis,* LeConte Stewart: The Spirit of Landscape *[Salt Lake City, Utah: The Church of Jesus Christ of Latter-day Saints, 1985], 62).*

PLATE 139: **Springtime in Peterson**, 1939
LeConte Stewart (1891–1990)
Oil on panel, 24" x 30" (61 cm x 76.2 cm)
Museum of Church History and Art

*The beautiful and fertile Morgan Valley, comprising farm land and several villages, was settled by the Latter-day Saints. Many sites there attracted LeConte Stewart. He painted one subject in Peterson, a small clapboard house surrounded by trees and several barns, scores of times over a sixty-year period, during every season and at every time of day. In all of those paintings, Stewart viewed the house looking south from across the pasture. He always included the same landscape elements, but within this narrow range of subject is a wide variety of expression and beauty. This painting provides evidence of what Stewart said were "those things that are introspective, that you peer into, and see, and feel." After he retired from university teaching, Stewart continued to instruct groups and individuals on location in the fundamentals of art until the last year of his life. Students gathered to sketch and learn in the Morgan Valley towns of Peterson, Milton, Stoddard, and Porterville. Some of those devoted students have continued Stewart's great legacy of landscape art.*

PLATE 140: **Eyes Wide Open, near Farmington, Utah**, 1939
LeConte Stewart (1891–1990)
Oil on panel, 16" x 20"
(40.6 cm x 50.8 cm)
Museum of Church History and Art

*The stark beauty of an apparently abandoned Latter-day Saint farmhouse is echoed in the bare autumn landscape that frames the house. The home takes on human characteristics as it looks out of the painting. Stewart's gentle wit is evident in the piece's title, Eyes Wide Open. LeConte Stewart was Utah's preeminent landscape painter. In a career that spanned more than eighty years, Stewart produced thousands of works of art that expressed in great depth the feeling of the rural landscape and habitations created by the Latter-day Saints. Stewart studied at the Art Students League in New York and returned home to become an influential teacher in the public schools and at the University of Utah.*

PLATE 141: *LDS Meetinghouse,
Clearfield, Utah,* 1935
LeConte Stewart (1891–1990)
Oil on canvas, 18" x 24" (45.7 cm x 61 cm)
Museum of Church History and Art

*Modern elements of telephone wires and railroad
tracks encroach on the stately dignity of this
pioneer Latter-day Saint chapel in northern Utah.
With directness and honesty, Stewart paints the
marks of change on the community. The
juxtaposition of symbols of modern life against the
chapel's embodiment of faith suggests both a
physical and spiritual clash between two times.
During the years of economic depression, Stewart
painted a number of works of the "American
Scene." Artists following this tradition depicted the
truth of everyday life in America, even though it
might not be particularly pretty or aesthetically
pleasing. The stark reality of this painting is typical
of Stewart's works in this tradition.*

PLATE 142: *The Creation of the Earth,* 1920
LeConte Stewart (1891–1990)
Oil on canvas, 108" x 65" (274.3 cm x 165.1 cm)
Creation room, Alberta Temple

*LeConte Stewart planned that his six Alberta
Temple creation room murals would visually
present the room's unique message in unity with the
temple's distinctive design. Throughout his work,
Stewart followed closely the Pearl of Great Price
and Old Testament accounts of the Creation.
Stewart's murals reveal and confirm God's creative
powers and are among the greatest monuments of
Latter-day Saint artistic expression. To capture
light and atmosphere, Stewart used daubs of color
methodically placed close together, much like the
style of some French Impressionists. In the six
murals, as the earth moves into focus and the
work progresses, Stewart's art becomes less
abstract and more defined. The limited color
range throughout the compositions maintains an
even decorative plane of vision. Primarily a
landscape artist, Stewart found a deep religious
meaning in painting God's creations.*

Stewart wrote: "In these pictures I'm trying to cut a slice of contemporary life as it is in the highways and byways, as I have found it."[17]

Paralleling this work was a lifetime of artistic service to the Church. LeConte Stewart's pen-and-ink artwork illustrated stories in the *Improvement Era* and in "A Review," an epic poem about the Mormon pioneers. In 1917 he was assigned for his mission to paint murals in the creation room and other areas of the Hawaii Temple. The Church then commissioned him at age twenty-nine to supervise several artists doing the extensive interior artwork for the Alberta Temple. Stewart himself painted panels representing *The Creation of the Earth* (PLATE 142) and five other murals for the creation room. The integration of architecture, interior design, and artwork with the religious purposes of the building is on the highest level of design and execution. In 1925 the artist painted large murals in the new temple in Mesa, Arizona. "One of my great joys has been painting in the temples in Canada, Arizona, and Hawaii. It was an inspiring opportunity," he said.[18] Stewart completed a half-dozen large murals for chapels in Utah and Colorado, using both landscape and biblical themes. A great teacher, he was head of the University of Utah Art Department from 1938 to 1956. In 1984 the Church Museum opened the memorable 240–piece retrospective exhibit "LeConte Stewart: The Spirit of Landscape."

LeConte Stewart was a deeply humble man beloved by his followers. Perhaps a glimpse of his being can be gained in these few words he gave during an interview at age ninety-three:

> When I encounter a tree, a personality comes forth which is wonderful. To see the growth and structure . . . causes me to bow down in humility. Many times I have come home bowed down with reverence, thankful that I am an artist. He created trees in a spirit form, and then here on earth, and this is so marvelous and beyond my thinking I just say to myself, "How did you do it, O Lord?" I am thankful also the Lord had a taste for beauty and art. When I go out to paint a tree I feel the Lord's spirit. I cannot do what He has done; the least I can do is paint it, but in painting it I have come to see Him in nature.[19]

Stewart's art always springs from the reservoir of nature, but for George Dibble (1904–1992), depicting rural Utah scenery was a point of departure for practicing conscious personal expression. His life was balanced among teaching, writing about, and producing artwork—primarily watercolors. Returning to Utah after receiving a master's degree at Columbia University, Dibble began a long tenure as a professor of art at the University of Utah. He wrote a popular textbook

*This watercolor is a personal interpretation in color and form of the towers and pinnacles atop the gothic-style Assembly Hall on Temple Square. It follows the artist's assertion that a picture is "not a portrait of what you would see, but a glimpse. Things are never as they look, anyway," he said. "What is real is pretty much a philosophical question."*

*Born in Laie, Hawaii, and raised in Utah, Dibble received his bachelor's and master's degrees in art from Columbia University. There he embraced modern viewpoints and practices such as Cubism, where forms are reduced into basic, geometrical shapes. Returning to Utah, he taught first at Utah State Agricultural College in Logan and then at the University of Utah, where he remained until he retired. For decades, his weekly column in the Sunday* Salt Lake Tribune *reviewed current exhibits.*

PLATE 144: *Latter-day Saint Chapel in Eureka, Utah,* 1985
ELLA PEACOCK (1905– )
OIL ON CANVAS, 20 1/4" X 24 1/2" (51.4 CM X 62.2 CM)
MUSEUM OF CHURCH HISTORY AND ART

*The steeple of the Eureka meetinghouse dominates the scene and brings a sense of order to the jumbled streets of this central Utah mining town. The weathered yet stately building seems to stand as a sentinel, protecting the homes of the town. Landscapist Ella Peacock is noted for her muted palette, loose brushwork, and distinctive, hand-carved frames. Since 1970 she has lived in Spring City, Utah, and turned her brush to capturing rural scenes of central Utah. She received her professional training at the Philadelphia School of Design.*

FIGURE 37:
ELLA PEACOCK

on watercolor painting and a weekly column of art news and evaluation for the *Salt Lake Tribune.* *Assembly Hall Details* (PLATE 143) explores the modern viewpoints that he advocated.

Ella Peacock (1905– ) (FIGURE 37) was another artist trained in an eastern U.S. painting tradition. She became a respected painter of the Utah rural landscape after she and her husband joined the Church in Pennsylvania in 1962 and subsequently settled in the quiet Mormon town of Spring City in Sanpete County, Utah. She depicted with pale earth colors in a sketchy, dry style the arid sagebrush settlements of her region, bringing out the character of this land. Focusing on subjects like an adobe pioneer home or an old ward building such as the *Latter-day Saint Chapel in Eureka, Utah* (PLATE 144), Peacock worked quickly on location and finished up canvases in her studio, where she hand carved her unique wood frames.

## ART AND THE SCRIPTURES

Another class of artwork used by the Church conveys teachings and doctrines contained in the scriptures. Besides the earlier-discussed murals made for meetinghouses, most of this was illustrational work used for teaching and audiovisual displays. Artists were involved with Church magazines such as the *Improvement Era,* the *Relief Society Magazine,* the *Children's Friend,* the *Contributor,* and the *Instructor.* Some did layout work or provided illustrations for articles or magazine covers. Jack Sears, for example, wrote an illustrated monthly column for Church youth. Others had their landscapes and personal artistic work reproduced with accompanying commentary in brief "art appreciation" vignettes. In leaner periods, as a cost-cutting measure, artwork was reduced or dropped altogether from Church magazines. There were also years when photographs provided nearly all of the visuals for publications.

Before producing artwork for The Church of Jesus Christ of Latter-day Saints, Harry Anderson (1906– ) was an illustrator for leading national magazines and calendar publishers. A Seventh-day Adventist, Anderson fulfilled numerous commissions of biblical illustrations for his church's

publications. Meanwhile, the LDS church was beginning to use quality illustrative art for displays in Church visitors' centers. The Mormon Pavilion at the 1964 New York World's Fair was a major effort to present Latter-day Saint beliefs to visitors through artwork in multimedia displays. The focal point was "Jesus Christ as the answer to man's needs and aspirations,"[20] and Anderson was commissioned to produce a large mural of Christ ordaining the Twelve Apostles (PLATE 145). Widely reproduced and admired, it became the first picture of many by the artist that defined for Church members the look and demeanor of the Savior. Over the next fifteen years Anderson completed more than a dozen original paintings that were placed in the North Visitors' Center on Salt Lake City's Temple Square. The first series, from the later 1960s, portrayed the great prophecies of the Old Testament. Some of those murals were painted by Anderson himself and demonstrate great skill and psychological penetration. Others were enlarged by copyists working from his smaller paintings. During the middle 1970s copyists completed a second group of murals on the life of Christ. One of those, *The Ascension of Christ* (PLATE 146), in Anderson's original is an expressive and light-filled work. As the paintings were completed, they were run on the cover of the *Ensign* magazine, at the rate of about one per year. Beginning in December 1973, the *Ensign* sponsored the "Gospel-in-Art Program," with the goal of providing good religious art for the home at low cost. Members were invited "to display in your home artwork that says something about your most cherished convictions."[21] The first offering was a twenty-by-sixteen-inch reproduction of *Gethsemane,* possibly the best known of all of Anderson's images of Christ. More than forty thousand were sold, leading to a second print, his *Christ and the Children.*

Anderson was also a very good portrait painter, as revealed by his likeness of Elder Nathan Eldon Tanner (PLATE 147). A sincere Christian, Anderson used his insight into people to produce works with lasting meaning. Wendell Ashton of Church Public Communications and liaison to the artist explained: "He keeps close to his Maker, and his own life comes through in his paintings."[22]

Harry Anderson's friend Tom Lovell (1909– ) was another non-LDS illustrator engaged by the Church because of his skill and experience. Lovell studied at the College of Fine Arts at Syracuse University in the 1920s and afterward was a freelance magazine illustrator. Later he portrayed the history of the Southwest in a series of paintings that carefully re-created the past. He took that realistic approach in the few paintings he did for the Church, including *Moroni Buries the Gold Plates* (PLATE 148) and *Moroni Appears to Joseph Smith* (PLATE 149).

PLATE 145: ***Christ Ordains His Apostles,*** 1964
HARRY ANDERSON (1906– )
OIL ON PANEL, 59" X 144" (149.9 CM X 365.8 CM)
MUSEUM OF CHURCH HISTORY AND ART

*This large, mural-sized painting of a scene seldom portrayed in religious art shows Christ ordaining one of His Twelve Apostles. The importance of the laying on of hands and the divine role of the Savior are emphasized by the light that radiates outward from Christ, who stands in the center of the painting. The white robes of Christ and three of His Apostles, probably Peter, James, and John, create a strong center of focus and stand in contrast to the common clothing of the other disciples. This painting was commissioned for the Mormon Pavilion at the New York World's Fair in 1964–1965. It was the first painting Harry Anderson, a Seventh-day Adventist, did for the Church. Subsequently he produced more than two dozen paintings of Old and New Testament themes for the Church. Many of his commissions have been enlarged by Latter-day Saint artist Grant Romney Clawson and displayed as teaching murals on Temple Square.*

PLATE 146: **The Ascension of Christ**, 1976
HARRY ANDERSON (1906– )
OIL ON CANVAS, 33 1/2" x 47" (85 CM x 119.4 CM)
MUSEUM OF CHURCH HISTORY AND ART

"He was taken up. . . . And while they looked
stedfastly toward heaven as he went up, behold,
two men stood by them in white apparel; which also
said, Ye men of Galilee, why stand ye gazing up
into heaven? this same Jesus, which is taken up
from you into heaven, shall so come in like manner
as ye have seen him go into heaven" (Acts 1:9–11).
The narrative qualities of this painting typify the
kind of art Harry Anderson has done throughout
his long career. Anderson, who enjoys painting art
that tells a story, began his commercial art career
in Chicago after studying art at Syracuse
University from 1927 to 1931. His commercial
illustrations for advertisements appeared in most of
the major magazines of the mid-twentieth century.

PLATE 147: **Nathan Eldon Tanner**, 1966
HARRY ANDERSON (1906– )
OIL ON CANVAS, 40" x 30" (101.6 CM x 76.2 CM)
MUSEUM OF CHURCH HISTORY AND ART

Portraits bring to life subtle inner qualities
and characteristics not always captured with
photography. Artist/illustrator Harry
Anderson completed this likeness while
President Tanner served in the First
Presidency with President David O. McKay.
Experienced in commercial and religious art,
Anderson has a realistic touch that creates a
soft and comfortable feeling.

DEVELOPING A REGIONAL LATTER-DAY SAINT ART, 1925–1965

PLATE 149: **Moroni Appears to Joseph Smith in His Bedroom,** 1977
TOM LOVELL (1909– )
OIL ON CANVAS, 84" X 60" (213.4 CM X 152.4 CM)
MUSEUM OF CHURCH HISTORY AND ART

*On the night of September 21, 1823, Joseph Smith called upon God in prayer. He later recalled, "A personage appeared at my bedside, standing in the air. . . . He called me by name, and said unto me that he was a messenger sent from the presence of God to me, and that his name was Moroni; that God had a work for me to do" (Joseph Smith–History 1:30, 33). This visit marked the beginning of a sacred relationship between the ancient Book of Mormon prophet Moroni and the young prophet Joseph. This rendering interprets Moroni's appearance to Joseph Smith in a photographic style, carefully following Joseph's description of the event. Although not a Church member, Lovell has done several works depicting Latter-day Saint scripture and Church history. A resident of Connecticut and New Mexico, he is best known for his illustrations of western scenes.*

PLATE 148: **Moroni Buries the Gold Plates,**
ABOUT 1970

TOM LOVELL (1909– )
OIL ON PANEL, 33" X 23" (83.8 CM X 58.4 CM)
MUSEUM OF CHURCH HISTORY AND ART

*As his people were being destroyed, Moroni, the last Nephite prophet, became the caretaker of the sacred records of his ancestors. To keep them safe for future generations, Moroni buried the plates in the Hill Cumorah. Fourteen centuries later, as a resurrected being, he revealed the location of the plates to Joseph Smith, who translated them and published them as the Book of Mormon. In this painting the artist has portrayed Moroni as a gray-haired warrior wearing tattered clothes from his years of lonely wandering, kneeling in prayer before depositing the plates in their hiding place. Tom Lovell's narrative paintings are meticulously researched and sketched before being set to canvas. Known as one of America's premiere illustrators, Lovell uses his realistic style to record historically accurate scenes.*

*Feeling that "the Gospel was too precious to myself to be withheld from the children," Richard Ballantyne organized the first Sunday School in the Salt Lake Valley in 1849. Each week children gathered in Ballantyne's home to listen to the Scottish emigrant teach lessons from the scriptures. The idea of Sunday classes for children later spread to other wards, becoming a Churchwide program in the 1870s. This centennial memorialization of the first Sunday School class was painted on commission from the Deseret Sunday School Union. It was the first of many official and semiofficial commissions of Church themes for Friberg, who became the most widely known Latter-day Saint illustrator of the twentieth century.*

FIGURE 38: ARNOLD FRIBERG WITH HIS WIFE, PRESIDENT MCKAY, CHARLTON HESTON, AND STEPHEN L RICHARDS

Although younger than Anderson and Lovell, Latter-day Saint artist Arnold Friberg (1913– ) (FIGURE 38) produced illustrative art for the Church a quarter-century earlier—art that for many Latter-day Saints has formed their visual image of the Book of Mormon. After moving to Utah in 1949, he was hired to paint a commemorative picture of the first Sunday School meeting, held by Richard Ballantyne in December 1849 (PLATE 150). Neighborhood children in period dress posed for the picture. This work has the qualities that make Friberg's paintings appealing: a friendly presentation of the story, attention to historic fact, carefully painted detail, a golden warmth, and focus on the hero or central person in the work. Those qualities are also visible in *First Mormon Missionaries in Denmark* (PLATE 151).

Adele Cannon Howells, the general president of the Primary organization, engaged Friberg to paint twelve large pictures portraying dramatic stories from the Book of Mormon, to be published serially in the *Children's Friend. Baptism in the Waters of Mormon* (PLATE 152) is a work of pictured beauty and drama from that popular set. The action-filled paintings were subsequently printed in millions of copies of the Book of Mormon and were installed in the South Visitors' Center on Temple Square.

PLATE 151: *First Mormon Missionaries in Denmark,* 1964
ARNOLD FRIBERG (1913– ), AFTER CHRISTIAN DALSGAARD
OIL ON PANEL, 35" X 48" (88.9 CM X 121.9 CM)
MUSEUM OF CHURCH HISTORY AND ART

A Mormon missionary preaches the gospel in the country home of a Danish carpenter in Friberg's copy of an 1856 Danish painting. About ten thousand Scandinavians, mostly Danes, joined the Church in the 1850s. The impact of missionary work and the gathering is reflected in Danish genre painter Christian Dalsgaard's painting, which shows Mormon missionaries as an aspect of daily life in Denmark.

Friberg copied the Dalsgaard painting on commission for a former Danish missionary. The original, which hangs in the State Museum of Art in Copenhagen, has been a favorite among missionaries to Denmark for more than a century. Friberg, himself a son of Scandinavian emigrants, has reinterpreted the original color and tone, giving it his own imprint.

PLATE 152: *Baptism in the Waters of Mormon,* 1953
ARNOLD FRIBERG (1913– )
OIL ON CANVAS, 43" X 61" (109.2 CM X 154.9 CM)
MUSEUM OF CHURCH HISTORY AND ART

The Book of Mormon prophet Alma, converted to the teachings of the Savior by the persecuted Abinadi, stands in the waters of Mormon to baptize a group of new converts. The magnificence of the setting, typical of Friberg's illustrations, reflects his desire to make the people and places in his art as grand as the teachings each story reflects. This painting is one in a series of twelve illustrations of Book of Mormon stories originally commissioned in the 1950s for the Children's Friend magazine. Friberg, whose Swedish father and Norwegian mother were both Mormon converts and immigrants to America, began drawing at a young age. By the time he was eight, he had aspirations to be a newspaper cartoonist, but after studying at the Chicago Academy of Fine Arts and later in New York, he went on to become a noted commercial artist and illustrator. He is best known for his work with Cecil B. DeMille's film The Ten Commandments and his nearly four decades as chief illustrator of the Royal Canadian Mounted Police.

About his Book of Mormon paintings, Friberg said, "I try to bring into reality the stories so often taught in Sunday school. These stories are not mere allegory; they happened to real people who had names, jobs, and grandchildren. . . . Through my paintings I bear witness to the truth as I understand it."[23]

Friberg also had extensive magazine illustrating experience. His 1952 *Improvement Era* cover, *Be Thou an Example* (PLATE 153), was intended to motivate youth.

These pictures led to contact with legendary Hollywood mogul Cecil B. DeMille, who commissioned Friberg to develop the artistic look and costuming for the classic film *The Ten Commandments*.[24] The artist provided large paintings along with drawings of actors with their individual dress. Because the movie schedule was tight and the Book of Mormon series was not yet finished, Friberg asked President David O. McKay for advice. President McKay replied: "*The Ten Commandments* can't wait. They are making it now. The Book of Mormon can wait.

PLATE 153: *I Timothy 4:12: Be Thou an Example,* 1952
ARNOLD FRIBERG (1913– )
OIL ON CANVAS, 40" x 29" (101.6 CM x 74 CM)
MUSEUM OF CHURCH HISTORY AND ART

*This motivational work produced for a July 1952* Improvement Era *cover illustrates young people of the Church progressing into adulthood as they follow the teachings and programs of the Church. Friberg blends the religious and historical ideas in this work. A specialist in Western, historical, and biblical studies, Friberg has said, "I have no purpose but to tell a story and to tell it as well, as eloquently, as I know how."*

PLATE 154: *Return of the Prodigal Son,* 1960
RICHARD BURDE (1912– )
OIL ON CANVAS, 35" X 32 1/4" (88.9 CM X 81.9 CM)
MUSEUM OF CHURCH HISTORY AND ART

*The parable of the prodigal son is one of the most powerful stories of repentance and forgiveness in the scriptures. Burde has appealed to the viewer by using the highly emotional technique of combining strong lighting with bold forms and strong compositional elements that emphasize the personal feelings of a repentant son and a forgiving father. Burde's art reflects both the academic training he received at the Academy of Fine Arts in his native Dresden, Germany, and the rich aesthetic tradition of Northern European art. As a convert to the Church, Burde left Germany in 1952 and immigrated with his family to Utah. His art displays his intense interest in themes from the Bible. In his work he expresses a sense of humanity by capturing moods of compassion, humility, and forgiveness rather than the heroic, proud, and powerful.*

Do *The Ten Commandments.*" DeMille later described Friberg and his work: "Among the living artists who have dedicated themselves largely to religious art, one stands out for his virility and warmth, dramatic understanding and truth. That man is Arnold Friberg."[25]

Taking a totally different approach to religious themes, Richard Burde (1912– ) worked in his Salt Lake City home producing highly original works drawn largely from the Bible. A native of Germany, he studied at the Dresden Academy of Fine Arts before World War II. He and his wife joined the Church in 1941, and in 1952 emigrated to the United States. His work depicts the downtrodden, the poor, the humble and repentant with great feeling and humanity, and his own beliefs are reflected in work such as *Return of the Prodigal Son* (PLATE 154).

## LATTER-DAY SAINT LIFE, PROGRAMS, AND ACTIVITIES

For the four-decade period beginning in 1925, key artwork showing the Latter-day Saints continued to focus on rural life. Here, the truth and nobility of the people are conveyed—their roots in time and the sense of place created by their setting. The small events that make up their history are depicted together with core gospel values. Images also illustrate the activities of Church auxiliaries.

PLATE 155: *Homeward,* 1950
J. GEORGE MIDGLEY (1882–1979)
BROMOIL TRANSFER PRINT, 10 1/4" x 10 1/4"
(26 CM X 26 CM)
MUSEUM OF CHURCH HISTORY AND ART

*In this bromoil transfer print a shepherd and his flock move homeward. With the Manti Temple posed on the hill, the photograph also becomes a metaphor for a heavenly journey led by another shepherd. The bromoil process provides a soft focus and allows the creator to manipulate the photograph before the transfer print is made. Elements can thus be brought out or restrained. In this image the sky and surroundings drop out of focus, allowing attention to center on the temple and the flock. By leaving out extraneous detail, the artist invites the viewer to bring her or his own imagination to the work. Midgley, a photographer by avocation, applied the art of the bromoil process to his prints for decades after its popularity waned, creating scores of evocative images of the Utah landscape.*

PLATE 156: *A Song of Summer,* 1953
J. GEORGE MIDGLEY (1882–1979)
BROMOIL TRANSFER PRINT, 13 3/4" X 10 1/4"
(35 CM X 26 CM)
MUSEUM OF CHURCH HISTORY AND ART

*J. George Midgley, a Salt Lake City native, spent nearly six decades photographing rural Salt Lake and Davis counties. Though this photograph was taken in 1953, its pioneer messages seem timeless. The stately poplar trees, a symbol of Utah's pioneer past, the rural lane, and the horse-drawn farming equipment reflect the farmer's dependence upon the land. Midgley was able to incorporate a sense of mood and message in his views, something often lacking in landscape photography.*

*His lifelong photography avocation began around the turn of the century, when amateur photography was thriving after the introduction of the Kodak camera. Using photography journals and the limited resources available nearby, he taught himself the highly manipulative bromoil transfer process, which he preferred above other methods because it allowed him to create images filled with mood and feeling. Besides his Utah work, Midgley also made bromoil and gum-bichromate prints of city and industrial subjects with a keen awareness of modernist styles. Throughout his life, he enjoyed mailing entries to photography exhibits and competitions around the world. In his later years, he was active in the Salt Lake Camera Club, and though he quit producing pictures when he was in his eighties, he continued to show his work until his death.*

J. George Midgley (1882–1979) was drawn to the image of the Mormon farmer quietly toiling on his land. These personal and visionary photographs allied interpretive artwork with the objectivity of the camera. He worked weekdays as an executive with the Heber J. Grant Company in Salt Lake City but seriously pursued photography as a fine art in his spare time.

Midgley began to practice the "bromoil process" about 1910, which allowed a photographic image to be altered and printed with lithographic ink on paper in a small press. With this technique he created soft, mood-filled images of the Utah rural landscape, recording a nostalgic era when man was closer to the land. Two typical prints in this mode are *Homeward* (PLATE 155) and *A Song of Summer* (PLATE 156). Midgley felt at one with this idyllic land, and though pictorial photography as a movement had died, he continued to produce such images even after he was eighty years old.

PLATE 157: **The Furrow**, 1929
MABEL PEARL FRAZER (1887–1982)
OIL ON CANVAS, 24" x 30" (61 CM x 76.2 CM)
MUSEUM OF CHURCH HISTORY AND ART

*This painting illustrates a Latter-day Saint emphasis on industry and self-reliance. "Life depends upon that furrow," Frazer proclaimed. "I have tried to concentrate that thought in the straining bulk of the horses and man, in the gulls repeating the rhythm of the man's motion, as they swoop down behind the plow." The artist believed that the idea of a painting should dictate technique. This is a modern expressionistic work with its hard-edged, broad, flat areas and distortion of form. The strong diagonal lines of the furrows and seagulls indicate action and activity. The vibrant use of colors repeated in the fields is echoed in the sky and fields beyond the foreground. Mabel Frazer was raised in Beaver, a farming community; thus she undoubtedly understood the effort of working the soil.*

Life on the land is also the subject of *The Furrow* (PLATE 157) by Mabel Frazer (1887–1982), long considered a regional masterpiece of Mormon agrarian life. In this painting she combined the human-interest theme with what she called "dynamic rhythm and color."[26] Frazer was not in favor of academic art training, and she revealed the beliefs that gave form to *The Furrow:* "I belong to no school. Schools set fashions in technique, but technique is not art. . . . The vitality of art is life. All great art must have its roots deep in a native soil. It can be neither borrowed nor lent. Things expressed without deep convictions can never be greatly convincing."[27]

Mabel Frazer believed in forging a new tradition of Latter-day Saint art. In a short article for the *Young Woman's Journal* titled "Latter-day Saint Artists," she wrote:

> I believe God sent us to the West to create a new commonwealth better than any we might copy, and I am determined to do my share to create an art of our own. I hope the time will come when our homes will all possess treasures of art, and that all our churches as well as our temples will be fittingly beautiful to house the glorious gospel. Art is my means of approach to the study of the things of God and its purpose should be to enrich the lives of His children.[28]

*Sego Lilies* (PLATE 158), a still-life painting portraying the Utah state flower, is a work that embraced forward art movements and emphasized Frazer's statement that "structure is a very part of me."[29]

Frazer is known as much for her forty-five years as a professor of art as for her work. Raised in Beaver, Utah, "the daughter of two lines of builders,"[30] she received an art degree in 1914, and studied at the Art Students League in New York City. Returning, she soon joined Professor Edwin Evans on the University of Utah art faculty. During the 1930s Mabel Frazer and an assistant, Lura Redd, retouched the garden room of the Salt Lake Temple (FIGURE 39), and Frazer also wrote commentaries on works of art pictured in the *Improvement Era* magazine. Twenty years later she finished a mural for the Salt Lake City Thirty-third Ward depicting Christ leaving the twelve disciples, from Third Nephi in the Book of Mormon. She traveled to Yucatan to study the ruins in her quest for authentic details to suggest the setting of that subject.

FIGURE 39: GARDEN ROOM
OF THE SALT LAKE TEMPLE

PLATE 158: *Sego Lilies,* ABOUT 1930
MABEL PEARL FRAZER (1887–1982)
OIL ON CANVAS, 20" X 16" (50.8 CM X 40.6 CM)
MUSEUM OF CHURCH HISTORY AND ART

*Tiny, delicate sego lilies take on heroic presence in this still life honoring the Utah state flower. During the lean years of pioneering in the Salt Lake Valley, some settlers combed the foothills in early summer, digging bulbs of the sego lily for food. Though bitter in taste, the bulbs are credited with providing sustenance for hungry families. Although Frazer's style was often exuberant in pure color and bold brushwork, she was adamant that technique should never dominate the message of the work. Frazer studied at the University of Utah under Edwin Evans and then pursued further studies at New York's School of Industrial Art, the Art Students League, and the Beaux Arts Institute of Design. She then returned to the University of Utah and a forty-five-year career as an art teacher.*

The decade of the 1930s found an increasing number of Mormon artists depicting farm workers. B. Y. Andelin (1894–1986) painted pleasant landscapes to adorn living-room walls, but his best work transcends the picturesque to record a way of life, such as men working in the fields in *Picking Potatoes* (PLATE 159). He was a regular contributor to the annual salon of the Springville Art Museum, for many decades the primary Utah exhibit for traditionalist art. Andelin also taught at Ogden High School and Weber State College for thirty-five years.

Dorothea Lange (1895–1965) was the foremost visual documentarian of the Great Depression. She first photographed Mormon life in 1933 on a two-month working trip with her husband, Maynard Dixon, in the area around Zion National Park. They boarded their two sons weekdays with a Mormon family in Toquerville, a pioneer village northwest of Zion. Using her square-format Rolleiflex camera, Lange photographed the town's older residents, including Maryann Savage (PLATE 161), who in 1856 as a child had walked across the plains. On a second Utah trip in 1936, Lange was employed by the Farm Security Administration (FSA), a New Deal agency set up to relocate farmers and aid the rural poor. Her main assignment was to record the impact of the Depression in the poverty-stricken Utah towns of Consumers and Widtsoe, but in Escalante, Lange brought out distinctive characteristics of Mormon life and the stability of the village people (PLATE 160). In 1941, Lange photographed Mormon farms as she traveled through Utah on a Guggenheim grant.

Lange's most important Utah work came during August 1953 when she and Ansel Adams worked together on a project recording the Mormons in three southern Utah towns: Toquerville, Gunlock, and St. George. More than 1,200 images were produced; today they are the finest existing record of Mormon village life at midcentury. The project resulted in a ten-page photo-essay in *Life* magazine in 1954, and an exhibit organized by the Eastman House, Rochester, New York. Some of the prints also appeared in the 1967 publication *Dorothea Lange Looks at the American Country Woman.*

Many documentary photographs of Latter-day Saint rural life in Utah were taken between 1935 and 1941 by photographers working for the FSA. Dorothea Lange in 1936, Arthur Rothstein in 1940, and Russell Lee in 1940–1941 were assigned to record the lives of clients for government officials in Washington, D.C., and to provide pictures for mass distribution through popular

PLATE 161: **Maryann Savage, Handcart Pioneer, Toquerville, Utah,** 1933
DOROTHEA LANGE (1895–1965)
GELATIN SILVER PRINT, 14" x 14" (36 CM x 36 CM)
MUSEUM OF CHURCH HISTORY AND ART
COURTESY THE OAKLAND MUSEUM
GIFT OF PAUL S. TAYLOR

*The chiseled face of Maryann Savage is representative of the strength, courage, and conviction of all Latter-day Saint pioneers. Maryann journeyed to Zion with her family in a handcart company at the age of six. Recalling a sister's death on the journey, Maryann later remembered matter-of-factly, "My mother wrapped her in a blanket and put her to one side." Maryann's character captured the attention of Dorothea Lange, who photographed Maryann at her home in Toquerville in 1933. Lange later published the image as a representation of a "faithful Mormon" in her tribute to the American country woman. She took several photographing trips through central and southern Utah that resulted in an impressive collection of images documenting Mormon life.*

PLATE 162: **Congregation Leaving Church after Sunday School, Mendon, Utah,** 1940
RUSSELL LEE (1903–1986)
GELATIN SILVER PRINT, 17 1/2" x 23" (44.5 CM x 58.4 CM)
MUSEUM OF CHURCH HISTORY AND ART
COURTESY LIBRARY OF CONGRESS

*The central placement of the chapel in this photograph emphasizes the important role of congregational worship in Latter-day Saint life. Religion and community are linked in this simple church that looks more like a large home—the house of the Lord, the home of His people. Church members reach out from a window to shake hands, to relish conversation and friendship enhanced by common values and hopes. They walk together through the fields and lanes to their separate homes, but the lines of the chapel roof leading into those of the background mountains reach out to embrace them all as a community of brothers and sisters in Zion. Russell Lee was one of the major documentary photographers employed by the Farm Security Administration (FSA) to portray the effects of New Deal legislation in rural Utah. In the mid-1930s, Dorothea Lange had preceded him with bleak works affirming the need for government intervention. In the 1940s, Lee's assignment was to produce optimistic photographs to counter growing congressional criticism of FSA projects. By 1940, however, both the economy and the hopes of the people had improved and Lee's work was an accurate reflection of the American mood. In Mendon, Utah, he found a blend of government cooperative effort coupled with deeply rooted Latter-day Saint beliefs in a community that bolstered his propaganda assignment.*

PLATE 163: **Sunday School Class, Mendon, Utah,** 1940
RUSSELL LEE (1903–1986)
GELATIN SILVER PRINT, 17 1/2" x 23"
(44.5 CM x 58.4 CM)
MUSEUM OF CHURCH HISTORY AND ART
COURTESY LIBRARY OF CONGRESS

*A class of Mendon's Sunday School children pose for this picture in the chapel choir seats. Three rows of girls are beside and behind the teacher, while the two rows of boys in front receive her greater scrutiny. Their faces reflect the diverse social and personal mosaic of the Mendon Latter-day Saint ward. Telltale signs in dress, grooming, posture, and expression indicate that Mendon, a small Mormon community in the Cache Valley, had citizens of modest means and affluence, innocence and experience, humor and seriousness. The four standard works of Latter-day Saint scripture rest on the pulpit visible in the foreground. Russell Lee's photograph shows another aspect of the same Mendon Ward Sunday School that he pictured in Plate 162.*

publications. The photography of Russell Lee (1903–1986), done just before World War II, centered on contented Latter-day Saints on farms. His works reflected the relative prosperity of selected small northern Utah towns in the Cache Valley and in Box Elder County, as well as in Santa Clara in the southwestern part of the state. One typical group of photographs was taken on a Sunday morning in August 1940, when Lee recorded priesthood and Sunday School meetings at the Mendon Ward. His *Congregation Leaving Church* (PLATE 162) and *Sunday School Class* (PLATE 163) are images filled with the spirit of community, suggesting the Great Depression was over.

## EVALUATION

The rural landscape of "Mormon Country" was one of the most distinctive areas of American habitation. Artists and photographers who worked there between the two World Wars were drawn together through a common desire to express the heritage and values of this region. The training the Latter-day Saint artists had received, mostly at the Art Students League in New York, reinforced that goal. Those artists responded to the national "American Scene" movement by expressing the experiences of common folk living on and working the land. That regional style was also heavily influenced by the Great Depression, which fostered in artists a social awareness and a yearning for the happier past and for a brighter future. LeConte Stewart's *Private Car* (PLATE 164) has become possibly the key example from this era to illustrate those concepts. The contrast of the peaceful rural environment with the dislocated hoboes on freight cars is a stark reminder that many Latter-day Saint families left their peaceful villages during the 1930s in search of greater economic opportunity elsewhere. As the Church expanded in the United States during succeeding decades, the regionalist spirit in Latter-day Saint art waned.

PLATE 164: *Private Car,* 1937
LeConte Stewart (1891–1990)
Oil on canvas, 30" x 48" (76.2 cm x 121.9 cm)
Museum of Church History and Art

*"Especially in his paintings from the Depression years, Stewart achieved a bleak clarity of vision that has been compared to [Edward] Hopper's. . . . Below the alluvial slopes where towns like Kaysville perch, both Union Pacific Railroad and the main north-south highway go by. And along these routes, below the shady sanctuary of Mormon villages whose community solidarity was being tested by the hard times and change, passed the homeless of the thirties, distinguished by misfortune, without even the frail support that home and community can give. Private Car . . . demonstrates how much power there still is in realism when realism is the expression of a passionate vision. . . . The desert light that gilds those uprooted ones seems also to threaten them. They are silhouettes before flames. . . . Unlike most of its competition [this painting] totally resists the temptation to sensationalize Utah scenery"* (Wallace Stegner, "The Power of Homely Detail," American Heritage 36 [August/September 1985]: 65, 68).

# CONTEMPORARY LATTER-DAY SAINT ART, 1965–1995

4

*by Robert O. Davis*

For the history of Latter-day Saint artwork, the era from 1965 to the present has been richly rewarding. New museums have opened and public exhibits of Latter-day Saint art have been organized, and artists have responded to those increased opportunities to share their work and receive recognition. During this period Latter-day Saint artists have produced art on a far wider range of topics about life. Art has become a means of individual expression for enjoyment, or a way of seeking greater meaning and purpose in life. Markets have developed for art to decorate the home, particularly landscapes and pieces depicting gospel values. There has also been an effort to organize a formal movement of Mormon art. The Church continues to commission portraits of Church leaders, art to decorate meetinghouses, temples, and other buildings, and illustrations for manuals, magazine articles, and instructional prints. It also acquires works for display in thematic exhibits for the Church Museum and visitors' centers.

The training of Latter-day Saint artists has shifted from specialized art schools, such as the Art Students League, to colleges and universities. The art department at Brigham Young University prepared two-thirds of the artists dealt with in this chapter. The addition of Franz Johansen and Alex Darais to its faculty in the 1950s solidified the contemporary view of art held there already by Professor J. Roman Andrus. In 1965 the sprawling Franklin S. Harris Fine Arts Center (FIGURE 40) opened, and the number of art majors at BYU expanded. The school hired Dale Fletcher, Robert Marshall, Trevor Southey, and William Whitaker, all skilled representational artists who understood the abstract substructure of traditional artwork. In 1972, Wulf Barsch became head of the printmaking depart-

FIGURE 40: FRANKLIN S. HARRIS FINE ARTS CENTER

ment. Other faculty members since that time who have made significant contributions include Frank Magleby, Wayne Kimball, Peter Myer, Bruce Smith, Brent Gehring, Jeanne Lundberg, Neil Hadlock, and Hagen Haltern.

## LATTER-DAY SAINT ART EXHIBITS

The origin of contemporary group consciousness for a "Mormon art" began in 1967 when faculty and students at Brigham Young University met weekly to discuss ideas about religious art. That same year Elder Spencer W. Kimball of the Quorum of the Twelve gave a faculty lecture, "Education for Eternity," at which he gave this clarion call: "The story of Mormonism has never yet been written nor painted nor sculpted nor spoken. It remains for inspired hearts and talented fingers yet to reveal themselves. [The artists] must be faithful, inspired, active Church members to give life and feeling and true perspective to a subject so worthy."[1]

*Facing page: Detail from* **Jordan River Temple, Salt Lake Valley,** *by Al Rounds. (See Plate 180, page 126.)*

Dr. Lorin F. Wheelwright, dean of the College of Fine Arts and Communications, set goals to meet this challenge. The university sponsored the "First Mormon Festival of Arts" in 1968, with a large, unjuried exhibition and seminars that discussed art as expression of religious conviction. In its second year the festival included a variety of the arts, not just visual artworks. It featured a juried show of forty works of the finest current Mormon art, together with a retrospective exhibit of outstanding Latter-day Saint art of the past. The "Third Annual Mormon Festival of Arts" in the spring of 1971 was a highly publicized, two-week-long celebration of Latter-day Saint identity. A brochure proclaimed, "Creative Latter-day Saints from all over the world join together in concerts, plays, musicals, readings, symposiums, recitals, art and photography exhibits to express Mormon values artistically!"[2] Nine events dealt with visual art, including invitational art and photography exhibits and seminars on Mormon art and photography. A book, *Mormon Arts, Volume One,* edited by Dr. Wheelwright and Dr. Lael K. Woodbury, presented excellent reproductions of the finest of the work from the first three festivals, together with ambitious discussions of what characterizes Mormon art. The bold text captures the fervor of the time.

The next festivals were scaled back. Faculty members and professionals interested in Mormon art juried the exhibits, and some attempted to recruit contributions from artists of greater status. In the fall of 1978 a separate juried "Mormon Illustration Exhibition" was held in conjunction with Church magazines. With the "Twelfth Mormon Arts Festival," held the year of the sesquicentennial of the organization of the Church, came a change in philosophy. The show catalog explained: "Rather than limiting our view to art with Mormon subject matter, we must include any art that serves to amplify high moral values visually, regardless of subject. . . . Therein lies the true Mormon art."[3]

Into the 1980s the festival's definition of "Mormon art" continued broadening to include "the best work of contemporary Mormon artists,"[4] but as the shows became more inclusive the thematic focus diminished, and they gradually became weaker and were supported less by segments of the Latter-day Saint art community. This trend continued in the 1983 festival, in which art was called for that "need not be limited to [Mormon] subject matter. We simply desire that it exemplify significance and excellence in art."[5] In 1984 the title was changed to "Brigham Young University Fine Arts Exhibition," and for the last show in 1987, titled the "18th Annual Fine Arts Exhibition," no criteria at all for artwork content were stated in the entry form. During those nearly two decades the festivals prompted many significant expressions that became part of the whole of Mormon art.

Another exhibit format on the BYU campus is Gallery 303 in the Harris Fine Arts Center. Sponsored by the university's Art Department, it has featured small, high-quality exhibits of contemporary art from a variety of sources.

FIGURE 41: MUSEUM OF CHURCH HISTORY AND ART

In 1984 the Church opened the granite-faced Museum of Church History and Art (FIGURE 41) across the street from Temple Square in Salt Lake City, and by the 1990s more than 300,000 people a year visited there. The purpose of this institution has been to strengthen the beliefs of Church members and inform nonmembers by depicting the history and heritage of the Church in interpretive exhibits containing artifacts, documents, photographs, and artwork. The Church collection of art is preserved, maintained, and tracked largely by the Museum.

Latter-day Saint artwork was once again nurtured when the Museum of Church History and Art sponsored its "1987 Fine Art Competition and Exhibition" to encourage new art about

Church history, beliefs, and ways of life. Artists competed for prizes and purchase awards donated by two benefactors who desired to have religious work fostered, to reward outstanding efforts, and to develop new talent. Of the more than 1,000 entries submitted by 600 Mormon artists around the world, 180 were exhibited. Three years later the Museum sponsored the "Second International Art Competition: Themes from the Scriptures." Artists were encouraged to create quality work in any medium, reflecting a theme, value, or story inspired by something in one of the four standard works of Latter-day Saint scripture. Of the 831 entries from forty-two nations, 220 were juried into the show, and twenty-seven cash and purchase prizes were awarded from a fund established by two generous benefactors. Many of the pieces have been pictured in Church magazines and have appeared in succeeding museum exhibits. In 1994 the "Third International Art Competition: Living the Gospel in the World Church" generated an exhibition of 150 new works. From financial gifts graciously made by the Silver Foundation of Denver, Colorado, and Alan and Karen Ashton of Orem, Utah, twenty-nine artists were awarded prizes. Through these competitions, the Church collection has been greatly enhanced with contemporary art from around the world, including many of the works pictured in this chapter.

The Museum of Church History and Art has also sponsored a series of contemporary art exhibits featuring Mormon subject matter. In 1984, "Paintings and Prints by Contemporary Latter-day Saint Artists" contained work from the Church collection on Mormon themes. A six-section exhibition in 1988, "Reflections on the Kingdom: Images of Latter-day Saint History and Belief," gathered the finest artwork from all periods, one-third of it contemporary. Two years later a massive exhibit of large photographs displayed work in forty different themes from infancy to death. An important 1992 exhibit showed twenty key Church artworks with texts explaining how the artists used images and elements of art to convey meanings symbolically.

Several shows at the Museum have been devoted to the thematic religious work of individual contemporary artists and photographers, including "Looking Toward Home: Recent Art by Wulf Barsch" and "Images of Contemporary LDS Life: Craig Law Photographs." Two group exhibits with 10,000 total international entries were mounted in 1991 and 1993 using the solicited art of children: "Through a Child's Eye: Scenes from the Book of Mormon," and "Through a Child's Eye: All Families of the Earth Be Blessed."

In recent years the Springville Museum of Art in Springville, Utah (FIGURE 42), has supported contemporary spiritual-religious art through its own ambitious exhibit schedule. The Museum's annual Spring Salon has shown

FIGURE 42: SPRINGVILLE MUSEUM OF ART

progressive, modern art as well as the traditional, representational art that has been an outlet for the narrative subject matter favored by many Latter-day Saint artists. This museum has focused on Utah art, artists, and subjects that overlap with religious or cultural Latter-day Saint themes.

The impressive new Brigham Young University Museum of Art (FIGURE 43) opened in 1993,

FIGURE 43: BRIGHAM YOUNG UNIVERSITY MUSEUM OF ART

and early exhibits there drew from the holdings of the university in art depicting Latter-day Saint subject matter. One exhibit, "C.C.A. Christensen's Mormon Panorama," contained all of the great pioneer artist's mural-sized paintings that portrayed the early history of the Church. A major emphasis of this institution is educational, serving the needs of the university as well as reaching out to the community.

PLATE 165: *President Howard W. Hunter*, 1995
WILLIAM WHITAKER (1942– )
OIL ON CANVAS, 40" X 32" (101.6 CM X 81.3 CM)
MUSEUM OF CHURCH HISTORY AND ART

*This portrait captures the likeness of the fourteenth President of the Church, a man who will be remembered for his lifelong service and his powerful message to "treat each other with more kindness, more courtesy, more humility and patience and forgiveness." Through lighting, the artist has created a strong center of focus on President Hunter's hands and face, conveying the love, kindness, and humility for which he was known. The viewpoint and low horizon serve to raise President Hunter's figure, as if to the measure of his sacred calling, while the somber greys of the cloudy world seem to yearn for the light of the gospel. The rolling hills of Judea, standing in silhouette against the amber sunset, represent the Holy Land, where President Hunter visited as an Apostle on several occasions. William Whitaker has distinguished himself as a painter of environmental portraits, and his manner here is reminiscent of the classical styles of the old masters he admires.*

PLATE 166: *Thomas S. Monson*, 1990
KNUD EDSBERG (1911– )
OIL ON CANVAS, 28" X 22" (71.1 CM X 56 CM)
MUSEUM OF CHURCH HISTORY AND ART

*The Church has a rich portrait painting tradition that commemorates its leaders. Edsberg, Denmark's best-known portrait artist, has depicted President Monson as counselor in the First Presidency, where he has served since 1985. A largely self-taught traditional artist, Edsberg acquired his style by studying the Danish masters. Darkening the canvas before beginning to paint, he strives for unity when combining color, surroundings, and subject.*

## PORTRAITS OF CHURCH MEMBERS AND LEADERS

In the 1980s the Museum of Church History and Art became the repository of official portraits of Church leaders in permanent exhibits, including "Presidents of the Church" and "Portraits of Church Leaders." These exhibits drew from existing commissioned portraits completed during the terms of service of most of the members of the Quorum of the Twelve Apostles and the First Presidency. To fill the gaps when no portraits existed, the Museum commissioned new work from life by Judith Mehr, Ken Corbett, Wilson Ong, Cloy Kent, Knud Edsberg, and William Whitaker; modern portraits of deceased leaders were painted from photographs by Mehr, Shauna Cook Clinger, David Ahrnsbrak, Ong, Kent, Corbett, and Marcus Vincent.

Just before President Howard W. Hunter's death in 1995, William Whitaker (1942- ) completed an officially commissioned portrait of the prophet (PLATE 165). Whitaker's work was well known by then; in 1970 his artworks commemorating the organization of the Church appeared in the premier issue of the *Ensign*. Ten years later, he produced a carefully researched new portrait of Joseph Smith for the *Deseret News*. A former professor of art at Brigham Young University, Whitaker taught the importance of drawing from life and working hard to achieve results.

Knud Edsberg (1911– ) of North Sjaeland, Denmark, a member of the Church since 1961, has done five portraits of Apostles, including Thomas S. Monson (Plate 166), and was selected to paint the official portrait of President Ezra Taft Benson. Over a long career he has completed several hundred portraits of notable people in business, government, academics, and the arts.

Seattle artist Judith Campion (1935– ) specializes in expressive portraits in pencil of individuals and families. Her portrait of President Spencer W. Kimball (Plate 167) captures his spiritual qualities. In the 1990s Brigham Young University-trained Wilson J. Ong (1958– ) (Figure 44) painted animated and lifelike commissioned portraits of Elders Dallin H. Oaks, Neal A. Maxwell, Richard G. Scott, and M. Russell Ballard, as well as posthumous portraits of Elders LeGrand Richards and Bruce R. McConkie. Ong's updated story of the prodigal son parable, *Genesis of Repentance: Realization,* and his *Pioneer Lady* (Plate 168), a modern interpretation of pioneer life, both won purchase award honors in the Museum's international art competitions.

PLATE 167: *Spencer W. Kimball,* 1984
JUDITH CAMPION (1935– )
GRAPHITE ON PAPER, 24" x 18" (61 CM x 45.7 CM)
MUSEUM OF CHURCH HISTORY AND ART

*The twelfth President of the Church, Spencer W. Kimball (1895–1985), was known as a tireless, hardworking man totally committed to the service of the Lord. He gave the Church such slogans as "Lengthen Your Stride." During his administration, the number of missionaries doubled and converts quickly increased. Rising above physical adversity, he personally took his message of the gospel to more than sixty countries of the world, doing so in the spirit of love and humility. Campion, an expert in her pencil medium, adeptly portrays the feelings and emotions of her subject. Her portrait of President Kimball captures his warmth, his joyous nature, and his approachable countenance.*

PLATE 168: *Pioneer Lady,* 1984
WILSON J. ONG (1958– )
OIL ON PANEL, 13 1/2" x 10 1/2" (34.3 CM x 26.7 CM)
MUSEUM OF CHURCH HISTORY AND ART

*"Blessed, honored pioneer" seems to be the refrain of this portrait of a pioneer lady. Transcending reality, the figure in its simple beauty reflects the ideals of faith, hope, courage, and purity. Memorialized in art, music, poetry, and drama, pioneers are role models for modern Latter-day Saints.*

*The artist has portrayed a friend as the ideal of a pioneer woman. She appears in profile before an arid landscape—a practice manifest in early Italian Renaissance portraiture. This gemlike work is successful in uniting the present with the past. Details such as the girl's sunburned nose and the frills on her collar add charm. Primarily a portraitist, Ong trained at Brigham Young University and at the Art Students League in New York and has worked in California and Utah.*

Mural painting in temple ordinance rooms was discontinued in the 1960s. Modern temples contain photographic reproductions of pictures of the Savior by artists such as Harry Anderson, as well as original paintings, especially restful landscapes. Artwork on specific themes enhances some temples, such as *The Transfiguration of Christ* by Greg Olsen in the Seattle Temple. Several murals removed from older temples have been conserved, reframed, and installed in new temples. Original artwork is no longer placed in ward chapels, but small prints of Delwin Parson's *The Lord Jesus Christ* and other framed art reproductions sometimes decorate the foyer area.

## THE HISTORY OF THE RESTORED CHURCH IN ART

After 1965, artists focused increasingly on an expanded pool of Latter-day Saint historical themes in a quest to create a specifically "Mormon" art. For example, major examples portraying the organization of the Church and the martyrdom of Joseph and Hyrum Smith were produced, not on the sesquicentennial anniversary years of these events, but by the artists' initiative or through commissions. These pieces show more originality and personal interpretation of the events than did earlier artwork.

PLATE 169: ***Benbow Farm and Pond, England,*** 1987
FRANK MAGLEBY (1928– )
OIL ON CANVAS, 36" X 48" (91.4 CM X 121.9 CM)
MUSEUM OF CHURCH HISTORY AND ART

*In 1840 Wilford Woodruff embarked on an extremely fruitful mission to England. A prosperous farmer, John Benbow, and his family and friends were Woodruff's first converts in Herefordshire. Elder Woodruff baptized more than six hundred individuals in the pond at the Benbow farm. The artist visited the pond and the farm almost a hundred and fifty years later, during the sesquicentennial of missionary work in Great Britain, before creating this commemorative work. Magleby has led a distinguished career as a landscape painter and as a professor at Brigham Young University.*

PLATE 170: *Martyrdom of Joseph and Hyrum Smith, Carthage,* ABOUT 1976
GARY ERNEST SMITH (1942– )
OIL ON CANVAS, 47" X 59 1/2"
(119.4 CM X 151.1 CM)
MUSEUM OF CHURCH HISTORY AND ART
GIFT OF ROBERT F. ORTON

*This painting depicts the final desperate moments in the assault on Carthage Jail on June 27, 1844. Hyrum Smith lies dead on the floor in the middle of the room. John Taylor, severely wounded by the gunfire, struggles to find cover near the bed, while Willard Richards raises a cane to deflect the guns of the attackers. As Joseph Smith reels toward the open second-story window of the jail, he is mortally wounded by volleys of gunfire and falls to his death on the ground below. The skewed perspective, the somber color, the presence of smoke in the room, and the facial expressions effectively convey the feeling of death and terror present there. This painting is part of a series Utah artist Gary Smith created portraying the events of the martyrdom.*

Frank Magleby (1928– ) (FIGURE 45), an art professor at Brigham Young University, continued the naturalistic, conservative, eastern United States tradition of landscape painting using tight

FIGURE 45:
FRANK MAGLEBY

detail and glazes. His *Benbow Farm* (PLATE 169) was a merit and purchase award winner in the 1987 fine arts competition. The artist painted it after visiting this site of successful British missionary work. Other historical paintings by Magleby in the Museum collection include *Nauvoo Landscape* and *The Sacred Grove.*

Gary Ernest Smith (1942– ) became conscious of rural life and local history growing up on a ranch near Baker, Oregon. He joined the burgeoning movement in Utah Valley to express Church historical themes by drawing on period styles of ancient Egyptian art and American regional art of the 1930s. The artful, narratively accurate *Martyrdom of Joseph and Hyrum Smith* (PLATE 170) is one of four works by Smith on this theme in the Church collection. Today Smith is noted for his evocative scenes of western rural life.

*Often called the "Lion of the Lord," Brigham Young is appropriately posed next to the carved stone lion that watches over his Lion House in Salt Lake City. This fine illustrative portrait with its strong lines, color, and lion imagery evokes the authority and leadership of this pioneer president. James Christensen, a professor of art at Brigham Young University, began his art career as an illustrator. Today he is considered one of the premier fantasy artists in the nation.*

FIGURE 46:
JAMES C. CHRISTENSEN

Artists sometimes take liberties in interpreting history to enable the viewer to make new connections. James C. Christensen (1942– ) (FIGURE 46), who teaches art at Brigham Young University, is known nationally as a painter of fantasy subjects carried out with detail and wit. *Brigham Young and the Lion* (PLATE 171) is almost photographically precise. By juxtaposing Brigham, the "Lion of the Lord," with the stylized sandstone lion from the entry roof of the Lion House, Christensen pulls meaning into a new realm through the interplay of the facial expressions. The artist's *Alma the Younger Called to Repentance* (PLATE 172) uses flat planes of leaded stained glass to create what has become a classic image derived from a Book of Mormon theme. Pino Drago (1947– ) is a native of Italy who worked for the Church as a graphic designer in Germany. *Monday, 24 June 1844, 4:15 A.M.: Beyond the Events* (PLATE 173), the second prize and purchase award winner in the Museum's first international art competition, is one of the most compelling symbolic works in the Church collection. This painting takes Joseph Smith's decision to face charges against him as the basis for a profound psychological study.

PLATE 172: **Alma the Younger Called to Repentance,** 1977
JAMES C. CHRISTENSEN (1942– )
LEADED STAINED GLASS, 73" X 52" (185.4 CM X 132.1 CM)
MUSEUM OF ART, BRIGHAM YOUNG UNIVERSITY

*"I went about with the sons of Mosiah, seeking to destroy the church of God; but behold, God sent his holy angel to stop us . . . and the whole earth did tremble beneath our feet; and we all fell to the earth, for the fear of the Lord came upon us" (Alma 36:6–7). After graduating from Brigham Young University, Christensen experimented with several different mediums and styles and also worked as an illustrator for national magazines and for the New Era, as a junior high school art teacher, and as a faculty member at Brigham Young University. After a trip to Europe in 1980, he decided to concentrate almost exclusively on fantasy art.*

PLATE 173: *Monday, 24 June 1844, 4:15 A.M.: Beyond the Events*, 1987
PINO DRAGO (1947– )
OIL ON CANVAS, 56" x 47" (142.2 CM x 119.4 CM)
MUSEUM OF CHURCH HISTORY AND ART

*With the realization that his earthly mission is almost over, Joseph Smith looks forward steadily, beyond the viewer, to eternity. The artist has grounded the event in time, choosing 4:15 A.M. three days before the martyrdom as Joseph's moment of truth. That moment is visible in the conflicting emotions of the figure. Joseph's left side is tense—his left hand grasps his knee in a futile attempt to hold onto life, and the left side of his face is cloaked in shadow. In contrast, the right side of Joseph's figure is relaxed and bathed in light, reflecting the peace that allowed him to declare, "I am going like a lamb to the slaughter; but I am calm as a summer's morning." The juxtaposition of Joseph's portrait with that of an Italian humanist thinker invites the viewer to compare the different sources of knowledge available to the two. Twenty-three layers of glaze, which the artist applied over a six-month period, intensify the focus on Joseph's face.*

Dean Millman (1948–1977) has conveyed historical information through a naturalistic still life, *LDS Scriptures and Brigham Young Letter* (PLATE 174). Millman painted freely and easily and was prodigious in his output during his short life of twenty-eight years. "He was a romanticist, creating a mood that transcends the commonplace and quietly beckons the viewer to experience and enjoy," said his sister, Lynne.[6] A 1977 article in the *New Era* featured the artist and his work. Millman's promising career was cut short when he died of leukemia.

The western art genre has attracted many Latter-day Saints, including Brigham Young University-trained Gary L. Kapp (1942– ). Descended from pioneers, Kapp said that their stories provided inspiration for his work. He researched his earlier pictures for authenticity of detail and costuming, but more recently his works have been freer, as in *Sunflowers and Buffalo Chips* (PLATE 175), purchased by the Museum from the 1987 international fine arts competition. John Jarvis (1946– ) is another BYU-trained western artist producing works for galleries. He is drawn to landscapes inhabited by Indians, and his point of view and gouache technique have much in common with the noted nineteenth-century American illustrator Henry Farny. *Jacob Hamblin and Chief Tuba* (PLATE 176) was commissioned for a room in the Church Museum devoted to the art of Latter-day Saint Native Americans. It depicts the Hopi chief and Hamblin when they crossed the Colorado River en route to Salt Lake City to meet Brigham Young. Tuba later was converted to the Church through Hamblin's efforts.

PLATE 174: **LDS Scriptures and Brigham Young Letter,** 1975
DEAN MILLMAN (1948–1977)
GOUACHE ON PANEL, 16" X 19" (40.6 CM X 48.3 CM)
MUSEUM OF CHURCH HISTORY AND ART

*This still life, worked primarily in brown tones, juxtaposes the Latter-day Saint scriptures with a statement by Brigham Young counseling, "Let every man and woman know by the whisperings of the Spirit of God to themselves whether their leaders are walking in the path the Lord dictates, or not." Together the scriptures and Church leaders' counsel, if followed as confirmed by the Spirit, will lead the Saints to salvation. Millman, who studied at Brigham Young University, focused his talents on creating still lifes filled with objects from the Old West. He tried to bring vibrancy to his paintings through exacting detail.*

PLATE 175: *Sunflowers and Buffalo Chips,* 1987
GARY L. KAPP (1942– )
OIL ON CANVAS, 20" X 30" (50.8 CM X 76.2 CM)
MUSEUM OF CHURCH HISTORY AND ART

*More than sixty thousand Latter-day Saint pioneers
journeyed over plains and mountains to Utah between
1847 and 1869. Although many of them began their
journey by ship, railroad, or steamboat, they made the
the main portion of the trek on foot with wagon or
handcart companies. Here, a mother gathers fuel for the
evening campfire while the wagons pause. Her daughters
pick the wildflowers nearby, bringing a touch of color to
the serious business of travel. The juxtaposition of
sunflowers with buffalo chips mirrors the placement of
the genteel-looking mother and daughters against the
harsh landscape of the journey. Kapp, from Provo, Utah,
is a painter of narrative western subjects.*

PLATE 176: *Jacob Hamblin and Chief Tuba,* 1984
JOHN JARVIS (1946– )
GOUACHE ON PAPER, 30" X 38" (76.2 CM X 96.5 CM)
MUSEUM OF CHURCH HISTORY AND ART

*Beginning in 1858, Jacob Hamblin, an Indian
missionary and scout, made many trips to visit the
Hopis. Chief Tuba and two other Hopis accompanied
the missionaries from Arizona to Salt Lake City to meet
Brigham Young in 1863. They are shown on that trip
just after they have crossed the Colorado River at Ute
Crossing. Another Latter-day Saint practitioner of
western painting, Jarvis paints in opaque watercolors.
He concentrates on desert landscapes and the Indians of
the desert country. Jarvis favors subtle effects of light
and shade, such as scenes illuminated at dusk or
subjects in shadow encompassing a narrow range of
color.*

PLATE 177: *Porter Rockwell, the Enforcer,* 1978
PETER FILLERUP (1953– )
CAST BRONZE, 19" X 8" X 13"
(48.3 CM X 20.3 CM X 33 CM)
MUSEUM OF CHURCH HISTORY AND ART

*The colorful Mormon frontiersman Orrin Porter Rockwell strikes a defiant pose in this bronze. Rockwell became a legend among Latter-day Saints for his rough and ready attitude, serving as a bodyguard to Joseph Smith, as a guerrilla soldier in the Utah War, and as a sheriff and marshal. This rugged hero of frontier Mormonism is a natural subject for Fillerup, a noted western sculptor. Fillerup studied art at Brigham Young University and with Avard Fairbanks before launching his career.*

PLATE 178: **The Saints Embark from Liverpool, England,** 1978
KEN BAXTER (1944– )
OIL ON CANVAS, 30" X 40" (76.2 CM X 101.6 CM)
MUSEUM OF CHURCH HISTORY AND ART

*For nineteenth-century European Latter-day Saints, joining the Church also meant joining the Saints in Zion. Nearly ninety thousand European Saints experienced scenes like this as they embarked on their journey to Zion. Of the 333 recorded voyages made by Latter-day Saint emigrant companies between 1840 and 1890, 209 began on the Mersey River at Liverpool, as portrayed here. Baxter, who studied at the University of Utah, is a noted landscapist. As in The Saints Embark at Liverpool, Baxter often transforms landscapes into their earlier historical setting.*

PLATE 179: *The Martin Handcart Co., Bitter Creek, Wyoming,* 1980
CLARK KELLEY PRICE (1945– )
OIL ON CANVAS, 36" X 48" (91.4 CM X 121.9 CM)
MUSEUM OF CHURCH HISTORY AND ART

*Early winter storms trapped the Martin Handcart Company in deep snow on the plains of Wyoming in October 1856. Burial scenes were common as almost a quarter of the company died from exposure. Here Scottish emigrant James Steele is laid in a shallow grave while his wife and infant son stand vigil. James, who was the artist's great-great-grandfather, starved to death, saving all of his rations for his wife and children. Price pays tribute to his ancestor who "died on the windswept plains, hundreds of miles from Zion, but it was in his heart." A wildlife and western artist from Wyoming, Price felt inspired to portray the scene that his mother had told him of as a child.*

The sculpture of Peter Fillerup (1953– ) (FIGURE 47) "brings to life the essence of the West."[7] After training at Brigham Young University, he apprenticed with master sculptor Avard T.

FIGURE 47: PETER FILLERUP

Fairbanks, working on the large Angel Moroni statue for the Seattle Temple. His bronze casting of a Mormon bodyguard, *Porter Rockwell, the Enforcer* (PLATE 177), maintains the legend that has grown up around that colorful personality; Fillerup explained, "Porter Rockwell is a hero type to me."[8]

Contemporary artwork sometimes attempts to carefully re-create the past. Such was the objective of versatile traditional artist Ken Baxter (1944– ) in his painting commissioned for a Church area office in England, *The Saints Embark from Liverpool, England* (PLATE 178). The artist researched a variety of visual and written sources for this painting. His earlier work depicted turn-of-the-century historical vignettes of downtown Salt Lake City, while more recently he has painted landscapes on site. Clark Kelley Price (1945– ) took a similar approach in *The Martin Handcart Co., Bitter Creek, Wyoming* (PLATE 179). Price related:

> The Church wanted more paintings depicting historical events. . . . It was then that the idea to paint the Martin Handcart Co. came to me and I set about with great fervor to bring it to life. . . . I spent one day out in the snowy desert in the wind and cold searching for the right setting and feeling. I felt a lot of help as I worked on this painting. I felt that it was a story that needed to be told.[9]

PLATE 180: *Jordan River Temple, Salt Lake Valley,* 1982

AL ROUNDS (1954– )
WATERCOLOR ON PAPER, 22" X 30"
(55.9 CM X 76.2 CM)
JORDAN RIVER TEMPLE

*The strong use of color along the diagonal canal draws the viewer into this painting to encounter the understated depiction of the Jordan River Temple. The sense of quiet discovery reflects the peace and introspection Latter-day Saints find in temples. Al Rounds spent a year studying the temple site and sketching before he discovered this scene and mood. The artist studied at Brigham Young University and the University of Utah, and is noted for his watercolors of significant sites from Latter-day Saint history nestled in their landscapes, both historical and contemporary.*

## RECORDING THE "MORMON LANDSCAPE"

From 1965 to the present day, the "Mormon Landscape" has become increasingly popular as subject matter for artwork. As rural farmland was replaced by housing, people longed for images of the peaceful country environment. Landscapes by early Utah artists became prized collector's items, and as the early work became scarce, new talents came forth.

Watercolor paintings of rural landscapes and Mormon buildings by Al Rounds (1954– ) have become well known among Church members through prints and *Ensign* magazine covers. Rounds's work is characterized by dramatic effects of sunset and weather, bold perspective created by irrigation ditches, wide roads, and rows of poplar trees cutting into the picture, and accurately rendered pioneer architecture. In *Jordan River Temple, Salt Lake Valley* (PLATE 180), the artist uses an unusual perspective and artistic license to isolate the subject from surrounding buildings. Rounds often evokes the past by picturing historic buildings but removing all vestiges of modern life from around them.

Working in a similar manner, G. Allen Garns (1954– ) created *Randolph Utah Tabernacle* (PLATE 181) as part of a project to document significant historical Latter-day Saint meetinghouses and tabernacles. His work for the Church has also included a series of *Ensign* illustrations.

PLATE 181: ***Randolph Utah Tabernacle,*** 1982
G. ALLEN GARNS (1954– )
OIL ON CANVAS, 32" x 42" (81.3 CM x 106.7 CM)
MUSEUM OF CHURCH HISTORY AND ART

*The impressive walls of this northeastern Utah
tabernacle dedicated in 1914 stand as a sentinel to
the Latter-day Saints in Rich County, calling them
together to worship. The tabernacle is a center for
congregational and recreational activities for the
entire stake. Although some tabernacles are still in
use, as this one is, stake centers now accommodate
most large congregational activities. The artist
here works with broad planes of color to
summarize the form, and infuses his work with a
static quality—a sense of timelessness uniquely
appropriate to portraying historic buildings. The
warm afternoon light pervades the painting, and
the artist's palette of orange, muted greens, and
purples is a hallmark of his work.*

PLATE 182: *Tithing House, Chesterfield, Idaho,*
ABOUT 1979
CRAIG J. LAW (1946– )
CARBON PRINT, 6 7/8" x 9 1/2" (17.5 CM X 24.1 CM)
MUSEUM OF CHURCH HISTORY AND ART

*Chesterfield, Idaho, was privately founded in 1879 by descendants of the original settlers of Bountiful, Utah. An LDS ward was organized, and in the 1890s the tithing house was constructed. Church members brought to the house a portion of the commodities they produced, and these were later distributed to the poor. This striking photograph of the now-abandoned town shows characteristics of the community and setting. The tithing house on the left is framed by a rainbow symbolic of blessing. To the right is the salt-box style home of Denmark Jensen, an early settler. Craig Law's photographic essay of Chesterfield was published to bolster efforts to preserve the remains of the town. In his work Law follows the example of photographer George Edward Anderson in documenting the daily life and history of the Latter-day Saints.*

FIGURE 48: CRAIG LAW

Craig J. Law (1946– ) (FIGURE 48) has photographed Latter-day Saint landscape, history, and life. *Tithing House, Chesterfield* (PLATE 182), is one of many images Law took for the book *Chesterfield: Mormon Outpost in Idaho.* Law has produced the finest documentation of modern small-town Mormon life in our day. In two series of beautiful archival photographs he also recorded the interiors of the Logan and Manti Temples before modernization. For twenty years in his roles as husband, father, bishop, teacher, and friend, he has recorded the history of his ward and his family's activities at home and at Church events. Law sensitively and accurately portrays ordinary Latter-day Saints without attempting to overstate for effect. He lets the subject speak for itself, as in the portrait of his grandparents holding his son, *Couple with Great-Grandson, Willard, Utah* (PLATE 183). Another commissioned collection of seven large exhibition photographs shows people and groups in front of the temple, suggesting its different functions. Those images appeared in the 1993 Salt Lake Temple centennial exhibit at the Church Museum.

PLATE 183: ***Couple with Great-Grandson,
Willard, Utah***, ABOUT 1976

CRAIG J. LAW (1946– )
GELATIN SILVER PRINT, 7 3/4" X 11 1/2"
(19.9 CM X 29.2 CM)
MUSEUM OF CHURCH HISTORY AND ART

*The links of generations are powerfully captured in
this image of an elderly couple standing in awe of
their great-grandson. The old family home and
manicured yard frames the setting of love
expressed in this photo. The relationship between
the human figures and the classic landscape is a
beautiful photographic investigation. In Law's
photographic work, the human landscape involves
exploring the aesthetic ties and the contrasts
between two classic subjects and then letting each
affect the other. Law uses the photographic medium
to express his belief that "making clear visual order
of the world is not necessarily how it is, but how I'd
like it to be." His prolific works have become
priceless for their historic value. Law teaches
photography at Utah State University.*

PLATE 184: *Staff among Spears,* ABOUT 1975
ALEXANDER B. DARAIS (1918– )
OIL ON PANEL, 30 1/4" x 24 1/2"
(76.8 CM X 62.2 CM)
MUSEUM OF CHURCH HISTORY AND ART

*Except for the lone shepherd's staff, the humble and peaceful earthly mission of the Savior is nearly lost behind an imposing shield of Roman spears at his crucifixion. By contrasting the spears and shepherd's crook, the artist highlights the difference between the kingdoms of the earth and the spiritual mission of the Savior, who yielded himself to the demands of his captors to fulfill his holy purposes. Darais is a Latter-day Saint expressionist whose art often conveys personal views of his life and his religious beliefs. His highly personal style also reflects the artistic traditions of the 1950s and 1960s. A respected art teacher, Darais influenced hundreds of students during his more than twenty-five years of teaching at Brigham Young University.*

## SCRIPTURAL STORIES AND PRINCIPLES

Many contemporary Latter-day Saint artists who work from scriptural sources do not attempt to illustrate the stories literally, but instead express what is meaningful to them, often in a present-day context. The "Second International Art Competition: Themes from the Scriptures" was a fruitful exhibit for Museum acquisitions. Artists especially responded to President Ezra Taft Benson's call for work on Book of Mormon themes.

Alexander Darais (1918– ) (FIGURE 49) has been one of the most respected teachers and philosophers of contemporary Latter-day Saint art. At Brigham Young University he offered his students the highest level of personal integrity and a thoughtful, penetrating approach to the ideas and execution of artwork. *A Staff among Spears* (PLATE 184) is at once a personal, reflective statement of the artist and a visual expression of the meaning of scriptures

FIGURE 49:
ALEXANDER DARAIS

relating to the Crucifixion. His poem of the same title, together with a reproduction of the painting, is found in his wonderful book *Little Bird: Selected Poems and Paintings.* A colleague of Darais at BYU, Franz Johansen (1928– ) (FIGURE 50), was also one of the fathers of new art that symbolically expressed scriptural beliefs. He saw the human form as the basis for religious expression and taught direct drawing from models. He contributed to a climate that enabled others to bring about a Mormon art movement. Among his primary works were commissions to create the two-story-high relief sculpture on the facade of the Museum of Church History and Art and the bronze doors on the Washington Temple. *The Rod and the Veil* (PLATE 185) is a masterpiece unsurpassed in the originality of its interpretation of a Book of Mormon theme.

FIGURE 50:
FRANZ JOHANSEN

PLATE 185: *The Rod and the Veil,* 1975
FRANZ JOHANSEN (1928– ), CAST BRONZE, 84" X 99 1/2" X 6 1/2" (213.4 CM X 252.7 CM X 16.5 CM), MUSEUM OF CHURCH HISTORY AND ART

*This landmark work of art depicts fundamental Latter-day Saint beliefs regarding the premortal existence, the Atonement, and the importance of the word of God. Stretching through both sides of the veil that separates mortals from the spiritual realms, the iron rod (identified in the Book of Mormon as the word of God) is the eternal principle linking God's children in all stages of existence. Bearing the marks of his crucifixion, and with outstretched arms piercing both the veil and the background plane of the work, Christ is the continuation of the rod that the young boy stretches to grasp. The boy's feet also leave the framework of the piece, emphasizing the effort he must make. In catching hold of the rod, the boy will be able to interact with Christ; the Savior's hand slipping through the veil indicates the clearer vision possible to those who study God's word. Franz Johansen is a founder of a new symbolic contemporary Latter-day Saint art movement, and this piece reflects the layers of gospel symbolism inherent in his work. A professor of art at Brigham Young University from 1956 until his retirement in 1989, Johansen has influenced serious artists in the Utah Valley region. He studied art at Brigham Young University, the California School of Arts and Crafts, and the Academie de la Grand Chaumiere in Paris. Primarily a sculptor, Johansen completed architectural sculpture for the facade of the Museum of Church History and Art, the bas relief on the Lee Library at BYU, and the doors on the Washington Temple.*

PLATE 186: *Jacob and Leah,* 1990

BRUCE H. SMITH (1936– ), OIL ON CANVAS, 71" X 64 1/2" (180.3 CM X 163.8 CM), MUSEUM OF CHURCH HISTORY AND ART

*The Old Testament story of Jacob and Leah was the inspiration for this modern allegory. Jacob worked for seven years to win the hand of Rachel, only to find that at the wedding her father had switched Rachel for Leah, her older and plainer sister. In this painting, the artist uses symbols to help communicate the feelings of emotional distance. The contrasting styles of furniture, the untied ribbon on the floor, the bisected arch on the wall, and the plant with daggerlike leaves help reinforce the feelings of a tenuous relationship. Bruce Smith studied art at Brigham Young University and the University of Utah. His paintings are strongly influenced by the religious elements of Renaissance art. He currently teaches art at Brigham Young University.*

CONTEMPORARY LATTER-DAY SAINT ART, 1965–1995

PLATE 187: *The Fourth Article of Faith*,
ABOUT 1975
M. CLANE GRAVES (1939– )
ACRYLIC ON CANVAS, 60" X 79" (152.4 CM X 200.7 CM)
MUSEUM OF ART, BRIGHAM YOUNG UNIVERSITY

*A series of symbols expresses the four concepts of conversion in the Fourth Article of Faith. The two white chevrons pointing upward represent faith. The X-shape represents a blotting out or repentance. Baptism is represented by the half-circle of blue with the descending white chevron. The squares in the same column suggest the laws of the gospel. The final figure is descending and resting, symbolizing the Holy Ghost. Clane Graves is a former graphic designer whose work has been exhibited throughout the world. He returned to Brigham Young University to obtain an advanced degree in painting; his MFA exhibit was held at the Harris Fine Arts Center in 1995.*

PLATE 188: *Jeremiah Contemplates the Destruction to Come*, 1980
HAGEN HALTERN (1947– )
WATERCOLOR AND GRAPHITE ON BOARD,
10" X 7 1/2" (25.4 CM X 19 CM)
MUSEUM OF CHURCH HISTORY AND ART

*The prophet Jeremiah is seen deep in contemplation while writing his prophetic vision of the future. The artist uses expressive physiognomy and bodily attitude to convey Jeremiah's feelings as he records scriptures of cataclysmic destruction. Haltern, who exhibited extensively in his native Germany, has more recently taught art and design at Brigham Young University. In his art, he utilizes a refined black-and-white technique, making use of graphite paste and wash on a highly polished white board. His work combines naturalism with abstract form. Haltern's art arises out of his complex aesthetic theories, rooted in German philosophy.*

One of Darais's and Johansen's best students was Bruce H. Smith (1936– ), who today continues their tradition at Brigham Young University as a teacher. Smith says, "If there's anything controlling art today it's a lack of the spirit. Most art has a fatalistic, nihilistic attitude."[10] *Jacob and Leah* (PLATE 186), with its beautiful craft, effective organization, and simplicity, is a contemporary allegory of the biblical story with lessons every beholder can apply.

FIGURE 51:
M. CLANE GRAVES

Clane Graves (1939– ) (FIGURE 51), a graphic designer and artist, was also enrolled in the university art department in the later 1960s when serious-minded students and faculty began a self-conscious quest for a distinctive Mormon art and iconography. By 1980 he was chairman of the Design Department at BYU, but later left to open a design office. Graves wrote that his approach in *The Fourth Article of Faith* (PLATE 187) "is simply a private and personal quest to come to an increased level of faith in and understanding of God, the Eternal Father of us all."[11]

Like his teaching colleagues at Brigham Young University noted above, Hagen Haltern (1947– ) has produced deeply thought-out, exquisitely crafted work with scriptural content. Haltern is a major theorist dealing with Latter-day Saint art issues. His publication *Art Integration: The Spiritual Foundation and Anagogical Level of Meaning of the Celestial Style* analyzes the principles that he believes lead to a unified art, which he identifies as being spiritual and visionary. He called his new artistic vision the "Celestial Style"; it is founded in the gospel of Christ and claims "integration" as its overarching principle. This style is an alternative to the "Dance of Death" engaged in today by much of the modern secular art establishment. *Jeremiah Contemplates the Destruction to Come* (PLATE 188), an early work more literal than most by the artist, is given as a voice of warning.

FIGURE 52:
NANCY GLAZIER-KOEHLER

PLATE 189: **Without Any Ire,** 1984
NANCY GLAZIER-KOEHLER (1947– )
OIL ON CANVAS, 35 1/2" X 50" (90.2 CM X 127 CM)
MUSEUM OF CHURCH HISTORY AND ART
GIFT OF THE SILVER FOUNDATION

*Several verses of scripture and a favorite Latter-day Saint hymn inspired this painting. Among the millennial scriptures referenced by the artist is Isaiah 11:9, "They shall not hurt nor destroy in all my holy mountain." The fourth verse of the hymn "The Spirit of God" by William W. Phelps begins, "How blessed the day when the lamb and the lion shall lie down together without any ire."*

*Nancy Glazier-Koehler is a largely self-taught artist who learned by studying the techniques of the masters. Now a resident of Montana, she has been painting for over twenty years, specializing in wildlife art.*

Nancy Glazier-Koehler (1947– ) (FIGURE 52) is an internationally recognized wildlife artist, but her two works in the Church Museum also have a scriptural foundation and are consistent favorites with visitors. She renders nature's surfaces with uncanny accuracy, but there is more: "The frightening aspect of painting in a place like Yellowstone is that it's so possible to have antlers and hooves and hides but have nothing inside," Glazier said. "That's the mystery to me [—]of reproducing substance."[12] Her Christian beliefs enable her to see God's will in nature. "I believe God created the earth to use with wisdom and thanksgiving and human stewardship. If my work says anything, it is a confirmation of that belief."[13] *Without Any Ire* (PLATE 189) is a naturalistic work that also literally signifies the peace of the Millennium. *Latter-day Daniel* (PLATE 190) came after the artist unsuccessfully struggled to paint the scriptural-historical Daniel in the lion's den. She wrote: "At last! The light broke forth! What was needed was a Latter-day Daniel! A painting flooded with light and meaning and reality—with a powerful mixture of relief, determination, renewed hope, and yes, some distress."[14]

Scriptural illustration has been important to the Church both for use in publications and as art to be displayed and contemplated. The recent history of Latter-day Saint illustration is a broad topic, and only a few works can be discussed here. Preston Heiselt (1941–1983) was a talented illustrator based in Powel, Ohio. He produced *Baptism in the New World* (PLATE 191) for a family home evening manual. The traditional Christian baptism has here been modified into a dramatic Book of Mormon conception reminiscent of the work of Maxfield Parrish.

PLATE 190: *Latter-day Daniel,* 1990

NANCY GLAZIER-KOEHLER (1947– )
OIL ON CANVAS, 60" X 48" (152.4 CM X 121.9 CM)
MUSEUM OF CHURCH HISTORY AND ART
GIFT OF THE SILVER FOUNDATION

*The ancient biblical story of Daniel and the lion's den comes alive in this contemporary symbolic setting that expresses the relevance of Daniel's experience to contemporary life. According to the artist, the gold watch symbolizes wealth, authority, and "the dispensation of the fulness of time." In the biblical story, King Nebuchadnezzar gave Daniel a gold chain. The red scarf is also a kingly gift representing the blood of Christ. Daniel is wearing his work clothes and has his sleeves rolled up, symbolizing the good works that have helped him overcome the trials and dangers of life symbolized by the mountain lions. Personal revelation is symbolized by the cleft in the rock, while the personal obstacles that sometimes get in the way of hearing the whisperings of the Spirit are represented by the small rock wedged in the cleft.*

PLATE 191: **Baptism in the New World,** 1977

PRESTON HEISELT (1941–1983)
MIXED MEDIA, 23" X 17 1/2" (58.4 CM X 44.5 CM)
MUSEUM OF CHURCH HISTORY AND ART

*This work demonstrates the effect of Latter-day Saint thought upon standard Christian imagery. The strong influence of the American illustrator Maxfield Parrish is evident, both in the color scheme used and in the purple-shadowed romantic setting. Heiselt's technique, utilizing Prismacolor colored pencils applied to a sandpaper surface, is excellent for detail and a wide range of tonal values. The artist created numerous designs for Church publications.*

In the last ten years one work, *The Lord Jesus Christ* (PLATE 192) by Delwin Parson (1948– ), has become the most reproduced Latter-day Saint picture of Christ, replacing the paintings by Harry Anderson. In 1983 the Church commissioned the work with instructions that it fit the Church's image of the Savior. *The Greatest of All* (PLATE 193) is a similar picture, reflecting a somewhat new visual conception of the Savior's appearance. Parson is now on the art faculty at Southern Utah University. Greg K. Olsen (1958- ) is a prolific illustrative artist who has found financial success with popular pictures of religious, fantasy, and sentimental subjects. He created *The Bible and Book of Mormon Testify of Jesus Christ* (PLATE 194) as a possible poster image for the Church Graphics Design division. He has also done a half-dozen covers for the *Ensign*.

Some of the most stirring scripture-related pictures in the Church collection are produced by Latin American artists. Jose R. Riveros of Santiago, Chile, is a commercial artist by profession. His moving painting *Amumn Petu, Go Ye Therefore* (PLATE 195) depicts the native Indians of Chile patiently waiting for missionaries to come to their region to teach them the gospel. It won an award of distinction and a purchase prize in the second international art competition.

PLATE 192: **The Lord Jesus Christ,** 1983
DELWIN PARSON (1948– )
OIL ON CANVAS, 28" x 20" (71.1 CM x 50.8 CM)
MUSEUM OF CHURCH HISTORY AND ART

*This image was developed in response to a request for a general picture of the Savior not connected with a specific scriptural story. It was hoped that such a picture could be used for many purposes, as a teaching aid, in publications, and for creating an ambience in the meetinghouse, workplace, or home. Parson worked thoughtfully to refine the tone, and his rendition has become the most recognizable image of Jesus now used by the Church. About the work the artist commented, "The number one thing I wanted was the feel of what I think the Savior would look like. Not a look, but a feel" (Steve Moser, "A World Wide Influence," Ricks College Summit [Spring 1993]: 8–9).*

PLATE 193: **The Greatest of All,** 1987
DELWIN PARSON (1948– )
OIL ON CANVAS, 40" x 30" (120.3 CM x 76.2 CM)
MUSEUM OF CHURCH HISTORY AND ART

*The artist painted this picture of Christ in the Garden of Gethsemane for the 1991 "Second International Art Competition: Themes from the Scriptures." To prepare, Parson looked at a variety of images of the Savior, including many that have appeared in recent Church publications. The painting is a new, original work continuing in this tradition, but the artist also desired it to be a remembrance of Jesus in feeling and attitude. Parson is one of the most utilized Latter-day Saint illustrators, with about 100 published works, including The Lord Jesus Christ, prints of which have been widely distributed around the world by the Church. Some of the more ambitious examples of the artist's work are among the dozen in the Museum collection. After living for years in Idaho, Parson recently joined the art faculty at Southern Utah University in Cedar City, Utah.*

PLATE 194: **The Bible and Book of Mormon Testify of Jesus Christ**, 1989
GREG K. OLSEN (1958– )
OIL ON PAPER, 37 1/2" X 34 3/4"
(95.3 CM X 88.3 CM)
MUSEUM OF CHURCH HISTORY AND ART

*"The testimony of two nations is a witness unto you that I am God. . . . Wherefore, I speak the same words unto one nation like unto another. And when the two nations shall run together the testimony of the two nations shall run together also" (2 Nephi 29:8). This work depicts the sacred relationship between the Bible and the Book of Mormon— both testify of the divinity of the Savior and his earthly mission. The painting was planned by Warren Luch of the Graphics Design Department of the Church and executed by Greg Olsen as a Latter-day Saint missionary/ meetinghouse-library picture. Olsen, trained as a commercial artist and illustrator at Utah State University, has in recent years painted full-time to fulfill commissions for his highly detailed works. His wide range of subjects includes Western art, religious and fantasy art, portraits, and statements on social issues.*

PLATE 195: **Amumn Petu, Go Ye Therefore,** 1990
JOSE R. RIVEROS
OIL ON CANVAS, 64" X 64" (162.6 CM X 162.6 CM)
MUSEUM OF CHURCH HISTORY AND ART

*Four Araucanian Indians of Chile, dressed in native costume and standing in the beauty of Chile's countryside, gaze into far-off places, unsure of what the future may bring. The artist, a native Chilean, originally intended to paint this group of Indians with two missionaries visiting them, but realized that not much missionary work was being done among the Lamanites of Chile. Instead, sensitively aware of the Book of Mormon promises to these people, he portrays them waiting and searching the horizon for hope of good news. Riveros, a professional artist trained in Australia, uses strong colors, bold designs, and often abstracted images that characterize much of the art of South America.*

Another Latin American painter adopting a serious approach is Panama native Antonio Madrid Hendricks (1949– ), a university art teacher trained in Spain. The apocalyptic *Battle of Gog and Magog* (PLATE 196) symbolically re-creates the Revelation account in which the sinister forces of evil mounted on steeds and the Christ of the Second Coming appear to be moving toward the great confrontation in which evil will be overcome.

Younger university-trained artists continued to be interested in making conceptual, symbolic statements about the scriptures. Bethanne Andersen (1954– ) (FIGURE 53) graduated in 1979 from Brigham Young University with a Master of Fine Arts degree. Her thesis project was a series of twenty pastel drawings on Jesus' parable of the sower. Her *Last Supper (Place Setting)* (PLATE 197) is a contemplative work about Christ knowingly "tasting bread and earth-grown vegetables for the last time, enjoying the moment, sitting with people he knew and loved—touching the plate, the glass—a frozen moment before the inevitable."[15] *Abraham's Sand* (PLATE 198), by Laurie Schnoebelen (1955– ) (FIGURE 54) of California, is based on a complex literary program derived from ideas contained in the book of Abraham. Schnoebelen has been a regular contributor and prize winner at the art competitions, and three of her works are now in the Church collection. The other two paintings portray the blessings of the gospel to the Polynesian peoples.

FIGURE 53:
BETHANNE ANDERSEN

FIGURE 54:
LAURIE SCHNOEBELEN

PLATE 196: *The Battle of Gog and Magog,* 1987
ANTONIO MADRID HENDRICKS (1949– )
OIL ON CANVAS, 44 1/2" x 55 1/2" (113 CM x 141 CM)
MUSEUM OF CHURCH HISTORY AND ART

*In this painting, the artist communicates with symbols the last great apocalyptic battle between the forces of good and evil. The menacing figures of Gog and Magog are mounted on steeds. By abstracting the figures, Madrid conveys the message that these are the collective forces of evil. By contrast, he paints the figure of the Savior in the familiar realistic style of Harry Anderson's* Second Coming of Christ *to draw attention to Christ's specific, literal role in vanquishing the forces of evil. The artist studied art in Spain, where he was widely exposed to abstract symbolism in twentieth-century European art.*

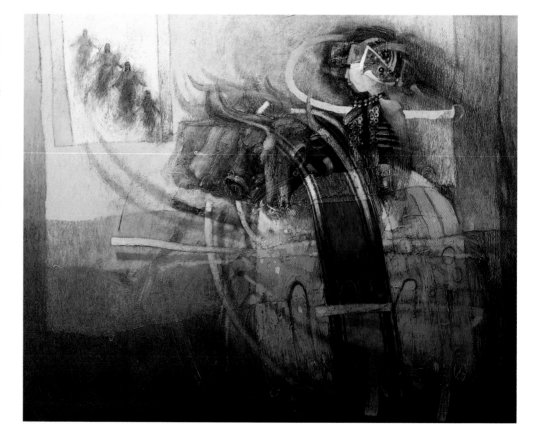

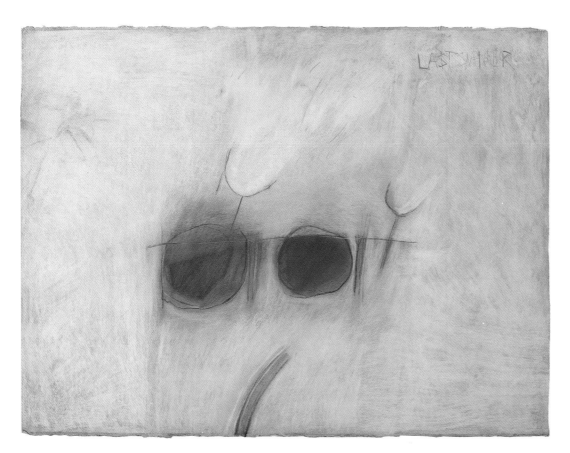

PLATE 197: **The Last Supper (Place Setting)**, 1982
BETHANNE ANDERSEN (1954– )
PASTEL ON PAPER, 22" X 30" (55.8 CM X 76.2 CM)
MUSEUM OF CHURCH HISTORY AND ART

*This unusual view of the last supper shows Christ's place setting at the table during his final meal before the crucifixion. His plate and goblet sit on the table. The work is an attempt to understand from Christ's point of view all that would go on before and after that famous meal. Many of Andersen's works are introspective and personal. In her work, she tries to understand the inner state of the soul. She has written, "In my drawings I use personal symbols to rethink an experience and create new ones."*

PLATE 198: **Abraham's Sand**, 1993
LAURIE OLSON SCHNOEBELEN (1955– )
OIL ON CANVAS, 56" X 56" (142.2 CM X 142.2 CM)
MUSEUM OF CHURCH HISTORY AND ART

*This highly symbolic painting deals with the covenants God has made with his children on the earth through the ancient prophet Abraham. God promised Abraham that his seed would be as numerous as the sand of the sea— hence the sand in the central recessed square of the painting. The hands are those of the children of the Abrahamic covenant, symbolically enacting and perpetuating the promises of the covenant. Lives are defined by the actions and work of the hands. The artist says, "We could say that we are the sum of the acts that our hands perform. Hands can do evil or loving deeds." Laurie Schnoebelen has exhibited in galleries in southern California. This work won a purchase award in the Museum's "Third International Art Competition: Living the Gospel in the World Church."*

PLATE 199: **Women in Christ's Line,** 1990
SALLIE CLINTON POET (1949– )
OIL ON CANVAS, 35 1/2" x 47 1/4" (90.2 CM x 120 CM)
MUSEUM OF CHURCH HISTORY AND ART

*In the various scriptural listings of Christ's ancestors, few women are mentioned. Of those who are, however, virtually all are remarkable women with a keen sense of family destiny. Sallie Clinton Poet's works reflect the role of women in society. In some ways her forthrightly executed paintings resemble those of Minerva Teichert, who also painted the women of the Bible. In style, both let a strong story and subject compensate for the lack of detail.*

FIGURE 55:
SALLIE POET

FIGURE 56:
MARCUS A. VINCENT

The life of Christ and parables from the New Testament have provided rich sources of subject material. Northern California artist Sallie Poet (1949– ) (FIGURE 55) explores themes of notable women in the scriptures. About *Women in Christ's Line* (PLATE 199), she stated: "I love these five women. They were just ordinary women functioning in their small spheres; yet in their choices and everyday events they shaped the face of all humanity by being the progenitors of the Savior. I wanted this work to have a feminine feeling, yet be powerful in message and design."[16]

*Epiphany* (PLATE 200), by Marcus A. Vincent (1956– ) (FIGURE 56), juxtaposes realistic elements with abstract forms and color to create further meaning. Vincent received an advanced degree from Brigham Young University in studio art and has been active as a museum registrar there, and as gallery director for the BYU Department of Visual Arts. Oregon artist David Hoeft (1961– ) was trained at the Art Center School. *The Price of Potters Field* (PLATE 201), a 1987 competition winner, reflects a quest to unite significant scriptural meaning with disparate symbols and values of design and artwork. The scriptural story of Judas's betrayal of Christ is told by symbolic elements such as the dead hawk, a noble predatory bird here hung upside down in shame. The art of Brian Kershisnik (1962– ) (FIGURE 57) is noted for its stark, enigmatic figures. The Museum commissioned him to design section logos and other work for its historical exhibit "A Covenant Restored." About his painting *Christ Healing a Man Blind from Birth* (PLATE 202), Kershisnik wrote: "In addition to the extraordinary need that we have in common for our eyes to be 'opened,' I wish to speak somewhat in this painting about the necessary vulnerability on the part of the recipient of the healing."[17]

PLATE 200: **Epiphany,** 1989
MARCUS A. VINCENT (1956– )
OIL ON PANEL, 51" x 20" (129.5 CM x 50.8 CM)
MUSEUM OF CHURCH HISTORY AND ART

*"By the power of the Spirit our eyes were opened
and our understandings were enlightened, so as
to see and understand the things of God" (D&C
76:12). This painting deals with the personal and
sudden realization of the divine origin of
mankind. The woman, dressed in the symbolic
white robes of purity, opens her eyes and gestures
as if suddenly receiving an insight into a teaching
previously uncomprehended. In a fleeting and
quiet moment, symbolized by the hummingbird,
she becomes aware of truths beyond her present
sphere. These truths, represented by the red lines
of the square, begin to encompass her as she
comprehends her heavenly origins. Marcus
Vincent often communicates abstract spiritual
and philosophical messages in his realistic artistic
style. His ability to capture portrait likenesses
and his drawing skills reflect his specialized
training in drawing the human figure.*

PLATE 201: **The Price of Potters Field,** 1987
DAVID HOEFT (1961– )
OIL ON CANVAS, 93" X 42" (236.2 CM X 106.7 CM)
MUSEUM OF CHURCH HISTORY AND ART

*In this painting, the artist represents the consequences of Judas's betrayal of Jesus as a warning of the dangers of pride, greed, and selfishness. Some time after receiving the thirty pieces of silver for betraying Christ, Judas took the coins back to the chief priests, threw the silver at their feet, and then went and hanged himself. The chief priests used the coins to purchase the "potters field" used thereafter for the burial of strangers. Pride is represented by the dead hawk, one of the noblest birds, hanging in an inverted cross signifying his role as the antithesis of Christ. The checkbook represents worldly wealth, while the pen suggests the element of choice. The yellow flag, which once warned sailing ships of the plague, identifies pride and greed as deadly spiritual plagues. The artist, who works as an advertising illustrator in Oregon, has used a super-realistic style and symbolic composition to express spiritual insights.*

CONTEMPORARY LATTER-DAY SAINT ART, 1965–1995

FIGURE 57:
BRIAN KERSHISNIK

PLATE 202: **Christ Healing a Man Blind from Birth,** 1990

BRIAN KERSHISNIK (1962– )
OIL ON CANVAS, 60" x 41"
(152.4 CM x 104.1 CM)
MUSEUM OF CHURCH
HISTORY AND ART

When Jesus spat on the ground and made clay to anoint the eyes of the blind man, the Savior called upon the man to trust Him by washing his eyes in the pool of Siloam to be healed. The blind man went forth, washed, and was healed. In this painting, the blind man represents each human being who must walk in faith and trust so that his spiritual eyes can be opened to heavenly teachings and understanding. Kershisnik's works are evocative in the sense that his simplified figures invite the viewer to question the meaning of the subject. His uncomplicated compositions usually contain jarring and contrasting elements intended to create a psychological and physical tension that provokes thoughtful inquiry.

The past three decades have seen a flowering of artwork relating to all aspects of the lives of the Saints, often in themes not expressed before 1965. It is partly in depicting this subject matter that the uniqueness of art done by Church members can be noted. The works collectively form a great visual testament of present-day experiences showing what it means to be a Latter-day Saint. Acquisitions from the "Third International Art Competition, Living the Gospel in the World Church," enriched the Museum collection with two dozen examples.

Women have created many recent pictures of motherhood and family life. After raising her family in Connecticut, Jeanne Leighton-Lundberg (1925– ) (FIGURE 58) joined the Church and subsequently obtained an advanced degree in studio art at Brigham Young University, where she is currently a faculty member. *Family: Dessert* (PLATE 203), a celebration of women and the family, expresses her belief that "a painting should have emotional content, evoke visions, edify, and possibly serve as a decorative element—a maximum personification of art theory, life philosophy and subjective license."[18]

The art life of Jill Hellberg (1939– ) accelerated when she was in her forties, after she raised her four children. She received her art education degree and her master's degree in studio art from Utah State University, and afterward taught on the university level. *Conflicting Choices* (PLATE 204) was exhibited in the third international competition and expresses "some of the trauma and trials of life."[19]

PLATE 203: ***Family: Dessert,*** 1980
JEANNE LEIGHTON-LUNDBERG (1925– )
OIL ON CANVAS, 48" X 54" (121.9 CM X 137.2 CM)
MUSEUM OF CHURCH HISTORY AND ART

*A feast of fruit sumptuous in its variety and color spreads in seamless profusion across this large canvas. Comfortable and ordinary as the images are, this work is highly symbolic. From the left a mother, crowned by background flowers, is bringing more fruit to the brilliant feast. Fruit and plants, symbols of abundance, burst through the crisscrossing geometry of patterns. In the background, lit by oranges and yellows, sits the family, bound together by their book and through their poses into a right triangle.*

*Although adhering to avant-garde expression, the artist rejects the oversimplified abstract representations associated with much twentieth-century work. "Our lives as women are complex," she maintains. "A minimalist art certainly cannot symbolize a woman's experience." Leighton-Lundberg therefore unites early modern trends with her own exuberant style.*

PLATE 204: **Conflicting Choices,** 1993
JILL HELLBERG (1939– )
OIL ON CANVAS, 48" X 48" (116.8 CM X 116.8 CM)
MUSEUM OF CHURCH HISTORY AND ART

*The artist painted her daughter and grandchildren to*
*illustrate the choices facing Latter-day Saint women*
*in the 1990s. "The symbols of dollar bills and family*
*fighting for dominance," she says, "form a visual*
*metaphor of the inner struggles of many of our*
*modern-day Eves who feel a need for success in both*
*areas." Jill Hellberg—mother of four, teacher of art*
*methods, and an artist juried into many shows—here*
*shows her strong feelings about the importance of*
*family. She sees a deterioration and peeling away if*
*the dollars receive predominant emphasis.*

Individual women in simple settings are central to the art of Lee Udall Bennion (1956– ) (Figure 59). Bennion reports that her work is not so much portraiture as it is "form, color, and feeling foremost,"[20] as in the portraits of Van Gogh or Gauguin. Iconlike, Bennion's paintings often show basic relationships of love, respect for home, and simple enjoyments. *Looking at Sarah* (Plate 205) illustrates her statement that "My figures are often slightly distorted, but hopefully reflect the warmth and goodness that exist with them."[21] Judith Mehr (1951– ) (Figure 60) has also painted families in such classics as *Family Garden* (Plate 206), a work reflecting her attitudes. "Art is a matter of love for me," Mehr wrote. "What subject matter I choose to paint is always linked to how much emotion I feel concerning it. That love is always influenced by the gospel."[22] Her other works about life show domestic topics such as women canning, baking bread, and sharing family photographs with children. Judith Mehr also created the twenty-three-foot-wide mural *Families Are Forever* in the lobby of the Family History Library in Salt Lake City, and four of her portraits of Church leaders, including one of President Spencer W. Kimball, are on display at the Museum.

FIGURE 59:
LEE UDALL BENNION

PLATE 205: *Looking at Sarah*, 1987
LEE UDALL BENNION (1956– )
OIL ON CANVAS, 44" x 32" (111.8 CM x 81.3 CM)
MUSEUM OF CHURCH HISTORY AND ART

*The human figures in Lee Udall Bennion's paintings are not so much portraiture as they are a personal expression. Bennion often uses herself and her children as models, and the subjects of this work are a close friend and her child, but the intent is to move beyond individuals and achieve a high objective. With a careful use of form, color, and feeling, she seeks to build a harmony between the subject and the viewer. Her pensive, elongated figures add a distinctive touch to her work and enhance the emotional atmosphere she hopes to create. The unique, hand-wrought frames serve as an extension of her paintings.*

# TWENTIETH-CENTURY INTERNATIONAL FOLK ART

# 5

*by Richard G. Oman*

I f the great Latter-day Saint epic of the nineteenth century was the pioneer experience of gathering to the West and building Zion, the epic of the second half of the twentieth century has been the establishment of the Church internationally. Over two-thirds of all Church growth is now happening outside of the United States and Canada. Most of the international growth is occurring in developing nations whose cultures are quite different from the Euro-American traditions of the nineteenth- and early twentieth-century Church. This massive international growth has had a major impact on Latter-day Saint art.

Defining Latter-day Saint art in terms of Utah art no longer works when Church members live in wards and branches in more than 150 different nations. Nor is it possible for long to focus on a particular style or medium when Latter-day Saint artists work in such divergent styles and mediums as batik, wood, tapa cloth, and Navajo weaving. With members working in so many places in so many styles, could we simply say that any art done by Church members is Latter-day Saint art? The problem with this definition is that its broadness drains it of meaning.

So what makes Mormon art in our time distinctive? A useful criterion for creating a currently functional definition of Latter-day Saint art would be to emphasize thematic content rather than style, technique, or geography. Using that definition, this chapter will look at twentieth-century Latter-day Saint folk art from the United States and abroad.

Folk art differs from fine art in several ways. Folk artists usually learn how to create art from their families rather than from formal academic art schools. Because the teaching and creation of folk art usually takes place in the home, there are literally thousands of Latter-day Saint folk art schools all over the world. Because the skills in making folk art are usually passed down from generation to generation, the styles and techniques are usually quite conservative. The emphasis is on continuity with the ancestral family artistic tradition. For example, the Migration pattern pot (PLATE 222) by Fannie Nampeyo Polacca (FIGURE 67) is very similar to pots done by her mother, her sisters, her children, and even her grandchildren.

Folk artists often use readily available local materials such as wood, clay, and wool. These accessible and inexpensive materials localize the art and link it with the immediate environment where it is created. For example, Leta Keith (FIGURE 68) made her Navajo rug *Missionaries on the Reservation* (PLATE 223) from local wool that she cleaned, carded, spun, and dyed.

One favorite medium of expression in folk art throughout the years has been the quilt. From the earliest days of the Church until the present, artists have created quilts that tell stories, depict beliefs, or simply bring color and warmth to a room. The examples chosen from the Museum collection (PLATES 224–230) demonstrate the broad range of purpose and style in this art form.

*Facing page: Detail from* **Presidents and Temple Rug**, *Ruben Ouzounian, Mary Ouzounian, and Josephine Ouzounian Ksajikian. (See Plate 256, page 183.)*

PLATE 222: **Migration Pot**, ABOUT 1952
FANNIE NAMPEYO POLACCA (1904–1987)
CERAMIC, 8 1/4" HIGH X 13 1/2" DIAMETER
(21 CM X 34.3 CM)
MUSEUM OF CHURCH HISTORY AND ART

*The lines on this pot depict the migration of the
ancient Hopi to the mesas where the Hopi now live.
The footprint of a bear represents the leadership of
the Bear Clan in the migration. Migration is a
spiritual concept for the Hopi. It means leaving the
wicked behind and experiencing the refining
influences of difficult travels. The Hopi remember
the prophecies of the ancient prophets in their
migrations that one day new leaders would come.
Many early Hopi converts viewed Latter-day Saint
missionaries as the ones expected to come. Tom
Polacca, the uncle of the artist, was strongly
influenced by early Latter-day Saint missionaries.
The artist's mother was Nampeyo, the mother of
the Hopi renaissance in pottery. Many generations
of Fannie Polacca's family have been Latter-day
Saints and artists. This pot is an example of their
work that synthesizes cultural, religious, and
artistic traditions.*

FIGURE 67: FANNIE NAMPEYO

PLATE 223: **Missionaries on the Reservation**, 1985
LETA KEITH (1923– )
TEXTILE, 48" X 60" (121.9 CM X 152.4 CM)
MUSEUM OF CHURCH HISTORY AND ART
GIFT OF PAMELA OMAN

*Latter-day Saint missionaries have been working
among the native peoples of the American
Southwest for almost 150 years. Leta Keith and her
family were baptized in 1966. Several of the artist's
own children have served as missionaries like those
depicted on this rug. The artist lives near
Monument Valley, also shown in this rug. Navajo
pictorial rugs are a late nineteenth-century
adaptation of traditional Navajo rugs and blankets.
This is a high-quality example of this style. To
make this rug Leta Keith sheared, carded, spun,
dyed, and wove the wool. The "bumpiness" of the
individual threads within the rug identifies this
handsome piece with the handmade process.*

FIGURE 68: LETA KEITH

PLATE 224: *Sesquicentennial of the Church Quilt,* 1980

Oakland California Stake Relief Society
Textile, 87" x 87" (221 cm x 221 cm)
Museum of Church History and Art

*This quilt was created to celebrate the 150-year anniversary of the
organization of the Church. The individual blocks depict well-known Church
beliefs and activities, including temple marriage, family home evening,
missionary work, welfare, and the Word of Wisdom. Church history is also
prominently featured, including several images of Latter-day Saint temples,
both historic and modern. Cooperative quilt making has been a Relief Society
tradition for more than one hundred years. Working together to create finely
crafted and artistic quilts has been a metaphor for sisterhood and for
cooperating toward the ideal of creating beauty and harmony in all activities.*

PLATE 225: *Kingdoms Quilt*, 1987
CHARLOTTE WARR ANDERSEN (1952– )
TEXTILE, 96" X 85" (243.8 CM X 215.9 CM)
MUSEUM OF CHURCH HISTORY AND ART

This quilt depicts the Latter-day Saint doctrine of eternal life. Bright rays of light of varying intensities illuminate angelic figures standing with hands prayerfully folded. These groups of people have received their eternal reward in the afterlife. The large group at the bottom of the pyramid, those inheriting the lower or telestial glory, stands in relative darkness compared to the two groups immediately above who have inherited greater rewards in the terrestrial and celestial kingdoms. The three personages standing at the top of the pyramid represent the godhead. Those who committed unpardonable evil deeds grope and struggle in the surrounding darkness. Charlotte Andersen is a nationally recognized Latter-day Saint quilter. She has received numerous awards for her work, including second prize in the prestigious Statue of Liberty quilt contest sponsored in 1986 by the Museum of American Folk Art in New York City.

FIGURE 69:
CHARLOTTE WARR ANDERSEN

PLATE 226: *Hmong Bedspread*, 1983
MANOLIE JASPER
TEXTILE, 114" X 96" (289.5 CM X 243.8 CM)
MUSEUM OF CHURCH HISTORY AND ART

This work is typical of Hmong textiles and designs created using appliqué, reverse appliqué, and cross-stitching. The six panels in the center of this coverlet display an intricately designed, cross-stitched checkerboard pattern that is common in Hmong textiles. The bright borders of the appliquéd border design are also typical. Hmong needlework usually employs complicated and controlled geometric designs combined with vibrant, bold colors. The Hmong are mountain-dwelling people of Southeast Asia. Many who immigrated to the United States after political difficulties in their homelands have found a ready market for their colorful, unique textiles. This coverlet was created by a Hmong member of the Church who settled in Utah.

PLATE 227: *Come, Let Us Rejoice*, 1992
CHARLOTTE WARR ANDERSEN (1952– )
TEXTILE, 96" X 85"
(243.8 CM X 215.9 CM)
MUSEUM OF CHURCH HISTORY AND ART

This piece, which was commissioned for the Relief Society sesquicentennial in 1992, celebrates ideals of faith in Christ, nurturing, compassion, sisterhood, serving our communities, and developing our talents, all within a context of being "women of covenant." It supports the goal of the Church to bring people to Christ through making and keeping sacred covenants at baptism and in the holy temple. The blue blocks at the bottom are an old traditional pattern called "Enigma" or "Puzzle." The gold row at the top is an old pattern called "Guiding Star." The message is that life, which is sometimes a puzzle, can lead to fulfillment if we follow the gospel as a guiding star.

PLATE 229: **Tahitian Quilt,** 1985
NINIREI KATOMEA TEKEHU MARO (ABOUT 1912– )
TEXTILE, 94 1/2" X 94 1/2" (240 CM X 240 CM)
MUSEUM OF CHURCH HISTORY AND ART

*The bold patterns and bright colors on this patchwork quilt are typical of Tahitian quilting. This is the Heifara pattern named in connection with an island tree known as the pandanus. The pandanus tree produces fruit with edible seeds. The yellow stars represent the ripened seeds.*

*The artist is a native Tahitian and lifetime member of the Church. She learned quilting from her mother and has spent hundreds of hours quilting at Relief Society and with women in her neighborhood. In Tahiti, as in other parts of the world, quilts are used as bedspreads and wedding gifts, but they are also often hung behind a bride and groom as a backdrop at a wedding.*

PLATE 228: **American Fork Relief Society Quilt,** 1952
AMERICAN FORK FIRST WARD RELIEF SOCIETY
TEXTILE, 75" X 85" (190.5 CM X 208.2 CM)
MUSEUM OF CHURCH HISTORY AND ART

*The tiny pieces salvaged and pieced together to create this quilt reflect the pioneer motto "Use it up, wear it out, make it do, or do without." This quilt top was already old when found by the president of the American Fork First Ward Relief Society. It was then finely quilted by the most expert quilters in the ward for use in the Joseph Smith home in New York. After more than ten years at the home, it was transferred to the Museum collection for preservation. This quilt illustrates the strong narrative content in Latter-day Saint art. With its stylistic unity from multiple creators, it reflects the century-old tradition among Latter-day Saint women of working together cooperatively.*

FIGURE 70: EMMA ALLEBES

PLATE 230: **To All Worthy Male Members,** 1990
EMMA ALLEBES (1931– )
TEXTILE, 100" X 75" (254 CM X 190.5 CM)
MUSEUM OF CHURCH HISTORY AND ART

*This quilt celebrates the revelation that extended the priesthood "to all worthy male members." The patterns of raised hands are tracings of actual hands of members from around the world. The artist picked fabric with African and Asian patterns to emphasize the international expansion of the Church into new areas for missionary work. The raised hands symbolically represent voting to sustain, the ordinance of baptism, and the making of priesthood covenants.*

PLATE 231: ***Becoming Self-Reliant,*** 1993
ABU HASSAN CONTEH (1964– )
TEXTILE, 35" X 38" (88.9 CM X 96.5 CM)
MUSEUM OF CHURCH HISTORY AND ART

*The artist, a convert to the Church living in the West African nation of Sierra Leone, depicts how Latter-day Saints in his native land become self-reliant through hard work. This appliqué picture cloth was created for the third Churchwide art competition.*

Folk art reflects and usually affirms the religious beliefs, traditions, values, and history of the artist's family and community. Most folk artists are closely linked with their intended audience.

The intellectual ideas in folk art are clear, bold, and unambiguous. Folk art can deal with some fairly complex beliefs, traditions, values, and stories because it can be stylized and simplified into symbolic forms. This simplification is possible because the artist and audience already share a knowledge of and commitment to the beliefs, experiences, and history depicted in the art. The artist can refer viewers to shared ideas through symbolism. Thus tight visual details usually don't need to be depicted because the intended audience already knows the "story."

These simplified forms that stand for broader stories or ideas are called symbols. Symbols often communicate several ideas at once. For instance, the Salt Lake Temple is a visual symbol that means many things to Latter-day Saints. It can symbolize the eternal nature of marriage and family. It represents the center of the Church. It is the House of the Lord. Its multilevel towers reflect on the order of the priesthood. The Angel Moroni on its top spire symbolizes the restoration of the gospel in this dispensation.

Folk artists usually use visual forms and symbols that are widely known by their intended audience. This is important because folk artists usually create art that is heavily laden with ideas, not just aesthetic form. Symbolism makes it possible to communicate rather complex ideas in a single work of art. The question most folk artists would ask is not "Does this work of art look like a photograph?" but "Does this work of art communicate an important idea or value?" Folk art narrows the distance between artist and audience by symbolically communicating shared beliefs and values.

PLATE 232: ***The Lamanites Blossom As the Rose in the Desert,*** 1993
MARIA GLADIS BARRIENTOS DE MONTERROSO
EMBROIDERY AND OIL PAINT, 24" X 18" X 2"
(61 CM X 45.7 CM X 5.1 CM)
MUSEUM OF CHURCH HISTORY AND ART

*The Book of Mormon records prophecies of future greatness and knowledge in the latter days for the descendants of the Book of Mormon peoples. Many Latter-day Saint Native Americans throughout North, South, and Central America consider themselves to be those descendants. Monterroso links this "blossoming" among her own people to their knowledge of the Book of Mormon and the covenants received in the temple at Guatemala City. Textile arts have been the main folk art of the highland Mayas of Guatemala for centuries. The artist combines this textile tradition with the painting tradition brought to Guatemala by Spanish conquerors. The combining of paint and embroidery allows for more texture and detail than either technique alone would produce.*

**PLATE 233:** ***The Lamanites Shall Blossom As a Rose,*** 1990

JOSELITO ACEVEDO GARCIA (1965– )
ACRYLIC ON CANVAS, 23 1/2" X 39 1/2"
(59.7 CM X 100.3 CM)
MUSEUM OF CHURCH HISTORY AND ART

*In this metaphorical folk art painting, the artist shows the spiritual journey of an Indian woman from the Peruvian highlands. She is dressed in her traditional costume and sits in front of her ancient stone house. The Book of Mormon she received from two local missionaries rests in her lap. In the background is the Lima Temple, symbolically placed in this mountainous landscape to represent her spiritual goals. The roses are a metaphor for the spiritual growth that comes to her people from accepting the gospel. Most folk art painting around the world is bold, bright, cheerful, and highly symbolic in composition. Often the colors and composition seem garish to persons with other cultural backgrounds. Yet the exuberance of this art provides a cheerful counterpoint for folk artists whose surroundings are natural drab colors.*

**PLATE 234:** ***Moroni and the Title of Liberty,*** 1967

RODOLFINA AND ROSINA, USTUPO, SAN BLAS, PANAMA
TEXTILE, 25" X 27" (63.5 CM X 68.6 CM)
MUSEUM OF CHURCH HISTORY AND ART
GIFT OF ELDER AND SISTER TED E. BREWERTON

*This mola combines two different stories. The center image depicts Captain Moroni raising the title of liberty. The secondary image depicts Helaman and his young warriors. Both images are based upon paintings by Utah artist Arnold Friberg that are reproduced in many copies of the Book of Mormon. Much folk art is very conservative and relies upon patterns and images already known to the artist's society.*

The symbolic elements in a work of folk art are frequently arranged in order to tell a story or communicate an idea, not necessarily to depict a naturalistic scene. For instance, in the painting *The Lamanites Shall Blossom As a Rose* by Joselito Garcia from Peru (Plate 233), the brilliant rose is enlarged and the temple is moved from a coastal metropolis to an inland site.

Folk artists tend to use strong, bright colors such as the day-glow greens used by the Latter-day Saint Haitian painter Henri-Robert Bresil (Figure 71) in his painting of Alma baptizing in the waters of Mormon (Plate 236). Some readers unfamiliar with folk art may see these colors as brash. But many folk artists would see the same colors as joyful and self-confident. In many cultures, color is the only luxury the people have.

The aesthetic elements of folk art are as bold and direct as the ideas that the art communicates. Folk art usually uses strong, simplified forms that are widely known, so it is not necessary to depict every tiny detail. "When the story is told, the picture is finished."

PLATE 235: ***Charity Never Faileth,*** 1966
RELIEF SOCIETY, CUNA ISLANDS, PANAMA
TEXTILE, 22 1/2" x 36" (57.2 CM X 91.4 CM)
MUSEUM OF CHURCH HISTORY AND ART
TRANSFERRED FROM THE
GENERAL RELIEF SOCIETY PRESIDENCY

*This is the oldest and largest mola with a gospel theme in the Church collection. It was made less than a year after the gospel officially arrived among the Cuna people. The Relief Society, with its ideals of loving watchcare, found enthusiastic support among these women who by long tradition love and serve each other and know that "Charity Never Faileth."*

*This mola is more than twice as large as traditional molas created for the front or back panel of a woman's blouse. The size and quality of craftsmanship speak of the makers' love of the gospel and of Relief Society. Some of the lettering is reversed. As a people, Cunas are not oriented to the written word. They have a long and rich oral tradition, but their language has been written only recently. In using the Relief Society seal as a pattern, the makers of this mola undoubtedly saw the letters not as words but as design elements that they were free to modify artistically.*

FIGURE 71:
HENRI-ROBERT BRESIL

PLATE 236: ***Baptizing in the Waters of Mormon,*** 1988
HENRI-ROBERT BRESIL (1952– )
OIL ON CANVAS, 36" X 24" (91.4 CM X 61 CM)
MUSEUM OF CHURCH HISTORY AND ART

*Bresil has painted Alma the Elder baptizing in the waters of Mormon. He has placed this familiar Book of Mormon scene in a lush tropical wilderness in his own region. The artist is one of the first Haitian converts to the Church. He is an important national artist working in a bright and exuberant Haitian tradition that draws from both folk art and European fine art. Colorful, stylized painting, in which detail is subordinated to brush strokes with high energy and rhythm, makes Haitian art an internationally acclaimed contemporary style.*

PLATE 237: *The First Vision,* 1990
JACINTA R. ZUMAETA (1940– )
WOOL EMBROIDERY, 52" X 32" (132.1 CM X 81.3 CM)
MUSEUM OF CHURCH HISTORY AND ART

*Joseph Smith's humble, straightforward prayer seeking truth and enlightenment is the foundation story of the restoration of the gospel of Jesus Christ. This story is a pattern for all who seek truth. Folk art of all types often takes familiar images and presents them in a new but still recognizable form. This piece from Chile is in that tradition. An oil painting by Greg Olsen has been reinterpreted by Rosales in very finely worked crewel embroidery. Across cultures and time, textile arts of many kinds are the most common art produced by women.*

PLATE 238: *Austrian Wardrobe, Linzer Style,* 1984
ROSALINDE LIPP (1927– )
POLYCHROMED WOOD, 90" X 68" X 26 1/2"
(228.6 CM X 172.7 CM X 67.3 CM)
MUSEUM OF CHURCH HISTORY AND ART

*The panels of this armoire display scenes from Church history, beliefs, and ordinances. Except for these Latter-day Saint vignettes, the patterns and decoration represent a rococo painting style used in Upper Austria around 1830 when the Church was organized. Rosalinde Lipp, a convert to the Church and former missionary in Austria, is among the world's most prominent twentieth-century practitioners of this traditional style of Austrian folk painting. She lives in Austria, where she continues to paint as well as teach this traditional Austrian folk art to new generations of artists.*

PLATE 239: *Seagull and Cricket*, 1990
TSHIPEPELE-KANDE
WOOD, 9" X 4" X 5 1/4"
(22.9 CM X 10.2 CM X 13.3 CM)
MUSEUM OF CHURCH HISTORY AND ART

*The pioneer story of crops being saved from hoards of crickets by the divine intervention of seagulls is known by Latter-day Saints worldwide. The appeal of this story lies in its assurance that God hears and answers the pleas of the righteous in their extremity. To the residents of the American West this folk art seagull hardly looks like a gull at all. Nevertheless this bird, patterned after one from the artist's own environment in Zaire, represents faith in God's care common to Saints everywhere.*

FIGURE 72:
ROGER W. OTIS

PLATE 240: *Queen Esther*, 1990
ROGER W. OTIS (1945– )
MAPLE, 68 1/2" X 40" X 7"
(174 CM X 101.6 CM X 17.8 CM)
MUSEUM OF CHURCH HISTORY AND ART

*The artist created this piece to remind the viewer of the important contributions of women throughout the history of the world. He explained that many courageous women like Queen Esther have put their own lives in jeopardy to save the lives of others. At times the courage of an individual woman such as Queen Esther has saved an entire nation. The image of Esther and the composition of this carving as a whole are reminiscent of Minerva Teichert's Queen Esther. Reinterpreting the familiar in new guises is a familiar folk art approach. The artist specializes in life-size wood sculptures.*

PLATE 241: *Parable of the Wise Virgins*, 1980
GERD BERGSTROM SJOKVIST (1936– )
WOOD, 22" X 46 1/2" (55.9 CM X 118.1 CM)
MUSEUM OF CHURCH HISTORY AND ART

*The parable from the New Testament of the five wise and five foolish virgins has often been used by Latter-day Saints to teach that simply being a member of the Church is not sufficient for salvation. Members have the individual responsibility to provide oil for their own lamps of righteous preparation. Long, dark, northern winters spent mostly indoors and the surrounding abundant forests have been factors in making wood carving one of the traditional folk art forms of the Swedish people. Even contemporary university-trained artists in Scandinavia feel the power of the traditional folk art of their native lands. Bergstrom, a native of Sweden, did this piece for her Master of Fine Arts program while attending Brigham Young University. She later sold it to help finance her return to Sweden to serve a mission for the Church.*

FIGURE 73: CHERYL WHITE

PLATE 242: *Joseph and Emma Smith Dolls*, 1983
CHERYL WHITE (1953– )
MIXED MEDIA, 30" X 14" X 13"
(76.2 CM X 35.6 CM X 33 CM)
MUSEUM OF CHURCH HISTORY AND ART

*Joseph Smith, the first prophet of the restoration, and his wife, Emma Hale Smith, who was named in revelation an "elect lady," were well matched in intelligence, energy, and commitment to the establishment of the Church. Theirs is also a great American love story, from their elopement in 1827 to his name on her lips as she died many years after his martyrdom. Fine doll making combines a wide range of artistic and research skills. The project took the Salt Lake City artist fourteen hundred hours. She sculpted the faces of these dolls using pictures of Joseph and Emma and the death mask of Joseph. The hand-sewn costumes were made of authentic fabrics using patterns accurate to the time, place, and background of the subjects. The artist used a lavender palette for Emma's clothing because research determined that lavender was Emma's favorite color.*

In understanding folk art, it is useful to consider two stylistic classifications. One comes from the naive rendering of a realistic western art tradition. The other comes from using more abstract forms that frequently are indigenous and ancient. Much Latter-day Saint folk art comes from each tradition. For example, Katya Estrada Lupitou's *The Gospel Comes to the Lamanites* (PLATE 243) represents the first tradition. The style of the Guatemalan artist reflects a naive, largely self-taught, rendering of a naturalistic art tradition that has its antecedents in earlier formal Spanish painting. In contrast, Les Namingha's bowl depicting the three degrees of glory (PLATE 244) uses ancient symbolic visual forms of the Hopi and Zuni tribes of the American Southwest. Though Namingha's piece is more abstract than Lupitou's painting, his bowl uses existing forms from within his culture. But his work requires some knowledge of Hopi and Zuni visual language for complete understanding.

There is a conceptual difference in the work of Namingha and much of contemporary abstract western fine art. Namingha's piece exhibits traditional forms that are widely understood from within his culture, while some modern western abstract artists create new symbolic forms with personal meaning. Namingha's work connects with the past and with a typical member of his culture. Some modern abstract artists make a conscious separation from the past and from a typical member of their culture. Folk artists do not exist in cultural isolation. Whether they create naive renditions of earlier western formal styles or draw upon ancient indigenous forms and symbols, they are concerned with making intellectual, emotional, and spiritual connections with typical members of their society. The emphasis is on communication with others.

This desire to communicate shows up in works of Latter-day Saint folk art depicting a wide variety of Church themes. Among those themes are the temples, missionary work, the First Vision, and Lehi's vision of the tree of life. These works of art enrich traditional visual experience through new interpretations of familiar themes; they are frequently done with techniques, styles, and materials new to many Anglo-Americans. This contemporary folk art from the United States and around the world is one of the great Latter-day Saint visual and spiritual celebrations of modern times.

PLATE 243: *The Gospel Comes to the Lamanites,* 1987

KATYA ELIZABETH ESTRADA LUPITOU (1969– )
OIL ON CANVAS, 21 1/2" X 28" (54.6 CM X 71.1 CM)
MUSEUM OF CHURCH HISTORY AND ART

*This painting of an Indian family from the highlands of Guatemala depicts their personal journey to greater spiritual understanding. They are first shown living as their people have lived for centuries (symbolized by the Mayan pyramid). Next, they are introduced to the gospel by missionaries, and finally they approach the temple in Guatemala City to be sealed together as a family. The temple is a symbol of new faith in an ancient land and among an ancient people. Although Lupitou has participated in Church activities since 1980, including graduating from seminary, receiving the Young Women medallion, and teaching various classes, she was not yet a member when she painted this folk-art-style piece in 1987. She was finally able to be baptized in 1988. She studied art for two years before painting this piece.*

PLATE 244: *The Three Degrees of Glory,* 1994

LES NAMINGHA (1968– )
POTTERY, 3 3/4" HIGH X 13 1/2" DIAMETER
(9.5 CM X 34.3 CM)
MUSEUM OF CHURCH HISTORY AND ART

*Namingha, a Hopi/Zuni artist, has used forms native to the American Southwest to depict the various kingdoms of glory promised by the Lord as a reward for valiancy in life. He has used the scriptural references to the glory of the sun, the moon, and the stars to represent these differing rewards. In the center stands Christ, dressed in priestly robes. His face is veiled because the artist felt that Deity was too sacred for him to depict accurately. The Zuni "souls" are depicted as small round faces emanating rays of light. Namingha shows an increasing light from the faces as the degrees of heavenly order ascend.*

PLATE 245: *Moroni Delivers the Plates,* 1973
MAX REZLER
INLAID WOOD, 24" X 21" (61 CM X 55.2 CM)
MUSEUM OF CHURCH HISTORY AND ART

*The coming forth of the Book of Mormon was a key event in the restoration of the gospel of Jesus Christ. Here Moroni, the book's final author and custodian, turns the golden plates containing this record over to Joseph Smith, who will translate the record "by the gift and power of God."*

*The marquetry or wood inlay technique used by the artist to create this piece goes back to Europe, particularly eighteenth-century France, Italy, and Germany. Brazil has had a substantial European presence, especially from Germany, for over a century. Rezler is part of that tradition. He used ten different kinds of wood, mainly from the Parana region of Brazil. All the wood colors are natural (no stains were used).*

PLATE 246: **The Last Supper,** 1990
INGETRAUT RIEMER (1938– )
FIRED CERAMIC, 38" X 29" X 6"
(96 CM X 74.3 CM X 16 CM)
MUSEUM OF CHURCH HISTORY AND ART

*The Last Supper of Jesus Christ has been rendered by artists for centuries. This expressionistic version, acquired from the "Second International Art Competition: Themes from the Scriptures," drew inspiration from European medieval sculpture and rustic folk art found in northern Europe. The "Pottery Group of Bremen"—Relief Society sisters from the Bremen Branch, Hamburg Germany Stake—worked to create this sculpture. Ingetraut Riemer headed the group; other sisters who made equal contributions were Gerlinde Gessell, Brigitte Hörstel, Ilse Selvarajah, Sieglinde Nowak, and Rosemarie Troche.*

We hear much in public discourse in today's world about "multiculturalism." There is a growing tendency to embrace cultures different from one's own. The appeal is obvious: the exotic, the new, the unknown. But the challenge in such an artistic and intellectual environment is in building "bridges" to hold such diversity together. Ethnic strife around the world today graphically illustrates the perils of burning the connecting bridges between people. On the other hand, if the multicultural nature of the world is ignored and all people are forced into exactly the same cultural mold, the richness of human and spiritual experience will be diminished. People from different cultures will feel ostracized or, at best, second class.

Latter-day Saint folk art from around the world demonstrates a unique response to this challenge and opportunity. A wide variety of materials, techniques, and styles are used by these folk artists. They are not forced to give up what is best and true in their respective cultures. But through the use of shared and overtly Latter-day Saint themes in their art, they reach out and bond with other Church members from around the world. These themes are found in the gospel of Jesus Christ and shared religious commitments and experiences.

The Museum of Church History and Art has been active in promoting spiritual communication through art in several ways. First, the Museum actively collects fine examples of Latter-day Saint folk art spontaneously created by the Saints. Second, the Museum occasionally commissions an outstanding artist to create a work of art that is uniquely Latter-day Saint in subject matter. Third, beginning in 1987 the Museum has sponsored Churchwide art competitions every three years, and many of the entries are folk art. Prizes have been awarded, and many works of art have been acquired for the Museum's permanent collection. Fourth, the Museum creates a continuing series of art exhibitions using folk art. Fifth, Church magazines and lesson manuals increasingly use these works. All of these actions encourage the production of Latter-day Saint folk art and then share that art with other members. The goal is to make a diverse membership "no more strangers and foreigners, but fellowcitizens with the saints" (Ephesians 2:19).

PLATE 247: *Three Degrees of Glory,* 1991
PHILLIP SEKAQUAPTEWA (1948– )
SILVER, LAPIS LAZULI, CORAL, TURQUOISE, AND GOLD,
14" x 1 1/2" (35.6 CM x 3.8 CM)
MUSEUM OF CHURCH HISTORY AND ART

Latter-day Saints believe that most people
will ultimately be saved in glory, although
there will be degrees of glory. The Doctrine
and Covenants compares these various
states of glory to the brightness of the sun,
moon, and stars as viewed from the earth.
The feather shape is often used by Hopis
to represent prayers or heavenly
communication. Taken together, the feather
shape and the emblems of the sun, moon,
and stars symbolically represent the
modern revelation explaining the three
degrees of glory and the importance of
prayer to receive divine guidance to return
to the Lord's presence. Precious metals and
imbedded semi-precious stones have been
used by Sekaquaptewa to enhance this
traditional Hopi silvermaking style. The
artist learned silversmithing from his
father, the late Wayne Sekaquaptewa, who
was one of the best-known innovators in
modern Hopi jewelry making.

FIGURE 74:
PHILLIP SEKAQUAPTEWA

PLATE 248: *In Our Lovely Deseret Sampler,* 1990
ELAINE THATCHER (1950– )
TEXTILE, 20" x 21" (50.8 CM x 53.3 CM)
MUSEUM OF CHURCH HISTORY AND ART

Deseret is a Book of Mormon term meaning
"honeybee." In the nineteenth century Latter-day
Saints adopted the bee and beehive as symbols of
industry and stewardship within a covenant
community. In our own time, Latter-day Saint
Young Women between the ages of twelve and
fourteen have been called "Beehives." The bees and
small beehives are the reverse of each other in this
original work. Cross-stitch ties the artist to women
and their arts across time and space and especially
to her own great-grandmother who was a pioneer in
Cache Valley, Utah. A sampler made by this great-
grandmother hangs in Thatcher's living room. An
aunt taught Thatcher to cross-stitch as therapy at a
traumatic time in her life. She says that cross-stitch
somehow seems to her to be an especially good way
to represent LDS subjects. The artist earned an
M.A. degree at Utah State University and is
employed as a professional folklorist.

FIGURE 75:
REID W. PARKINSON

PLATE 249: *Maughan's Fort,* 1981
REID W. PARKINSON (1914– )
PAINT ON TIN, 30" x 30" (76.2 CM x 76.2 CM)
MUSEUM OF CHURCH HISTORY AND ART

Peter Maughan, for whom Maughan's Fort was
named, was the leader of the earliest pioneer group
to settle in Cache Valley in northern Utah. The fort
site was the largest settlement in the valley until
troubles with the federal government in 1857 led to
the temporary abandonment of many outlying
communities. When settlers returned to Cache
Valley, Logan became the largest and most
important community. The site of Maughan's Fort
is now known as Wellsville.

The artist has created a folk-art-style winter scene
at a pioneer fort. Activities are represented by the
man fishing and the three men carrying a deer back
to the fort. The rounded structures in front are
dugouts, one of the earliest forms of shelter for
pioneer settlers in many communities.

PLATE 250: **The Modern Prophet,** 1987
BERNADETTE B. PEREZ (1950– )
OIL ON CANVAS, 63" X 54" (160 CM X 137.2 CM)
MUSEUM OF CHURCH HISTORY AND ART

*President Ezra Taft Benson was beloved of Filipino Latter-day Saints who honored and followed his instruction to read and study the Book of Mormon. The artist used a number of techniques and symbols to heighten her message: (1) President Benson has features and coloring similar to many Filipinos; (2) the light-colored suit represents both the purity of his soul and the dignity of his calling; (3) the large overstuffed chair and its bright purple color show honor and prestige and celebrate the importance of his position as prophet; and (4) the shelf of books reinforces President Benson's call to study the Book of Mormon.*

FIGURE 76:
LUCY LUEPPE MCKELVY

PLATE 251: **Echoes of the Ancient Ones,** 1988
LUCY LUEPPE MCKELVEY (1946– )
CERAMIC, 11 1/2" HIGH X 12 7/8" DIAMETER
(29.2 CM X 33 CM)
MUSEUM OF CHURCH HISTORY AND ART
GIFT OF RICHARD G. OMAN

*The artist explains that this pot relates the story of the Book of Mormon peoples to her own people, the Navajo. The gold plates of the Book of Mormon appear in the center of a whirlwind with clouds spreading out from two places bringing rain and prosperity. Laman, Lemuel, Sam, and Nephi travel to the promised land on whirling bamboo logs like the whirling logs of the Nightway Chant. Their promised land is shown as the four sacred mountains of the American Southwest. Two of the sacred plants (corn and squash) and clouds indicate happiness, peace, and prosperity. The plumed serpent, a common symbol for Christ in the Americas, also comes out of the whirlwind. McKelvey's pottery is unlike either the traditional Navajo or Hopi pottery. It represents a unique blending of old and new traditions with the additional influence of the gospel of Jesus Christ. The usual Navajo pottery is crude and utilitarian, while Hopi pottery is finely formed, polished, and painted. Hopis and Navajos were traditional enemies. At Brigham Young University, McKelvey became friends with Hopis who taught her new pottery techniques. Many of her designs are based on Navajo sandpaintings. However, since completed sandpaintings have sacred meanings for Navajos, McKelvey has only adapted and borrowed elements from these ancient symbols.*

PLATE 252: *St. George Temple*, 1980
MARGARET EULETA HOFF (1909– )
ACRYLIC ON CANVAS, 40" x 30" (101.6 CM x 76.2 CM)
MUSEUM OF CHURCH HISTORY AND ART
GIFT OF THE ARTIST

*This painting symbolically depicts the important and connected activities of genealogy and the performing of vicarious temple ordinances. The small hearts turning toward each other refer to the "hearts of the children turning to the fathers" through family history research. The small inset images depict some of the sacred ordinances done by the living on behalf of the dead. Temples are the favorite subject of the artist, who says, "Having the restored gospel without going to the temples is like reading in the twilight and guessing at the meaning, not knowing what the words are. Temples give light to our lives, our souls, and free us of doubts, clarify and make simple the whole of the Gospel Plan if we are in tune with God." A convert to the Church and a self-taught artist, Hoff has done many symbolic paintings of Latter-day Saint temples. Each of her paintings focuses on a distinctive aspect of temple worship or the unique history of that particular temple.*

FIGURE 77:
MARGARET EULETA HOFF

FIGURE 78:
ADA R. RIGBY

PLATE 253: *St. George Temple*, 1983
ADA R. RIGBY (1929– )
CUT PAPER, 11" x 8 1/2" (27.9 CM x 21.6 CM)
MUSEUM OF CHURCH HISTORY AND ART

*Temple marriages unite families for eternity. The artist expresses this concept of eternal love and commitment through a cutout that resembles an old-fashioned valentine. Ada Rigby learned this art technique from a neighbor who was a convert to the Church from northern Europe. Rigby is a past recipient of the Governor's Folk Art Award for Utah.*

These accomplishments can be illustrated by looking at just one theme in Latter-day Saint folk art—temples—to see the different spiritual insights folk artists have communicated. Margaret Hoff (FIGURE 77), an artist living in Vancouver, Washington, created a painting of the St. George Temple (PLATE 252). She wanted to celebrate the importance of "turning the hearts of the fathers to the children and the children to the fathers"—in other words, genealogy and temple work. The temple is surrounded by an inverted heart made up of small hearts turning toward each other to represent family history. In the two upper corners, baptism and confirmation are used to represent temple work. The artist selected the St. George Temple because of revelations about work for the dead that Wilford Woodruff received in that temple.

Lourdes Samson of the Philippines created an embroidery piece called *Families Are Forever* (PLATE 254). She shows a family from the Philippines standing under a palm tree and looking toward the Salt Lake Temple. The Savior is shown descending to the temple. The artist is telling us that families are sealed together for eternity in temples. The descending Christ reminds us that temples are also the House of the Lord. Her choice to depict the Salt Lake Temple instead of

PLATE 254: *Families Are Forever*, 1990
LOURDES D. SAMSON (1960– )
EMBROIDERED TEXTILE, 20 1/2" x 30"
(52.1 CM X 76.2 CM)
MUSEUM OF CHURCH HISTORY AND ART

*The artist uses symbolism in this work to communicate important spiritual ideas. For example, she represents a family in the Philippines standing next to a palm tree and looking toward the Salt Lake Temple, which in reality is thousands of miles away. This communicates their spiritual identification with this sacred building. The Savior is depicted above the temple because the temple is his holy house, and it is through his authority that the sacred temple ordinances are performed. Both the folk quality and the textile medium of this piece place it squarely in the Philippine folk tradition. Folk artists place themselves fully in the middle of the tradition of which they are a part. Samson's two-culture symbiosis is clearly shown in this work.*

the Manila Temple reminds the viewer that Salt Lake City is the spiritual center of the Lord's kingdom on earth. The bright colors reinforce the joy of families being together for eternity, joy that can come through temple marriages and sealings.

Hadi Pranoto (FIGURE 79) from Indonesia has created a batik of the Salt Lake Temple (PLATE 255). He has visually encrusted the temple with dynamic, complex, flowing patterns. In Indonesian art, an artist tells us what matters most by decorating the surface of the featured object with much ornamentation. Pranoto is saying that the Salt Lake Temple is very important to him.

FIGURE 79:
R. M. HADI PRANOTO

PLATE 255: *Salt Lake Temple,* 1985
R. M. HADI PRANOTO (1932– )
BATIK ON COTTON, 36" x 40" (91.4 CM X 101.6 CM)
MUSEUM OF CHURCH HISTORY AND ART

*Sacred ordinances performed in temples bind families together for this life and the life to come. The artist lives in Indonesia, a country that does not yet have a temple; however, Latter-day Saints everywhere revere and look forward to temple attendance and blessings. Batik is the national art form of Indonesia. Yogyakarta is the center of that tradition. Hadi Pranoto, a former branch president in Yogyakarta, is a third-generation batik artist.*

THE GLORY OF THE CHURCH OF JESUS CHRIST OF LATTER DAY SAINTS — COME TO THE HOUSE OF THE GOD OF JACOB HE WILL TEACH US OF HIS WAYS — AND THE DESERT SHALL REJOICE AND BLOSSOM AS THE ROSE

PRES. JOHN TAYLOR · SALT LAKE TEMPLE · PRES. JOSEPH SMITH · ST GEORGE TEMPLE · PRES. BRIGHAM YOUNG

LOGAN TEMPLE · SEA GULL MONUMENT · PRES. DAVID O. MCKAY · LOS ANGELES TEMPLE · MANTI TEMPLE UTAH

PRES. LORENZO SNOW · UTAH THE ✦ OF THE WEST · PR. WILFORD WOODRUFF

LAIE OAHU T.H. · L.D.S. PIONEERS, O HOW WE'LL MAKE THIS CHORUS SWELL—ALL IS WELL! ALL IS WELL! · CANADIAN TEMPLE

PRES. HEBER J. GRANT · IDAHO FALLS TEMPLE · PRES. GEORGE A. SMITH · ARIZONA TEMPLE · PRES. JOSEPH F. SMITH

PLATE 256: *Presidents and Temple Rug,* 1952–1955

RUBEN OUZOUNIAN (1892–1974),
MARY OUZOUNIAN (1908–1991), AND
JOSEPHINE OUZOUNIAN KSAJIKIAN (1939– )
TEXTILE, 143 1/2" x 107 1/2" (364.5 CM x 273.1 CM)
MUSEUM OF CHURCH HISTORY AND ART
GIFT OF MARY OUZOUNIAN

This tapestry is woven of a combination of manufactured and handspun threads. Between each line of weft is a line of cocoon silk. The weavers tied 2,750,000 knots and produced 6,575 lines of weave to create this tapestry by hand. The weaving took from twelve to sixteen hours a day for three years. The Ouzounian family depicted prophets and symbols significant in Latter-day Saint history. These images symbolize their efforts as "modern day" pioneer Saints.

As a growing community of more than two hundred Armenian Latter-day Saints developed in part of the Ottoman Empire (modern Syria), they faced persecution by other Armenians in the form of physical threats of violence, disruption of Church services, eviction from their homes, dismissal from jobs, and loss of income. In response, Church members learned rug and lace making in an effort to become economically self-sufficient. For many, to be a Latter-day Saint in their everyday lives meant making rugs, lace, and fine needlework on textiles. The Ouzounians migrated to the United States in the 1950s.

FIGURE 80: RUBEN AND MARY OUZOUNIAN

PLATE 257: *Beauty of the Seoul Korea Temple,* 1993

YU-SEON KIM (1961– )
CRYSTAL, 7" x 10" x 13 1/2"
(17.8 CM x 25.4 CM x 34.3 CM))
MUSEUM OF CHURCH HISTORY AND ART

From the earliest days of the Restoration, Latter-day Saints have gathered together to build temples where sacred ordinances could be performed and covenants made. Today temples dot the earth, making temple blessings increasingly available to Saints everywhere. For this Korean artist, the refraction of light by this crystal representation of the Seoul Korea Temple is symbolic of temple experiences for Latter-day Saints. He further says that the crystal suggests a "taste of eternity because of its colorless brilliance, refined light, and its clear ringing sound. But above all the temple is remarkable in its cleanness and refinement."

PLATE 258: *Salt Lake Temple,* ABOUT 1980
CUNA INDIANS, PANAMA
TEXTILE, 12 1/2" x 16 1/2" (31.8 CM x 41.8 CM)
MUSEUM OF CHURCH HISTORY AND ART

*The Salt Lake Temple is recognized in many parts
of the world as a symbol of the Church. Even
though a temple has not yet been built among the
Cuna, they understand the importance of being
grounded in covenants, and look with great respect
to the temple.*

*Molas are the quintessential art form of the Cuna
people of the San Blas Islands in Panama. The most
common mola-making technique is "reverse
appliqué." This is done by layering several different
colors of fabric and then cutting through the upper
layer(s) of fabric to reveal the desired color. The
upper layers are then neatly turned under. Details
are sometimes added by using small amounts of
overlay appliqué and embroidery. The Cuna do not
traditionally sketch out their designs. They cut and
sew from spontaneous ideas. Traditionally molas
formed the front and back panels of women's
blouses. Today they are often made and sold as art.*

PLATE 259: *Happy Family of Six Sealed
for Time and All Eternity,* 1993
AGRIPPA NDONGWE (1953– )
OPAL STONE, 11" x 6" x 4"
(27.4 CM x 15.2 CM x 10.2 CM)
MUSEUM OF CHURCH HISTORY AND ART

*Most people long for a family circle that is complete
and joyful. The joy and animation of this piece give it
a broad appeal. The artist, who is from Zimbabwe,
has produced numerous versions of this piece,
customizing them to family size and even color (black,
brown, or white) in addition to this more universal
representation of a family in soft greenish opal stone.*

ORELAND JOE (1958– )
UTAH ALABASTER, 29" X 20" X 10 3/4"
(73.7 CM X 50.8 CM X 27.3 CM)
MUSEUM OF CHURCH HISTORY AND ART

*The continuation of family bonds for eternity is one of the most appealing teachings of the gospel of Jesus Christ to many people. Sacred ordinances performed in temples bind families together for this life and the life to come. The New Mexico artist is half Navajo and half Southern Ute. Much of his work reflects his Native American background; however, he has moved far beyond being only an ethnic artist. His work has won national and international acclaim. Oreland Joe is best known for the quiet dignity that he imparts to his figurative sculpture. Much of his work focuses on the relationships of parents and children. He is a mostly self-taught artist, developing many of his own techniques and tools. Those techniques and tools often give such varied texture to a piece that it is amazing to realize that the work is created from a single piece of stone.*

PLATE 261: **Turning the Heart of a Child to Her Ancestors**, 1993

MARGERY SORENSEN CANNON (1926– )
CLOTH, 13 1/2" X 19 1/2" X 11"
(34.3 CM X 49.5 CM X 28 CM)
MUSEUM OF CHURCH HISTORY AND ART

*Family history is not just names, dates, and places. "As we teach children to turn their hearts to their ancestors through stories and songs we encourage their love, respect, and future service in the temples," says Cannon. These dolls are made of cloth over a wire armature. Hundreds of tiny stitches shaped the figures. A second fabric over the needle modeling hides the stitches and softens the overall look. The artist, who has won many doll-making competitions, is self-taught. She says that all of her many experiences in painting, drawing, sewing, and decorating were brought together in this piece.*

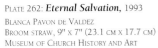

PLATE 262: *Eternal Salvation*, 1993

BLANCA PAVON DE VALDEZ
BROOM STRAW, 9" X 7" (23.1 CM X 17.7 CM)
MUSEUM OF CHURCH HISTORY AND ART

*For Latter-day Saints everywhere, ordinances performed in temples and honored in daily living become stepping-stones to eternal salvation. Although many temples have now been built around the world, the Salt Lake Temple remains important to all Latter-day Saints. This folk art representation of the Salt Lake Temple is constructed of colored broom straw. Many art forms around the world evolve from humble materials readily available to all.*

Alfred Wright lived near Salt Lake City. In his elaborate wooden sculpture *Plan of Life* (PLATE 266), he gives gospel advice to the youth of the Church. He depicts a young couple, just getting married, standing on the book of life. Included in this sculpture are twelve oxen and a baptismal font symbolizing the importance of temple ordinances. The four standard works remind us of the importance of the revealed words from the Lord. The stars, moon, and sun hold up the promise of heavenly glory if we live righteous lives. The sculpture is capped with the Salt Lake Temple, reminding us that it is in the temple that we receive the sacred ordinances and covenants that will enable us to return to the Lord and be exalted if we live worthily.

Joselito Garcia from Peru painted *The Lamanites Shall Blossom As a Rose* (PLATE 233) to show how the native population of Peru learns about the gospel and how it can bring joy to their lives. Garcia shows a highland Indian family and two missionaries with the Book of Mormon. This tells us about the importance of the Book of Mormon message for these ancient people. In the background is the Lima Temple, which has been placed on the mountainside. This reminds us that once one has learned about the gospel and become a member of the Church, one must go to the temple. In the lower right-hand corner is a huge pink rose. This symbolizes the Lamanites blossoming as a rose when they read the Book of Mormon, become members of the Church, and go to the temple. The use of bold forms and exuberant colors reinforces the joy and "blossoming" that comes to these descendants of ancient American people.

None of these works of art is a photo document of the temple. Temples don't have gigantic hearts around them. You can't shoot a single-exposure photograph that has the Philippines and the Salt Lake Temple on the same film frame. The temple is not encrusted with dynamic curvilinear decoration. The temple does not sit on a pile of scriptures. Yet the symbolic nature of folk art considerably broadens the interpretive meaning of the temple in the lives of Latter-day Saints.

PLATE 263: *The Family as a Central Unit in the Church,* 1993
LAWRENCE O. EHIGIATOR (1957– )
WOOD, 48" X 24" X 12" (121.9 CM X 61 CM X 30.5 CM)
MUSEUM OF CHURCH HISTORY AND ART

*As bishop of the Oliha Ward in the old royal capital of Benin City, Nigeria, Ehigiator understands the Church emphasis on strong and eternal families. Such families are grounded in the teachings of Jesus Christ as conveyed by the scriptures and living prophets. The son carries a copy of the Book of Mormon. Latter-day Saints in many lands have responded to the prophetic call to read and study this book as families. These family members are dressed in their "Sunday best."*

*Ehigiator is a professional artist in Benin City, a place known for its artistic traditions going back many centuries. Sculptures of wood, clay, and bronze are all representative of the artistic tradition of West Africa. This piece is crafted of "royal" okheum wood, which is very hard and heavy. The artist spent nine months completing this sculpture.*

PLATE 264: *Family Is Forever,* 1979
BAXTER QUESEDA (ABOUT 1950– )
WATERCOLOR, PEN, AND INK, 28" X 22"
(71.1 CM X 55.9 CM)
MUSEUM OF CHURCH HISTORY AND ART
GIFT OF THE BAXTER QUESEDA FAMILY

*Although the artist is not a Latter-day Saint, he used references from the Doctrine and Covenants to ground the ideas of this piece. He created the work to help finance his son's mission. The message "Family Is Forever" refers to sacred eternal family ties.*

*The Queseda family are Apaches from Arizona. The Arizona landscape appears along the bottom of the painting. The Lamanite family in the center heart and other symbols are important in both Apache and Latter-day Saint cultures, such as the arrow (representing straitness and honor) and roses (representing the "Lamanites blossoming as the rose").*

DOCTRINE AND COVENANTS 49:24

**PLATE 265: _Book of Genesis, Chapter One,_ 1985**
C. DEAN DRAPER (1923– )
CERAMIC, 34" HIGH X 10" DIAMETER
(86.4 CM X 25.4 CM)
MUSEUM OF CHURCH HISTORY AND ART

This ceramic cylinder symbolically depicts the six creative periods as recorded in the first chapter of Genesis. Adam and Eve are set apart as the crowning achievement of creation by their position on the sphere on top.

Draper taught at Fresno State University in California for over thirty years. Ceramic has been his favorite medium. He has been especially intrigued with exploring the "functionality of ceramics." After Draper retired as an art instructor, he and his wife served as missionaries in Kenya and Uganda in eastern Africa.

**PLATE 266: _Plan of Life,_ 1949**
ALFRED RAYMOND WRIGHT (1890–1962)
WOOD AND ACRYLIC, 41" X 17" X 30"
(104.1 CM X 43.2 CM X 76.2 CM)
MUSEUM OF CHURCH HISTORY AND ART
GIFT OF THE ARTIST

The temple is the earthly symbol of the celestial goal for Latter-day Saints. In this work the artist symbolically lays out the spiritual odyssey of all who seek to become Saints. A bride and groom, just starting out together, stand on the book of life. Baptism as the gateway to heaven is symbolized by a temple baptismal font on the backs of twelve oxen. Prominently displayed are the scriptures, which provide the road map for life's journey, and building God's kingdom on earth, which is represented by the beehive. The heavenly kingdoms of glory are represented by stars, the moon going through its phases, and the temple representing the sun or the celestial kingdom, where God dwells. The artist won the sweepstakes award in the 1949 Salt Lake County Fair for this folk-art carving. He also used it as a visual aid for explaining the plan of salvation in both formal and informal settings.

This joyful painting likens the journey toward the
tree of life to an exuberant Mexican festival
parade. The central female figure of the painting
points down the path of the rod to the tree and
beckons the viewer to join the procession. Joseph
Smith is shown as the first partaker of the fruit in
this dispensation. In the middle left of the painting
is a woman still shrouded by her past, seeking to
break free. In the lower left she has left her burden
behind and grasps the rod, which can take her
safely to her goal. In the lower right, the burden has
returned to another woman who has left the path.
Around the tree the cosmos as a rainbow spins,
signifying worlds without end and also the
multitudes of people drawn toward the tree of life.
The unaffected and primitive style of this painting
reinforces the honesty of Juan Escobedo's personal
testimony. Escobedo attended Brigham Young
University, then became an art teacher in Caliente,
Nevada. He has consciously embraced the folk style
of painting of his native Mexico.

The tree of life is an image that appears in many
widely dispersed cultures around the world. It has
special appeal to Latter-day Saints because of its
connection with the prophets Lehi and Nephi in the
Book of Mormon. In this account the tree represents
the love of God, and the exceedingly white fruit of
the tree was "most sweet" and "filled [the] soul with
exceedingly great joy" (1 Nephi 8:11–12). Although
Begay is Navajo, he works in New Mexico in a
traditional Santa Clara blackware pottery style
that he learned from his wife's family. His wife,
Marie, is a member of the Naranjo family of Santa
Clara potters. Blackware pottery is made black by
using an oxygen reduction technique at the end of
the firing process that thoroughly impregnates the
clay with black carbon. The shiny surfaces were
polished with a smooth stone before firing.

PLATE 270: **Lehi's Vision of the Tree of Life**, 1990
ROBERT YELLOWHAIR (1937– )
OIL ON CANVAS, 30" x 48" (76.2 CM X 121.9 CM)
MUSEUM OF CHURCH HISTORY AND ART

Yellowhair has depicted Lehi's vision in Native American terms. The people in the painting are dressed in Native American costumes, representing several groups, including the Hopi, Shoshoni, Zuni, Comanche, Apache, and Sioux. The tree of life in this representation is a piñon pine, which according to Yellowhair is the "most important to the birds, the human beings, and the animals that travel on the earth." Yellowhair grew up in the Indian Wells area of the Navajo reservation in Arizona. He is a largely self-taught artist who has been painting his people since childhood. He is also a silversmith. The Book of Mormon played an important part in his conversion to the Church.

PLATE 269: **Lehi's Vision of the Tree of Life**, 1987
VICTOR DE LA TORRE (1929– )
WOOD, 39" DIAMETER (99.1 CM)
MUSEUM OF CHURCH HISTORY AND ART

Depicted prominently in this carving are persons holding safely to the gospel iron rod as they move toward the tree of life, which symbolizes the love of God. Others are lost in the mists of darkness or in the filthy river. The masses of humanity in the background still need to make choices about their future destiny. The mocking worldly crowds in large modern urban buildings without foundations are seen in the upper right. As a boy Torre was apprenticed to a carpenter and later to a wood-carver in his native Ecuador. He studied art at the university in Quito and established himself as an artist in Ecuador. Later he moved his family to Venezuela. This carving reflects the meeting of three cultures in the life of the artist: a traditional rural culture with strong ancient Native American roots, a more recent cosmopolitan urban culture, and his adopted faith of Mormonism.

FIGURE 81:
VICTOR DE LA TORRE

FIGURE 82:
ROBERT YELLOWHAIR

189

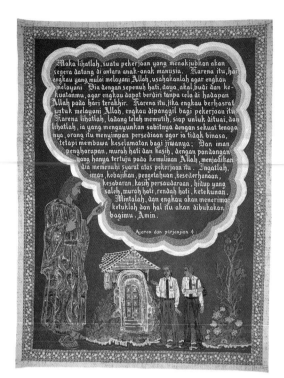

PLATE 271: *Fourth Section of the Doctrine and Covenants*, 1989

JONI SUSANTO (1961– )

BATIK ON COTTON, 88" x 65 1/2" (223.5 CM x 166.4 CM)

MUSEUM OF CHURCH HISTORY AND ART

*This batik portrays the Lord Jesus Christ reciting the revelation recorded in Doctrine and Covenants, section 4, to two missionaries standing in front of the Yogyakarta chapel in Indonesia. This revelation is addressed to all who desire to serve the Lord. It begins, "Now behold, a marvelous work is about to come forth among the children of men." Batik is a term that refers to the resist-dye textile technique, as well as to the cloth decorated by that technique. Batiks have been made in Indonesia since at least the sixteenth century and are the most famous Indonesian art form. Several Latter-day Saints are acknowledged masters of this art form, including Susanto and his father-in-law, Hadi Pranato. Susanto has served a mission in Indonesia and is the branch president in Yogyakarta.*

FIGURE 83:
JONI SUSANTO

Another important Latter-day Saint theme is missionary work. Because so many Church members, particularly outside of the United States, are converts, it is not surprising that this becomes a major theme in international Latter-day Saint folk art. A typical painting about missionary work done in Utah might depict young elders in an exotic location talking to someone. Folk art usually presents a much more complex set of ideas.

In Joni Susanto's *Fourth Section of the Doctrine and Covenants* (PLATE 271), we see the spiritual imperatives for doing missionary work. Susanto (FIGURE 83) has written out the entire text of section 4, which is the Lord's revelation requiring Latter-day Saints to do missionary work. To one side of the scripture is depicted the Savior himself, the author of the missionary scripture. The lower corner of the batik shows two missionaries before the chapel door in Yogyakarta, Java, Indonesia, in obedience to the Lord's command. The artist himself was a convert to the Church, a missionary, and is currently a branch president in Yogyakarta.

Erick Duarte, from Guatemala, created a painting about missionary work showing how a convert first gained her testimony (PLATE 272). He depicts a young Mayan Indian woman reclining on a couch, reading the Book of Mormon. A little clay Guatemalan bird, representing the Holy Ghost, is above her, testifying of the truthfulness of the book. The story is extended backward and forward by showing through an open window two missionaries coming toward her home to first bring her news of the gospel, and also showing a little insert of a baptism near the bottom of the painting. The painting thus celebrates the Book of Mormon as the central element in the young woman's conversion, how she got the book, and the important imperative for action when one receives a testimony.

From the Philippines comes Godofredo Orig's *Teach Me to Walk in the Light* (PLATE 274) about the impact of missionary work on the family of the artist. Five small paintings are combined into one to show the growth of hope, joy, and unity that comes to a family as they are introduced to the gospel and move through conversion to temple worship.

PLATE 272: *Ready for the Covenant*, 1990

ERICK DUARTE

PASTEL ON PAPER,

30 1/2" x 40 1/2" (77.5 CM x 102.9 CM)

MUSEUM OF CHURCH HISTORY AND ART

*The artist explains that this work depicts a Lamanite woman from Guatemala reading the Book of Mormon. She has accepted the scriptural message and awaits a visit by missionaries who are seen through the window. White birds signify the Holy Spirit. The woman in the lower right part of the painting is being baptized. Duarte received some training in Guatemala as a graphics artist but has drawn upon native Mayan Indian traditions for his images.*

PLATE 273: **Early Morning Baptism near Belgrade,** 1990

LJILJANA CRNOGAJ FULEPP (1952– )
OIL ON GLASS, 16" X 20"
(40.6 CM X 50.8 CM)
MUSEUM OF CHURCH HISTORY AND ART

*The message of this painting is that the gospel of Jesus Christ calls everyone to love and peace. The artist, a Croat national, depicts a Serbian branch president performing a baptism. Through this theme she suggests that the gospel makes it possible for people to transcend the cultural and ethnic divisions that commonly separate them from each other. Fulepp was the first Relief Society president in Zagreb, Croatia. She and her family felt impressed to leave Yugoslavia before civil war divided her homeland. Backpainted glass was developed centuries ago in eastern Europe as a religious art form. Many worshipers in a spirit of adoration kissed religious paintings, thus wearing the paint off. To protect the images from being "loved to death," the technique of backpainting on glass developed. This technique requires that the smallest details be painted first and requires great attention to planning on the part of the artist. Fulepp painted this religious piece in Utah in the old tradition of her people.*

PLATE 274: **Teach Me to Walk in the Light,** 1990

GODOFREDO ORIG
OIL ON PAPER, 24" X 29 3/4"
(61 CM X 75.6 CM)
MUSEUM OF CHURCH HISTORY AND ART

*This piece suggests that families grow in light as they learn about the gospel, join the Church, and grow spiritually in preparation to be sealed in the temple. Each step is filled with more light than the previous one. The stages of one family's conversion are shown in this painting, moving from lower left to upper right. This painting is autobiographical. The artist has used his own life and family to represent the growth toward the light experienced by converts.*

FIGURE 84:
FANGA TUKUAFU

PLATE 275: **Even to the Isles of the Sea,** 1989
FANGA TUKUAFU, TAPA AND PAINT, 30" X 36" (76.2 CM X 91.4 CM)
MUSEUM OF CHURCH HISTORY AND ART

*For more than 150 years, Polynesians in great numbers have joined the Church. According to the Church Almanac for 1992–1993, one in three Tongans is a Latter-day Saint. Today virtually all missionaries in Tonga are from Tonga. The white shirts, ties, and name tags are like those of Latter-day Saint missionaries everywhere. The lava-lava wraps and sandals are practical accommodations to local custom and conditions. The use of tapa cloth in this picture reinforces the ethnicity of the scene. Made of beaten mulberry tree bark, tapa cloth is used in almost all South Pacific islands for ceremonial occasions. This "painting" is a creative application of this old art and craft form. Individual pieces of tapa have been layered to create dimensionality. All the colors in this piece are derived from natural plant dyes commonly used in Tonga.*

PLATE 276: **Confirmation in Sierra Leone,** 1992
EMILE WILSON (ABOUT 1968– )
TEXTILE, 34 1/2" X 30" (87.6 CM X 76.2 CM)
MUSEUM OF CHURCH HISTORY AND ART

*The principles and ordinances of the gospel are the same for Latter-day Saints worldwide. This representation of a confirmation in one of the newest areas of the Church is familiar to Latter-day Saints everywhere. Wilson is a professional artist who specializes in batiks (resist-dyed fabrics).*

PLATE 277: **Strength, Color, Spirit in the Gospel,** 1993
IRENE BECERRIL, PASTEL ON PAPER, 24" X 32" (61 CM X 81.3 CM)
MUSEUM OF CHURCH HISTORY AND ART

*The vibrancy of "strength, color and spirit" that comes from accepting and living the gospel is the message of this art. The artist says that the missionaries and others in this picture are depicted in many hues to represent the gospel truly being for all the peoples of the earth. The Spirit is symbolically represented as a being hovering over all who seek and love the truth. Becerril is a convert to the Church. She is a professional artist who has had many exhibits of her works in both the Western Hemisphere and Europe.*

PLATE 278: **Restoration of the Melchizedek
Priesthood,** ABOUT 1980

USTUPO RELIEF SOCIETY, SAN BLAS ISLANDS, PANAMA
TEXTILE, 14" X 15 3/8" (35.6 CM X 39.6 CM)
MUSEUM OF CHURCH HISTORY AND ART

*The bestowal of the Melchizedek Priesthood by
Peter, James, and John on Joseph Smith and Oliver
Cowdery in 1829 is one of the most important early
events of The Church of Jesus Christ of Latter-day
Saints. Foundational stories and principles such as
this bind Latter-day Saints together throughout the
world. This mola is in one sense nontraditional, in
that embroidery and appliqué, rather than reverse
appliqué, dominate. Even though the Cuna Indians
seem to be traditional in outlook and activity, no
tradition is truly static. This mola is an example of
stylistic evolution within a broad traditional
framework.*

**PLATE 279: *Salt Lake Temple Square*, 1935**
VAVAU RELIEF SOCIETY, TONGA
TAPA CLOTH, 111 1/2" X 156"
(283.2 CM X 396.3 CM)
MUSEUM OF CHURCH HISTORY AND ART
GIFT OF VAVAU RELIEF SOCIETY

*Respect for the temple and a longing to have access to full gospel blessings seem to be poignantly represented in this piece. The words on the tapa cloth translate to "The great temple in Zion," "The great organ in Zion," and "The great Tabernacle in Zion." In this work of many hands, feelings of love and longing speak across the years and miles. Today the Saints in Tonga have a sacred temple in their own islands. The Polynesian peoples are notably generous. Missionaries and other visitors often leave the islands laden with gifts. This tapa is one of those gifts of love. It is the largest and finest tapa cloth in the Church collection. Artistic individualism is not the focus of traditional people who live in cultures where customs are handed down by word of mouth or example. Instead they often work together to create a statement of their shared feelings.*

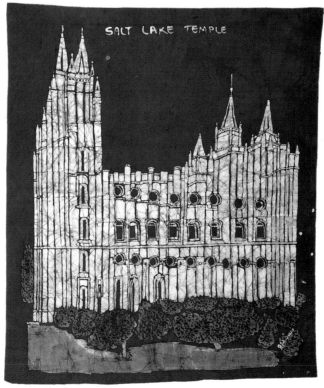

**PLATE 280: *Salt Lake Temple*, 1992**
EMILE WILSON (ABOUT 1968– )
BATIK TEXTILE, 35 1/2" X 30 1/2" (90.2 CM X 77.5 CM)
MUSEUM OF CHURCH HISTORY AND ART

*Living in West Africa, thousands of miles from Salt Lake City, the artist depicts the Salt Lake Temple as a symbol for all Latter-day Saints. This temple represents to many far-distant Latter-day Saints the geographic center of their faith, the covenants made at baptism, with the sacrament, and in temples. The artist lives in Sierra Leone, where he earns a living making batiks, a traditional art form.*

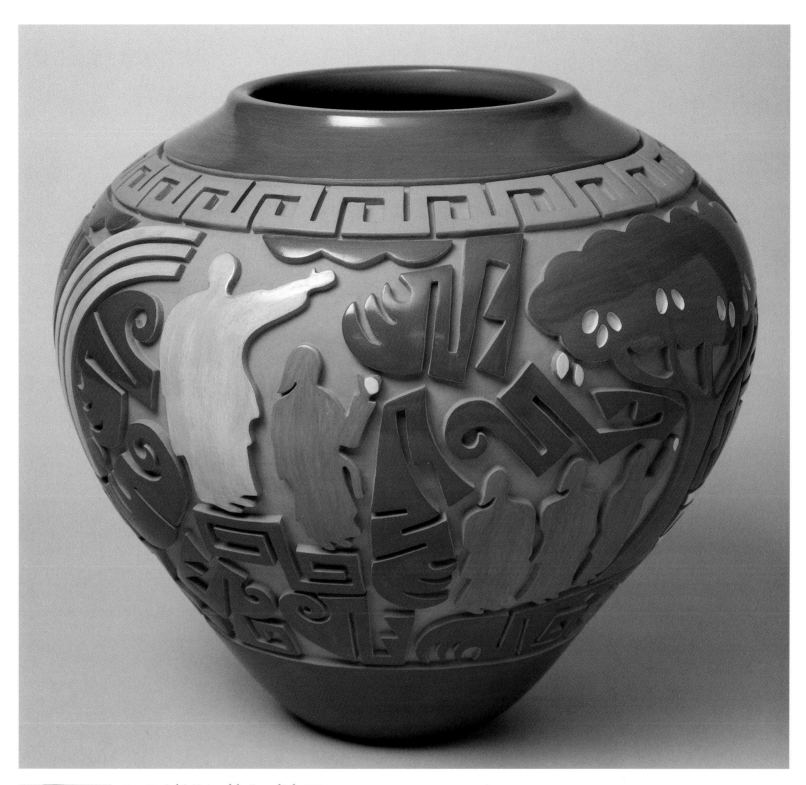

FIGURE 85: TAMMY GARCIA

PLATE 281: *Lehi's Vision of the Tree of Life*, 1994

TAMMY GARCIA (1969– )
FIRED CLAY, 14" X 15" (36 CM X 38.1 CM)
MUSEUM OF CHURCH HISTORY AND ART

*Lehi's vision of the tree of life offers an important message about the journey of life. This Book of Mormon story uses metaphor to outline responsibilities and potential rewards in following the word of the Lord in this life. Tammy Garcia, a leading Santa Clara Pueblo artist living in Taos, New Mexico, has blended traditional Pueblo techniques and forms with a few more naturalistic forms to convey the essential elements of this important story. By expressing the story within the framework of her own culture, she has followed the admonition of the prophet Nephi to "liken all scriptures unto us" (1 Nephi 19:23). The artist makes her pots using the coil method without the aid of a potter's wheel and then fires them under a wood fire. She digs the clay from the hills surrounding the Santa Clara Pueblo in the Rio Grande Valley of New Mexico. Few Native American artists are capable of making pots of this size using such methods.*

Why missionary work is imperative, how testimonies are developed, and what impact conversion has on a family are visually communicated through these works of art. Symbolism and radical readjustment of composition to include multiple paintings within a painting made it possible for these artists to transcend time and space in their works of art and focus on the why, how, and result of missionary work. These visual expressions of faith and testimony come primarily from the point of view of the convert and thus provide an important voice in the celebration of missionary work. Folk art as a form and the international Church as an important source of ideas made these works possible.

This same exercise could be done for many Latter-day Saint themes using international folk art. Such are the possibilities of Latter-day Saint folk art. Such are the testimonies of these folk artists.

As the Church becomes ever more international in membership, the vast sweep of art depicting Latter-day Saint themes is made by artists without formal university art school training. This visual communication is more like a testimony meeting than a formal sermon. But it reinforces and broadens our understanding of important gospel experiences, values, beliefs, and commitments and helps unify us as a religious people. Much of this folk art expands our aesthetic experiences with bright, bold symbols and forms, new styles, and a wide variety of mediums. This art tradition has a great variety of styles and forms while maintaining its cohesive Latter-day Saint identity. These visual images of faith and shared religious commitment can cut across linguistic boundaries and help build a united sense of fellowship for Latter-day Saints around the world.

FIGURE 86:
THOMAS POLACCA

PLATE 282: *The Faithful History of Tom Polacca,* 1990
THOMAS POLACCA (1934– )
CERAMIC, 12" HIGH X 11" DIAMETER (30.5 CM X 28 CM)
MUSEUM OF CHURCH HISTORY AND ART

*This piece uses both ancient and modern ideas to explain ideas and experiences from the family history of the artist. The kneeling figure represents the artist's grandfather, who was the first of his family to join the Church. The feather coming out of his mouth suggests that the grandfather is praying. The eagle indicates the presence of the Holy Spirit. The tree is a representation both of the literal trees on the artist's ranch in Arizona and of the tree of life. The concentric sun figure expresses the idea that the Lord blesses all his creations. The footprints "belong" to President Spencer W. Kimball, who as an apostle used the Polacca ranch in Arizona as a retreat and place of recuperation during a time of many illnesses. Thomas Polacca is descended from both the Polacca and Nampeyo branches of the Hopi tribe. People from both sides of his family were early converts to the Church.*

# NOTES

## Notes to Chapter 2

1. John Hafen, "An Art Student in Paris," *Contributor* 15 (June 1894): 485.

2. John Hafen, "An Art Student in Paris," *Contributor* 15 (September 1894): 690.

3. B. F. Larsen, "The Meaning of Religion in the Life of John Hafen," *Improvement Era* 39 (January 1936): 6.

4. John Hafen, "The Gospel in Art," *Improvement Era* 13 (December 1909): 177–78.

5. John Hafen to President Joseph F. Smith, Nashville, Indiana, 4 August 1909, research files, Museum of Church History and Art.

6. Larsen, "John Hafen," 5.

7. Hafen to Joseph F. Smith.

8. John Hafen, "Mountains from an Art Standpoint," *Young Woman's Journal* 19 (September 1905): 404.

9. John Hafen to unidentified individual, undated, research files, Museum of Church History and Art.

10. Rell G. Francis, *Cyrus E. Dallin: Let Justice Be Done* (Springville, Utah: Springville Museum of Art, 1976), 68.

11. George Henry Taggart, "Art in Utah," *Salt Lake City Deseret Evening News* (21 December 1901).

12. Alice Merrill Horne, "The Utah Painter—Lee Greene Richards," *Young Woman's Journal* 21 (May 1910): 262–63.

13. Ibid., 265.

14. Ibid., 266.

15. Alice Merrill Horne, "Utah's Sculptor, Mahonri M. Young," *Young Woman's Journal* 21 (April 1910): 196.

16. Mahonri M. Young to Bill, 1 June 1949, research files, Museum of Church History and Art.

17. Art Students League of New York, Bulletin, undated, 2.

18. Robert S. Olpin, *Dictionary of Utah Art* (Salt Lake City: Salt Lake Art Center, 1980), 292.

19. Florence Gifford Fairbanks, "A High Ambition Realized," in "History of John B. Fairbanks," undated type-script, 72.

20. Olpin, *Dictionary*, 74.

21. John Henry Evans, "Some Men Who Have Done Things," *Improvement Era* 13 (February 1910): 349.

22. Robert S. Olpin, introduction and notes, *A Basket of Chips: An Autobiography by James Taylor Harwood* (Salt Lake City: Tanner Trust Fund, University of Utah Library, 1985), 125.

23. *Journal of Discourses*, 26 vols. (London: Latter-day Saints Book Depot, 1856–1886), 8:83.

24. Olpin, *Dictionary*, 75.

25. J. Leo Fairbanks, "Frontispiece," *Improvement Era* 37 (December 1934): 733.

26. Pauline White Fairbanks, *Catalog of Paintings by J. Leo Fairbanks* (Corvallis, Oregon: Memorial Union, Oregon State College, n.d.), 2.

27. Exhibit text, "In Service to Church and Community: Pioneer Artists in Zion," research files, Museum of Church History and Art.

28. "Young Utah Artists: Herman Hugo Haag," *Young Woman's Journal* 15 (June 1904): 266.

29. Linda Jones Gibbs, *Harvesting the Light: The Paris Art Mission and Beginnings of Utah Impressionism* (Salt Lake City: The Church of Jesus Christ of Latter-day Saints, 1987), 28.

30. George Q. Cannon to Lorus Pratt, 12 September 1891, research files, Museum of Church History and Art.

31. "George Edward Anderson (1860–1928)," *Gallery Notes* (Fort Worth, Texas: Amon Carter Museum, n.d.).

32. Rell G. Francis, "Views of Mormon Country: The Life and Photographs of George Edward Anderson," *American West* 15 (November/December 1978): 15.

33. Hafen, "Mountains from an Art Standpoint," 403.

## Notes to Chapter 3

1. "Frontispiece," *Improvement Era* 36 (July 1933): 520.

2. Minerva K. Teichert, handwritten manuscript, 1947, research files, Museum of Church History and Art.

3. Ibid.

4. Minerva K. Teichert, eulogy, funeral service for Alice Merrill Horne, 1948, research files, Museum of Church History and Art.

5. Teichert, handwritten manuscript.

6. Reed Dayton, speaker, funeral service for Minerva K. Teichert, 7 May 1976, research files, Museum of Church History and Art.

7. Minerva K. Teichert, transcription of autobio-graphical sketch, 1937, research files, Museum of Church History and Art.

8. Frank Stevens, interview by Dr. Marian Johnson, 3 November 1986, research files, Museum of Church History and Art.

9. *Cope,* exhibition brochure (San Francisco: Maxwell Galleries, Ltd., 1971), 4.

10. Torlief S. Knaphus, "Description of the Hill Cumorah Monument," unpublished typescript, research files, Museum of Church History and Art.

11. Eugene F. Fairbanks, *A Sculptor's Testimony in Bronze and Stone: Sacred Sculpture of Avard T. Fairbanks* (Salt Lake City: Eugene F. Fairbanks, 1972), 42.

12. Ibid., 7.

13. Ibid.

14. Mamie Platt Dixon, "The Work of LeConte Stewart, Painter, Lithographer, Etcher and Designer," master's thesis, University of Utah, 1955, 14.

15. LeConte Stewart, interview by Richard G. Oman and F. Edward Bennett, Kaysville, Utah, November 1978, research files, Museum of Church History and Art.

16. Quotation distributed at LeConte Stewart Festival, Bountiful Art Center, Bountiful, Utah, 1982, research files, Museum of Church History and Art.

17. *Salt Lake Tribune,* 3 March 1935.

18. "Artist's Skill Enhances Beauty of Sacrament Gem," *Church News,* 14 February 1976.

19. LeConte Stewart, interview by Robert O. Davis, Kaysville, Utah, May 1984, research files, Museum of Church History and Art.

20. See Raymond H. Woolsey and Ruth Anderson, *Harry Anderson: The Man Behind the Paintings* (Washington, D.C.: Review and Herald Publishing Association, 1976), 119.

21. "Announcing the *Ensign* Gospel in Art Program," *Ensign* 3 (December 1973): 45.

22. Woolsey and Anderson, *Harry Anderson,* 121.

23. Ted Schwarz, *Arnold Friberg: The Passion of a Modern Master* (Flagstaff, Arizona: Northland Press, 1985), 142.

24. Ibid., 65.

25. Ibid., 75.

26. Mabel Frazer, "Latter-day Saint Artists," *Young Woman's Journal* 39 (December 1928): 785.

27. "Frontispiece," *Improvement Era* 36 (November 1933): 773.

28. Frazer, "Latter-day Saint Artists," 785.

29. Ibid.

30. Ibid.

## Notes to Chapter 4

1. Spencer W. Kimball, "Education for Eternity," address to faculty and staff, Brigham Young University, Provo, Utah, 12 September 1967.

2. *Third Annual Mormon Festival of Arts,* exhibit brochure (Provo, Utah: College of Fine Arts and Communications, Brigham Young University, 1971).

3. *The 12th Annual Mormon Festival of Arts,* exhibit brochure (Provo, Utah: Brigham Young University, 1980).

4. *Let Your Good Works Show at The Mormon Festival of Arts,* exhibit call for entries (Provo, Utah: Brigham Young University, 1982).

5. *Let Your Light Shine: Mormon Festival of Arts,* exhibit brochure (Provo, Utah: Brigham Young University, 1983).

6. Lynne Millman-Weidinger, *Dean Millman & Lynne Millman-Weidinger,* exhibit brochure, 1983.

7. *Peter M. Fillerup, Sculptor,* promotional brochure, undated.

8. Carole Bourget Legg, "Peter M. Fillerup," *Southwest Art* 14 (December 1984): 65.

9. Clark Kelley Price to Margot, 18 November 1985, research files, Museum of Church History and Art.

10. Bruce Smith, statement with artwork for the Second International Art Competition, 1991, exhibit files, Museum of Church History and Art.

11. Michael Graves, typewritten statement about a group of paintings including *The Fourth Article of Faith,* undated, research files, Museum of Church History and Art.

12. Todd Wilkinson, "Discovering the Soul of Nancy Glazier," *Wildlife Art News,* March/April 1991, 67.

13. Ibid.

14. Nancy Glazier to Richard G. Oman, September 1990, research files, Museum of Church History and Art.

15. Bethanne Andersen, statement, 1984, research files, Museum of Church History and Art.

16. Sallie Poet to Robert O. Davis, August 1994.

17. Brian Kershisnik, statement with artwork for the Second International Art Competition, 1994, exhibit files, Museum of Church History and Art.

18. Jeanne Leighton Lundberg Clarke, "A Considered Proposition of Reality: The Maximum Statement," MFA project, Brigham Young University, 1980, 5.

19. Jill Hellberg to Robert O. Davis, August 1994.

20. Lee Bennion, *The Art of Lee Udall Bennion,* exhibit invitation, Overland Trail Gallery, 1991.

21. Lee Bennion, statement submitted for group exhibit, "1986 Invitational: Latter-day Saint Artists in Utah," exhibit files, Museum of Church History and Art.

22. Judith Mehr to Richard G. Oman, 28 April 1980, research files, Museum of Church History and Art.

23. Kimball Warren, "I Want to Surprise People," *Art of the West,* March/April 1990, 58.

24. Judith McConkie,*Wulf Barsch: A Stranger in a Strange Land,* introduction by E. Frank Sanguinetti (Provo, Utah: Wulf E. Barsch, 1984), 2.

25. Hugh Nibley, "From the Earth Upon Which Thou Standest," *Wulf Barsch, Looking Toward Home* (Salt Lake City: Museum of Church History and Art, 1985), 13.

26. Florence Hansen to Robert O. Davis, June 1994.

27. Dennis Smith to Robert O. Davis, September 1994, research files, Museum of Church History and Art.

28. Article of Faith 13.

29. Minerva K. Teichert, eulogy, funeral service for Alice Merrill Horne, 1948, research files, Museum of Church History and Art.

30. Joseph Smith, *History of the Church of Jesus Christ of Latter-day Saints,* ed. B. H. Roberts, 7 vols. (Salt Lake City: Deseret Book Company, 1980), 3:295.

31. Spencer W. Kimball, "The Gospel Vision of the Arts," *Ensign* 7 (July 1977): 5.

# LIST OF ARTISTS